Notebooks of the Mind

Notebooks of the Mind

Explorations of Thinking

REVISED EDITION

Vera John-Steiner

New York   Oxford
OXFORD UNIVERSITY PRESS
1997

**To Sophie Polgar and Stan Steiner,
for they have built the houses of my thought.**

Oxford University Press
Oxford   New York
Athens   Auckland   Bangkok   Bombay
Calcutta   Cape Town   Dar es Salaam   Delhi
Florence   Hong Kong   Istanbul   Karachi
Kuala Lumpur   Madras   Madrid   Melbourne
Mexico City   Nairobi   Paris   Singapore
Taipei   Tokyo   Toronto

and associated companies in
Berlin   Ibadan

First published in 1985 by
the University of New Mexico Press, Albuquerque, NM 87131

First issued as an Oxford University Press paperback, 1997

Oxford is a registered trademark of Oxford University Press

Library of Congress Cataloging-in-Publication Data
John-Steiner, Vera, 1930–
Notebooks of the mind : explorations of thinking / Vera John-
Steiner.—Rev. ed.
p.   cm.   Includes bibliographical references and index.
ISBN 0-19-510896-5
1. Creative thinking. 2. Creation (Literary, artistic, etc.)
I. Title
BF408.J5   1996
153.3'5—dc20
96-31307

1 3 5 7 9 8 6 4 2

Printed in the United States of America
on acid-free paper

Contents

Foreword

Reading *Notebooks of the Mind* recalled an incident, a peaceful moment in World War II. During a long voyage on a troopship, a few people who liked poetry somehow met each other and found in the ship's library Edna St. Vincent Millay's *Conversations at Midnight*. We read it aloud, taking turns with the different voices. The long poem presents a fascinating and varied array of people gathered in Millay's mind to reflect upon the great questions of life.

This memory was awakened by Vera John-Steiner's book. For she has assembled a company of "experienced thinkers" (to use her wise and modest phrase) as conversationalists in a quiet and comfortable, yet disciplined reflection on the creative process. Of course, these conversationalists, numbering over fifty, do not ever gather together in the flesh. These are dialogues orchestrated by the author of the book, bringing out certain features of the creative process: the long apprenticeships, the continuous interaction of person and society, the varied languages or modalities of creative thought, and the importance of character in sustaining patient, disciplined hard work.

The author's idea of uniting these reflections differs from anthologies on creativity in which each contributor takes his or her turn and disappears, a rapidly fading memory quickly outshone by the next luminary. In *Notebooks of the Mind*, speakers appear and reappear, as the author reorganizes their reflections into a serious and many-sided examination of a set of unifying themes. It becomes clear that being creative is a self-reflective process. This is almost self-evident in the case of scientific creativity, because scientific thought must justify itself and explain its methods. Recent research has shown that older conceptions of *the* scientific method slight the intuitive, imagistic side of creative thought and entirely omit consideration of the passionate dialogue through which it is carried forward. *Notebooks of the Mind* is valuable in illuminating these points and in showing that they apply not only in the sciences but in all the arts.

Implicit in the book is a respect for the interplay of creative process and creative product. The person at work may use private languages and modes of thought, but these must then be translated into forms others can comprehend. Public and private are distinct, but they must be commensurate and transposable. Among the many examples John-Steiner uses to illustrate this point, I particularly liked her account of the playwright-turned-actor-turned-playwright. From the deep immersion in the actor's craft comes the knowledge of what the playwright must do. Similar examples can be found in the sciences: we think of Newton as a theoretician, but he was also a great maker of scientific instruments.

From a number of recent studies we have come to understand how a long and well-worked-through apprenticeship is vital to the development of a creative life. Teachers and mentors may be imposed upon the young person, or sought out, or discovered in a lucky accident. They may be physically present or far away, living or long dead models. But models and mentors there must be, as well as the disciplined work necessary to profit from them. This point emerges in my work on Darwin, in David Feldman's studies of prodigies, and repeatedly in the present volume.

In a refreshing reversal of more customary formulations, John-Steiner treats the skills and languages of thought of the creative person as ways of being, permeating the life. But in addition the creative person possesses a set of "invisible tools," which are matters of character—courage, discipline, openness to collaboration, ability to go it alone—without which the skills would come to naught. The key point is that creative aspiration must capture the whole life; thus it is that the skills, the languages, and the character are each indispensable.

In modern cognitive psychology, a continuing battle rages between the proponents of propositional thought and those who favor imagistic thought, each side aiming to show that the other can be "translated" out of existence. John-Steiner enters the fray with three important points to make. First, the set of alternatives numbers more than two. In addition to her examination of visual and verbal modes of thought, she gives a particularly rich and thorough presentation of the languages of emotion and of the body—music, dance, and theater. Second, the product must not be confused with the process. Among choreographers, for example, she shows how George Balanchine's thought is fundamentally musical, Merce Cunningham's spatial and geometric, and Martha Graham's poetic and mythic. Yet all produce dance, all appear on the same public stage, all contribute to and learn from the same world of dance. Finally, the fact that one language of thought can be translated into another by no means devalues either one. Indeed, this work of translation is a large part of the creative process.

Nowhere is this idea more clearly brought out than in the exchange between the physicist Richard Feynman and the mathematician Freeman Dyson—two characters who do not appear in this book's mighty cast, but who might well be waiting in the wings. A point came when Feynman had already worked out his system for representing quantum electrodynamic processes (now known as "Feynman diagrams"), but his colleagues could not understand him. Dyson's intuition told him that Feynman really had something. So the two men set to work, the distinguished mathematician to learn from the pioneering physicist. After months of collaboration they understood each other, and Feynman had an exponent who could teach the world. It is all well and good to say that Feynman had already had the basic insight. But without the hard work of collaboration, translation, and public rendering, the job is not done. So both parts are indispensable to the creative process, and among indispensables none must yield to another in vying for importance.

In previous discussions of the modalities of thought, too much emphasis has been placed on the choice between visual and verbal thinking. Now we can see how this Hobson's choice is unnecessary and almost beside the point. There are many modalities available, each person must struggle to develop his or her own patterns of thought, and the movement from modality to modality is the central issue on which we should be focusing our attention, rather than the choice of one or the other dominant "language of thought." Moreover, a relatively loose coupling exists between the forms of thought involved in the creative process and those displayed in the final public product. In *Frames of Mind*, Howard Gardner has recently revivified our knowledge of the multiplicity of these modes of thought. It remains now for us to work out in some detail the complex arrangements that evolve among different modes in different phases of the creative process.

Professor John-Steiner has made a wise choice of the term "experienced thinkers" to characterize the figures in her book. It permits her to introduce into this many-sided dialogue all sorts of people who might not qualify for a place in the Pantheon of creativity—lesser known artists, social scientists with something to say about the creative process, people from the media world of television, and so on. Depending on one's criterion level, they might or might not qualify as creative individuals—but they do each have something to say about the subject, something born of their own struggles and experiences. This enlargement of the cast of characters in the conversation makes it possible to introduce findings from experimental and developmental psychology into the discussion of creative work. By the same token, we can see how workers in these branches of knowledge can learn from reading the notebooks of the mind.

In "One Word More," Robert Browning wrote:

> Does he paint? he fain would write a poem,—
> Does he write? he fain would paint a picture.

These incessant dialectical movements—between process and product, person and society, one modality and another, intention and expression—are the core of the creative process. When you march, music captures your feet, when you sing it captures your heart. *Notebooks of the Mind* is like conversations; not at midnight, but say at a civilized hour of the morning, when each of the participants has already made good progress in the day's work, and wants to stop to reflect on it.

Howard E. Gruber
University of Geneva
and Rutgers University

Acknowledgments

Some books are part of one's life for many, many years. This is such an enterprise, and its slow but steady growth was helped by my family, my friends, and my students. I owe a special debt to Professor Howard Gruber, who shared his vast knowledge of cognition and creativity with me during many talks, and to the later writer Anaïs Nin, who read an early chapter and provided much needed encouragement. My colleagues in New York, California, and New Mexico arranged introductions to potential interviewees, and discussed ideas with me. Many of them are listed in the back of this book among the names of those interviewed.

The staff of the University of New Mexico press has been supportive and committed to this work, and my editor, David Holtby, applied the right mixture of pressure, thoughtful suggestions, and caring to get a busy professor to finish her favorite, but often neglected, task. A fellowship from the Office of Education (a Mina Shaughnessy Scholars program) helped me to devote some concentrated time to write about writing. My thanks to Joan Bossert, my editor at Oxford University Press, whose belief in this book made the revised edition possible. Finally, Nancy Gage, Carolyn Panofsky, and Teresa Meehan were among the many individuals at the University of New Mexico who gave me assistance with editing, typing, and other necessary chores in preparing this manuscript for the publisher.

Introduction to the Revised Edition

When I was a child in Budapest, Hungary, in the 1930s, the most valued human activity was developing and working with ideas. In those precarious years before World War II, nothing was certain. Yet the adults around me had the courage to continue addressing themselves to the great traditions of human knowledge. In the midst of their fears for the future, they still carried on impassioned conversations about Thomas Mann or the new physics. I wanted to understand how thinking and creative transformation can sustain life in the face of war and extermination. That was why I chose to study psychology. Part of this book has been a journey to try to understand the life-affirming power of intellectual endeavors.

That power was beautifully exemplified by a recollection of the Hungarian mathematician Pal Turan. In 1940, he was serving in a Hungarian forced-labor camp. While at labor, he thought of a new mathematical problem—counting the edges of a particular type of graph. Thirty-six years later, while suffering from a fatal illness, he recalled the pleasure this problem gave him: "I cannot properly describe my feelings during the next few days. The pleasure of dealing with a quite unusual type of problem, the beauty of it, the gradual approach of the solution, and finally the complete solution made these days really ecstatic."[1]

As a graduate student in the 1950s, I was taught the positivist model of psychological research: a focus on precise, limited problems of behavior. Broader human questions that motivated me were put aside as unscientific. As time went on, however, I found that narrow focus constricting. My desire to understand how human beings at the edge of danger could find freedom in the life of the mind remained unsatisfied. Yet I couldn't escape the positivist model while I was at the university where that model was shaped. Twenty years later, I moved to the Southwest and encountered the vastly different ways Native Americans visualize thoughts. Here, at last, I became ready to explore the issues that had motivated my choice of a profession.

It is quite a leap from Budapest to Rough Rock, Arizona, but the diversity of thought and the impact of culture as part of thought were vividly manifested in both places. For Navajos, the creation of beauty in paintings and ordinary artifacts has a life-sustaining power in the midst of harsh conditions they often face. Seeing this power, I asked myself: What sustains creative and intellectual endeavor?

When I started this book, my questions—about diversity of thinking, about the sustained efforts of creative individuals, about the move from intent to realization—seemed to be at the margin of what was being studied in cognitive psychology. And the little literature that was available was fragmented. Therefore, I decided to interview creative thinkers from a variety of backgrounds who agreed to talk about how they work. In these interviews the intensity with which creative people live their work was unmistakable. Many of them echoed Albert Einstein's belief that people come to art and science to create "a simplified and lucid image of the world," hoping in this way to attain some peace and serenity amid the cruelties of daily life.[2]

Powerful common themes emerged from the words of these one hundred very different creative individuals. Their voices contributed to the shape of this book. They also made me see that no single exploration can answer a question as ever-present and intriguing as the nature of creativity.

Since *Notebooks of the Mind* was first published in 1985, thinking about thinking and research on creativity have blossomed. Most significant in this expansion are the scholars who address the complexity of the human mind. There is a growing "thought community" of creativity researchers, cognitive psychologists, and neuroscientists who reject reductionist approaches,[3] or what Jerome Bruner called "ways of thinking that grew out of yesterday's physics."[4] The focus of these scholars is on the transforming possibilities of creative work. They also study how knowledge is passed from one generation to the next. The result is not a single, unified theory of creativity, but a shared framework of connected ideas. This book is part of this broader effort. It is part of an important shift in creativity studies, from a purely person-centered approach to one that includes the dynamic and social aspects of creative cognition.

This change of perspective is demanding because it challenges the image of the lonely creative genius that has been part of the Western mindscape for generations. This image of a solitary person influences our conception of human nature and the way we try to measure creativity. And for most of this century, creativity was studied by identifying the traits, abilities, and thinking styles of creative persons.[5] In this approach the investigator compares individuals using a battery of tests. In contrast, the emerging framework, and the one governing this book, no longer focuses narrowly on the creative personality as a set of traits, but sees creativity as a dynamic system. One of the architects of this framework, the psychologist Howard Gruber, sees creative work as an evolving system that is developmental, pluralistic, and interactive. In his groundbreaking study of Charles Darwin, Gruber analyses this scientist's notebooks as a springboard for studying the many aspects of his creative trajectory. In the recent *Creative People at Work*, co-edited by Gruber and Doris Wallace, the creative lives of artists and scientists are studied in an effort to uncover what sustains their creativity over a lifetime.[6] There is a deep, continuing kinship between their work and mine. We share a commitment to document the complex traces of creative thought, and we favor notebooks, journals, letters, scientific records, and interviews as resources for understanding the creative process.

Another approach that is similar in spirit comes from creativity research Mihaly Csikszentmihalyi. In 1965 he began a longitudinal study of several hundred young art students, marking the beginning of his influential career. He and his co-workers hoped to predict the success of the participating young artists over the ensuing decades, but they found that individual characteristics (including the researchers' own interesting notions of problem finding) could not explain why some artists "produced work that in the course of time would be judged creative while others did not."[7] A broader, more comprehensive approach was needed. Csikszentmihalyi subsequently suggested a dynamic model in which creativity is the result of the interaction of three shaping forces: (1) the domain, an organized body of knowledge about a particular topic; (2) the field, which selects promising variations from a domain; and (3) the person, who brings about changes in the domain. To illustrate this systems approach to creativity, Csikszentmihalyi drew on the history of art, particularly the first glimmers of the Renaissance in Florence.[8]

Over the years, like many of my colleagues, however, I have found that the study of creativity requires tools not furnished by psychology. Creativity demands multiple perspectives, including those of historians of science, literary critics, sociologists, and *experienced thinkers* engaged in creative work. This book is based on many such accounts. From a positivist point of view, such a combination of objective and subjective approaches may be seen as lacking scientific rigor. In fact, at the time of its first publication, *Notebooks of the Mind* was considered by some to be at the margin of traditional psychology. But now it is part of a powerful new paradigm of qualitative research, sharing interdisciplinary, interactive approaches of a growing community of creativity researchers.

Howard Gardner, a leading member of this community, was confronted with marginalization when he first developed his theory of multiple intelligences in 1983.[9] His thesis that human cognition is multidimensional was originally resisted by psychometric experts of intelligence, only to be embraced a decade later by thousands of educators. He addressed the issue of marginality again in his book *Creating Minds* in 1993, where he wrote of works at the edge of a domain and of their ensuing impact. There he described the ways that creative individuals are driven by a tension between their emerging perspectives and the constraints of established paradigms. To bring his theory to life, he profiled seven creative thinkers from the modern era, each of whom embodied a different cluster of intelligences—for example, Sigmund Freud, who exemplified intrapersonal intelligence, and Martha Graham, who exhibited bodily-kinesthetic intelligence.[10]

The theme that links Gardner's work with this book is a shared emphasis on the breadth of human competencies. A central claim in *this* work is that there is a diversity of representational codes or languages of the mind—a position I have recently called "cognitive pluralism."[11] In both theories, language is but one of several codes (or symbol systems) that constitute human thought. Our approaches contrast with theorists who favor imagistic thought or verbal thought to the exclusion of other modalities. These are important commonalities since the two theories were developed independently of each other. At the same time, there are significant differences in the way Gardner and I view the social, cultural, and individual sources of cognitive diversity. My approach is based on a Vygotskian, sociocultural theory of the mind, while Gardner's theoretical roots are in Freud and Piaget. I will next look at the way these different perspectives inform current debates in the cognitive sciences.

Cognitive pluralism

Thinking about the nature and diversity of mental representations reaches back to the Greeks. It is also a hotly debated contemporary concern. Aristotle believed that we think and remember in images, and many cognitive theorists favor such a "monistic" stance which ascribes an exclusive role to language, or images, or a "computational mentalese"[12] while ignoring other symbolic codes. The psychologist Rudolf Arnheim argues that thinking is primarily visual, and that thinking and seeing are dynamically interconnected. The neuroscientists Antonio Damasio proposes that "images are probably the main content of our thoughts, regardless of the sensory modality in which they are generated."[13]

Other theorists favor pluralistic models. Steve Kosslyn includes verbal and auditory images, verbal propositions, musical and mathematical notational systems as part of the content of thought.[14] Gardner bases his pluralistic position on neurological, evolutionary, and cross-cultural evidence. He writes: "To my way of thinking the mind has the potential to deal with several different kinds of *content*, but a person's facility with one content has little predictive power about his or her facility with other kinds. In other words, genius (and *a fortiori*, ordinary performance) is likely to be specific to particular contents: human beings have evolved to exhibit several intelligences and not to draw variously on one flexible intelligence."[15]

In reflecting in 1993 on the development of his pluralistic position—a decade after the first publication of *Frames of Mind*—Gardner suggests that he "centered the multiple intelligences far more within the skull of a single individual" than he would today,[16] pointing out that there has been a shift in the field toward a more social conception of human thinking and creativity.

Notebooks of the Mind anticipated this shift. It is shaped and sustained by the sociocultural approach to human development, thinking, language, and creativity. The ideas of L. S. Vygotsky (1896–1934)—the originator of the sociocultural framework—provide the foundation for this exploration of creativity. But as in many structures, this foundation is visible only to those looking for it. In the first edition of this book, many complex Vygotskian notions were kept in the background. They were discerned by knowledgeable readers without being fully explained. My reasons for such a strategy included the nature of Vygotsky's writing. His ideas are often cryptic. The reader must work through them again and again. This quality can be explained in part by the conditions of his short life. He contracted tuberculosis at an early age and, during his terminal illness, worked with fitful bouts of energy, leaving many unpublished manuscripts. For thirty years after his death, his work was largely ignored both in the West and the East.

This situation changed in 1962 when his classic *Thought and Language* was published in the United States.[17] Since then, Vygotsky's ideas have become increasingly available to a worldwide readership. Central to his approach is a view of the mind which extends beyond the "skull," which does not situate thinking in the confined spaces of the individual brain or mind. Instead, he proposes a sustained dynamic between other humans both present and past, books, the rest of our material and nonmaterial culture, and the individual engaged in symbolic activity. For Vygotsky, interaction with caregivers, peers, teachers, and the material world is the basis of intellectual development. As I show in this book, shared experience is crucial in the development of creative individuals. I explore the relationship between interdependence and the fashioning of a personal voice in the varied contexts of literature, music, and science.

While interest in Vygotsky's social and participatory views of learning has grown steadily, few of his notions have been applied to the study of creativity. The primary arena for testing his analyses is in education, particularly literacy studies. Although my involvement with Vygotskian theory goes back to the sixties, I found it a complex task to extend his theory to include creativity. Part of my challenge back then resulted from my participation in two groups which traditionally ignored each other. Creativity researchers gave limited recognition to sociocultural ideas, and Vygotskians were generally reluctant to discuss creativity. This book is a bridge between these two thought communities, each of which has grown in size and influence in the last ten years.

During this period of rapid growth, starting in the 1980s, the connection between these two independent "networks of enterprises"— creativity researchers and sociocultural theorists—became clearer to some participants. During this same period, some of Vygotsky's writings on imagination were translated into English. And recently David Feldman, a student of prodigies and an influential creativity researcher, acknowledged the profound impact of Vygotsky on his own work and on the field. At first, Feldman as well as most of his colleagues based their work on Piaget's epistemological framework. But his theoretical focus began to change as he considered the concept of novelty in thought and domain-specific development. Yet the change was slow. Up to this time most influential theories in psychology had focused on individual development (Piaget, for example) or on the dynamics of motivated thought within the human organism, following Freud. These preeminent theories served as starting points for many theorists studying development and creativity. But once creativity researchers began to examine creative lives in depth (including Feldman's own work on prodigies), they became increasingly constrained by theories that limited them to an individual focus. In 1993, in the preface to the second edition of *Beyond Universals in Cognitive Development*, Feldman writes that the enormous growth of interest in the sociocultural writings of the Russian psychologist L. S. Vygotsky in the last decade "and a decline in Piaget's hold on the field of cognitive development" were linked to broad concerns with diversity.[18] Moreover, he detected a relationship between theories of multiple intelligence and a decline in "all-purpose" universalistic theories, since these pay scant attention to cultural and cognitive pluralism.

In theories which posit universal stages of growth, development is seen as fueled primarily by biological forces. In contrast, sociocultural theories stress the constant dynamic between internal and external forms of human activity. One interesting example of such an interaction can be seen in philosopher Hannah Arendt's account of the role of language in thought. As she sees it, "discursive thought is inconceivable without words already meaningful."[19] It is a depiction that resonates with philosophers, writers, and social scientists for whom the inner voice is ever-present in thinking. Yet she adds that there are cultural variations in the forms and roles of language and their connections to other symbol systems. Her example is the highly visual character of Chinese writing, in which "the power of words is supported by the power of the written sign, the image."[20] By including images in her conception, Arendt differs from Arnheim, as well as the team of linguist Jerry Fodor and psychologist Zenon Pylyshyn, who developed a computational language of thought[21]—or to put it another way, a single, internal code. Arendt, while favoring language, also proposes a link between external forms of symbol systems—alphabetical or hieroglyphic writing systems—and internal codes. In doing so, she broadens her monistic approach and goes beyond a single, universal concept of a language of thought.

I take a similar stance in this book, and claim that there is a relationship between external and internal forms of symbolization. In constructing meaningful representations of experience, children and adults appropriate culturally patterned modes of reflection and expression. I describe some of these verbal, kinesthetic, and visual modes in the early chapters of this work. The development of this pluralistic model of thinking was first motivated by my observation of Native American children in the Southwest. Their reliance on visual symbols in play and in communication with others—frequently across language barriers—differs sharply from my own upbringing in the highly verbal culture of Central Europe. The search for a theoretical framework that could accommodate these varied modes of thought is described in this work. The resulting approach, cognitive pluralism, addresses contemporary concerns about diversity. It also structures my discussion of creative development in visual, verbal, musical, mathematical, and scientific domains.

I make the claim that diversity of inner representational modes exists, just as there is a diversity of expressive means by which thinkers convey their discoveries to others. Such diversity is critical to our understanding of thinking and creativity. In addition, I claim that there is a commonality among these diverse codes, a shared dynamic that transforms modes of thought into communicative forms.

My understanding of Vygotsky's approach to such diversity was deepened during the writing of this book, and during the subsequent decade. When I first read *Thought and Language*, like many other readers, I interpreted his statement, "Words play a central role not only in the development of thought but in the historical growth of consciousness as a whole," to mean that language and *only* language is critical to human symbolic endeavors.[22] Such an interpretation is not surprising, because Vygotsky did consider language as the *primary* vehicle of conscious thought. His focus on language in thinking is linked to his own life as a young Jewish man in Russia. His daughter recently recalled the rich verbal culture of his home and his love of poetry.[23] But his early interests and achievements were in the humanities, social sciences, and philosophy, in addition to psychology. To his analysis of the relationship of language and thought, he brought scholarly breadth, creative insights, and a deep love of words. The resulting work is inspiring. *Thought and Language* is one of the classics of the human sciences.

In the present book, Vygotsky's influence is strongest in Chapter 5, which looks at verbal thinking. He saw inner speech as serving a variety of functions: planning, reflection, and reordering and transforming the known into new perspectives and insights. Vygotsky focused on the spoken forms of this process; I add in this book new evidence drawn from the notebooks of creative individuals of what I have come to call "inner speech writing." This is a condensed, even cryptic form of written language, which allows "experienced thinkers" to keep abreast of their rapid bursts of thought. Such notes exemplify the packed, telegraphic features of inner speech described by Vygotsky. This chapter, with its applications and additions to Vygotsky's thinking, has been widely used by teachers to help students understand his complex notions.

As I worked on other chapters in this volume, I started to see a broader pattern of cognitive dynamics, of condensation and expansion, beyond those characterizing language as described in Chapter 5. I found planning notes, drawings, and a generative use of mathematical notations in the personal documents of creative individuals. I called these varied jottings for the self "notebooks of the mind." Some of them were later expanded and refined into accomplished works.

At the first publication of this book, my expansion of Vygotskian theory met with bafflement from some colleagues. The pluralistic stance in this book, concerning diverse languages of the mind, was disturbing to their interpretations of Vygotsky's position about the primacy of language in thought. I understood their concern, as my own early interpretation of his theory had been akin to theirs. But since then, several developments have supported the pluralistic position of this work. One is Howard Gardner's continuing work in multiple intelligence. Another is the theory of psychological tools (such as language, scientific diagrams, etc.) proposed by a leading Vygotskian, James Wertsch. And third is the work of several cross-cultural researchers who have documented culturally diverse modes of symbolization. We have already looked at Howard Gardner's multiple intelligences, so let's turn now to James Wertsch's theory.

Borrowing a metaphor from Ludwig Wittgenstein, Wertsch writes of the "tool kit" of psychological processes that mediate mental functioning.[24] While physical tools are directed toward the external world, psychological tools are symbol systems used by individuals engaged in thinking. Wertsch sees these psychological tools as symbol systems that mediate activities and represent their meanings. In describing these tools, Wertsch quoted a passage from Vygotsky I had not seen when writing this book:

> The following can serve as examples of psychological tools and their complex systems: language; various systems of counting; mnemonic techniques; algebraic symbol systems; works of art; writing; schemes, diagrams, maps and mechanical drawings; all sorts of conventional signs; and so on.[25]

My findings support this view of varied psychological tools. I write of *languages* of the mind, where Wertsch writes of psychological tools. Both formulations view human thinking as varied and adaptive to historical and cultural circumstances.

The pluralistic ideas of *Notebooks of the Mind* have also been used and expanded by scholars engaged in cross-cultural research. The developmental psychologist Barbara Rogoff offers an argument close to those in this book:

> Each generation of individuals in any society inherits, in addition to their genes, the products of cultural history, including technologies developed to support problem solving. Some of the technologies that have received attention as inherited tools for handling information include language systems that organize categories of reality and structure ways of approaching situations, literate practices to record information and transform it through written exercises, mathematical systems that handle numerical and spatial problems, and mnemonic devices to preserve information in memory over time. . . . Japanese abacus experts, for example, evidence specific but powerful consequences of their skill in the use of the abacus as a tool for mathematical operations. They use interiorized representations of the abacus that allow them to mentally calculate without an abacus as accurately as with an abacus, and often faster.[26]

This description of psychological tools is informed by a Vygotskian perspective. It demonstrates the way in which a socially constructed artifact—the abacus—becomes part of internalized thinking processes, even shaping them in significant ways.

There is a useful complementarity between cross-cultural studies and research in creativity. Cross-cultural researchers identify specific contexts in which development takes place, describing the various ways of knowing. And in many ways, cross-cultural work sets the stage for our study of cognitive pluralism. But in any culture only a subset of human possibilities are fully realized.

Those studying creative lives, on the other hand, look at more specific details. They study ways that different technologies, characteristic psychological tools, and scientific and artistic symbol systems are internalized and expanded in the works of creative individuals over the course of a lifetime. The study of creative lives provides specificity to our understanding of the languages of the mind. In Chapter 4, for example, I describe the many kinds of pictorial models and their impact on the development of young painters. I write of their voracious visual appetite, of their studying early and contemporary masters, their fascination with photographic illustrations, their immersion in art books. In short, I write of their internalization of visual conventions and culture, which for many artists is necessary for their subsequent transformation of the known into new forms and expressions.

These processes of internalization do not take place in isolation. They are embedded in apprenticeships with parents, mentors, and distant teachers. Vital relationships across generations and between peers are documented throughout this book. When these collaborations are successful, novices develop fluency, and learn how experienced artists and scientists think. At the same time, such collaborations offer renewal for the experienced individual and the use of shared knowledge for the novice's development of self. From a Vygotskian point of view, these interactions are central to the transformation of the novice into an experienced thinker. His well-known concept of the zone of proximal development is relevant in this context: he proposes that what a child can do with assistance today, he or she will be able to do independently in the future. The primary application of this concept has been to learning and development among school children. In this work, I broaden his approach to include creative apprenticeships. Some of the best-depicted examples of the transformation of joint experiences into the foundation of an individual's creative development are drawn from the lives of composers in Chapter 6. These musical apprenticeships reveal the productive tension that exists between social connectedness and individual voice—a recurrent theme in many creative lives.

Notebooks of the Mind challenges narrow interpretations of Vygotsky's work. I hope this book can inspire new readings of some of Vygotsky's key ideas and provide an entry for the newcomer to Vygotsky's thinking.

Introduction

What is thinking? How much will we ever know of the ever-present but changing human mind? When we ask about its nature, we ask questions of concern to all men and women. Interest in the processes of thought is an ageless one. It is linked to the search for an understanding of our species, *homo sapiens*. Today this inquiry is shaped by the tools and quests of this age, by preoccupations of the last decades of the twentieth century.

Human beings are characterized by a great plasticity of body and mind; however, this plasticity can be narrowed by habit and by the fears of the unknown. The philosopher Hannah Arendt has suggested that habitual responses (a certain kind of thoughtlessness) protect one from the burdensome aspects of reality, "against the claim on our . . . attention that all events and facts make by virtue of their existence. If we were responsive to this claim all the time, we would soon be exhausted."[1] While the power of thought is threatened by trivia, by the enormous spill of information present today, such power is necessary for our survival as a species. As we approach the limits of the abundance of the earth, and our tenure is threatened by nuclear war, we need to learn anew how to plan and construct a humane and lasting world. To do that, we need to mobilize fully the creative possibilities of the mind.

But our knowledge of thinking is still limited. While we are awed by the accomplishments of the gifted in the arts and sciences, our study of thought has largely ignored them. The basic assumption that governs *this* work is that a powerful resource for the understanding of thinking is provided by the self-knowledge of the creative individuals among us.

The diverse thought processes of artists, scientists, philosophers, and historians are gathered and analyzed in these pages. Their thoughts on thinking were elicited in the course of more than a hundred interviews. Beside these conversations, the reading of letters, journals, biographies and autobiographies, as well as works in progress, have formed the basis of this study of the notebooks of the mind. In the past, these promising materials were neglected by behavioral scientists, a neglect that was noted by the American psychologist, Jerome Bruner, when he wrote that "we know little about the use of the notebook, the sketch, the outline in reflective work."[2] These reflective sources are extensively used in this study of the mind, and their inclusion distinguishes this inquiry from the growing number of experimental studies of thought in the cognitive sciences.

Some aspects of human thinking can be studied effectively in the laboratory. These include investigations of short-term memory, perceptual and verbal comprehension tasks, and certain kinds of problem-solving activities. Investigators as disparate as Herbert Simon and Jean Piaget have obtained valuable records of the covert processes of thought when they encouraged their subjects to verbalize while engaged in diverse, problem-solving tasks. These methods, now called "protocol analysis," are widely used by cognitive scientists, students of writing, as well as developmental psychologists. The neurophysiological studies of hemisphere specialization have also enriched our knowledge of the mind by helping to differentiate between the dynamics of verbal and visual thought processes, and their respective linkage to the left and right sides of the brain. Morton Hunt describes these rapidly developing fields of study as follows:

> Only within the past generation has there appeared the
> empirical discipline called cognitive science—a hybrid
> of psychology, computer science, psycholinguistics, and
> several other fields—that uses experimental methods
> to explore those unseeable processes and events that are
> at once the most commonplace and yet the most
> marvelous of human accomplishments.[3]

The astonishing increase in number and sophistication of the studies of the mind within the last two decades attests to the compelling nature of this subject. But the search for ... roots of thought primarily through works of experimental scientists imposes an undue limitation on this endeavor. It is beyond the reach of these methods to specify the cognitive dynamics of slowly elaborated, complex, or creative mental work. To unravel such sustained efforts is the focus of this work.

My approach has been to combine theoretical analyses with descriptive accounts of what Jerome Bruner has described as "the swift flight of man's mind at its best." Although a considerable portion of this book is based upon reports and documents obtained from artists and scientists—letters, notebooks, and interview materials—a sole reliance upon them would result in a mere catalogue of the many ways of knowing. The objective of this work is to delineate the similarities and differences between thought in its mundane and creative forms, and to complement and extend the analyses of thinking obtained from laboratory studies with a broad, theoretical, and interdisciplinary approach to thought.

The theoretical writings of the cognitive psychologists L. S. Vygotsky, Jerome Bruner, and Howard Gruber have provided me with the beginnings of a framework for this endeavor. Each of these psychologists has addressed boldly the exploration of the mind. And although their work and their ideas differ in many ways, they have in common their opposition to the widely held belief within psychology that the study of the mind is beyond the resources of twentieth century science. Their view stresses the processes of thinking rather than its products; a developmental approach that focuses on the many transformations of thinking; and exploration of the ways in which humans are engaged in the construction of integrated and generative systems of thought. The premise that underlies their work is well expressed by Stephen Toulmin, who has written that Vygotsky's writings offer:

> a novel unification of Nature and Culture that acknowledges the variety and richness of historical and cultural differences, without ignoring the general processes involved in socialization and enculturation.[4]

A similar commitment governs this inquiry: I am interested in discovering the shared dynamics in the various processes of thought, while recognizing and exploring developmental, cultural, and historical differences in the mastery of thinking.

Thoughtful Accounts of Thinking

To attempt to answer the question *What is thinking?*, I have turned to experienced and productive thinkers. These individuals devote many hours each day to intellectual labor, the success of which is dependent upon their self-knowledge. Their insights are of great value in illuminating the largely hidden processes of the mind. In this inquiry, experienced thinkers have been asked to address some of the issues raised by the many students of thought: How do human beings achieve both continuity and novelty in their thinking? How can one pull together into a whole, fragments of reality that have previously been experienced as separate in space and time by the thinker? And what nourishes sustained productivity in the lives of creative individuals?

While such questions are important in shaping a broad exploration of the mind, one has to be careful not to impose too rigid and prescribed a structure upon individuals chosen for an interview. I tried to design a flexible format for my conversations with the participants, and also to provide them with an experience of some use. In the latter objective I was encouraged by the comment of Nevitt Sanford, who wrote:

> How do people benefit from being interviewed? They have
> a chance to say things for which there had not
> previously been an appropriate audience. They can put
> into words some ideas and thoughts that had been only
> vaguely formulated. . . .[5]

My first interviews were with physicists and mathematicians, for it was their accounts that have highlighted for me the importance of visual thinking in the course of discovery. I had already learned that to ask a person "How do you think?" blocked any ease in self-report. A more effective approach was to introduce early during a session an account furnished by someone else in the participant's profession. A successful paragraph to use in this way was Albert Einstein's answer to the French mathematician Jacques Hadamard, in which he describes some of his ways of thinking:

> The words or the language, as they are written or spo-
> ken, do not seem to play any role in my mechanisms of
> thought. The physical entities which seem to serve as
> elements in thought are certain signs and more or less
> clear images which can be voluntarily reproduced or
> combined.[6]

Some of the physicists were able to use this self-description by Einstein as a starting point for discussing their own inner processes of thought. As my work progressed, I used a variety of means to initiate discussion: I paraphrased self-reports by other participants; at times I sent a few questions in advance to an interviewee, who asked for a chance to think ahead. The sessions became longer: once interviewees became involved in sharing memories, ideas, anxieties, and successes, they volunteered more elaborate descriptions of their habits and processes of work. I learned to move the talk from the specificity of each individual's experience to eliciting broader descriptions. Some questions addressed whether an individual kept records of his/her promising ideas. At times I quoted Stephen Spender, who has written, "My method . . . is to write down as many ideas as possible, in however rough a form in notebooks. (I have at least twenty of these, on a shelf beside my desk, going back over fifteen years.) I then make use of these sketches and discard others."[7]

In preparation for my talk with the English writer Jessica Mitford, I had read most of her books and previous interviews conducted with her. She agreed to speak to me after a common friend called her, an approach that was helpful in establishing contact with a number of participants. I prepared a number of questions in advance. One of these was specific to Mitford's reported reliance upon her friends as readers and critics of her works in progress. After ten to fifteen minutes of talk based on the prepared questions, Mitford started to speak freely, recalling some of the events in her childhood which contributed to her becoming a writer:

> I used to write a fair amount as a child. We were all tremendous letter writers. I mean if one was away from home, one would write to one's sisters two or three times a week, all of them, and parents and such. We would illustrate them, the letters and everything else. . . . People used to say when I started doing *Hons and Rebels*, you write such good letters, so why don't you write a book?

In describing her methods of work, Mitford sketched an approach that was shared by others: "The first thing to do is to read over what you have done the day before and rewrite it. And then that gives you a lead into the next thing to do, and then it sort of goes. . . ." Her description illustrates "the dialogue between the thinker and his written words"[8] of which Jerome Bruner has written, and which is also vividly sketched in D. N. Perkins's *The Mind's Best Work*.

It was not always easy to ask relevant questions of individuals who treasured their time, and were somewhat weary of social scientists. I often sought the assistance of friends when preparing to work with an individual whose field I knew but slightly; they introduced me to the language that characterized discourse within such a field, and sometimes gave good suggestions for questions to ask of individuals I did not know.

The settings in which I spoke to the participants varied. Most of my interviews took place in the home or office of the interviewee, but there were some interesting exceptions: the choreographer Eliot Feld was rehearsing his company for a performance at the Delacorte Theater in New York's Central Park when we met. His assistant worked with the dancers while we sat on the hard bleachers, and Feld spoke of his work. The sight of the dancers furnished an interesting but at times diverting counterpoint to his words. Another memorable interview was one conducted with Aaron Copland in Santa Fe. He was between rehearsals with the Santa Fe Chamber Music Orchestra, enjoying walking through the plaza with his life-long friend, Harold Clurman, the director. We were given a quiet office in a downtown hotel for the interview, and while I addressed most of my questions to the composer Copland, some of the most interesting answers came from Clurman, who had observed his friend at work and play for more than fifty years. When I asked how he started a new work, the composer hesitated. Clurman suggested that the start was frequently a single musical phrase that the composer repeated many, many times. Copland smiled and commented, "It sounds rather dull the way you put it, [but] each time you repeat it you have different ideas as to where it might go."

These talks were always exciting for me: they provided an opportunity for the person being interviewed to express new ideas about him/herself and were full of surprises and unexpected turns of thought. All of these conversations included several themes: the earliest developments of the person's interests; the nature of his or her training and apprenticeships; the shaping of "invisible tools"—that is, their craft and creative intensity; some descriptions of daily routines; the biography of a recent work and reports of collaborative endeavors. There were questions about the individual's sources for new and generative ideas, and I probed, sometimes with difficulty, for the participant's insights concerning the more hidden, covert processes of thinking.

The hundred creative individuals who cooperated in this endeavor were not selected through traditional sampling methods. Instead, I relied on personal contacts, and the writing of many letters. And at times I was helped by chance in finding individuals who consented to be interviewed. (A list of those interviewed can be found at the end of the book.)

In one area, though, I was determined to create a balance—that between male and female participants. Traditionally the study of thought has been the domain of men; women were considered to be too subjective and lacking in the sustained commitment necessary for distinguished achievements, to be taken seriously as thinkers. These beliefs were unwittingly symbolized by the great French sculptor, Auguste Rodin. His well-known *Le Penseur* (The Thinker) is a seated, male figure. In the larger-than-life model exhibited in the garden of the Rodin museum in Paris, one sees the heavy head resting on a fist; the statue reveals taut and compact energy. In one of the rooms inside the Rodin museum there is another statue. It is a small head which bears the title *La Pensée* (Thought): the face is soft, the eyes are luminous, the brow is clear. The difference in the scale and the power of these two figures captures well the relative importance assigned to men and women in the traditional literature of the intellect, and the odd separation of "The Thinker" and the "Thought."

Notebooks of the Mind attempts to overcome this legacy of the traditional view of thought as a primarily masculine occupation. Women and men were interviewed in nearly equal numbers to form the descriptive accounts of thinking. The female as well as the male imagination in the arts and sciences was explored. The thrust for diversity and balance is part of the general approach in this book, where I seek to follow the advice of the British scientist P. B. Medawar:

> The analysis of creativity in all its forms is beyond the
> competence of any one accepted discipline. It requires a
> consortium of the talents: psychologists, biologists,
> philosophers, computer scientists, artists, and poets
> will all expect to have their say. That "creativity" is
> beyond analysis is a romantic illusion we must now
> outgrow.[9]

One form of Medawar's "consortium of talents" is provided by the many thinkers interviewed for this examination of the life of the mind. But the study of transcribed interviews affected my thinking as well, for it forced a shift in my focus as I wrote this book. My first working title was *The Leap*. I had hoped to penetrate those rapid moments of insight and discovery that have fascinated so many previous writers on creativity. As the work of analyzing the interviews proceeded, a different conception of sustained and productive work emerged: while some thought processes are indeed rapid and condensed, the transformation of those inner shorthands into artistically and intellectually convincing achievements requires craft, logic, mastery, and commitment. Ben Shahn, the painter, described the dialectics of creativity as "the long artistic tug-of-war between idea and image." It is this tension between idea and its realization, between an individual's "network of enterprises" (Howard Gruber's term) and the limitations of a single work—a tension which propels much of thinking—that became the new focus of *Notebooks of the Mind*.

The Languages of Thought

A new work of an artist may start with a phrase or that of a scientist may begin with an image, but each represents a nucleus of understanding that painstakingly unfolds through labor, craft, inspiration, and the careful nurturing of time that separates the beginner from those with experience. Great variations exist between artists and scientists, and even within a single field such as writing, in the ways in which experienced thinkers embark upon their work. But in all cases, the beginnings of creative endeavors are linked to one of the many "languages of thought."

The choice of such a language, or inner symbol system, is not always a conscious one. It is embodied in the history of an individual, beginning with his or her efforts at reflection that first developed in childhood. But the transformation of what is heard, seen, or touched is dependent upon the individual skill of the human mind in representing experience as images, as inner speech, as movement ideas. Through these varied languages of thought, the meanings of these experiences are stored and organized.

Experienced thinkers' reports and recollections aid in the depiction of the varied transformations that lead from the young child's play to the formation of a powerful, internal mode of representation. Of central importance to the formation of a language of thought, and to the development of one's talent, are the varied apprenticeships of intellectual and rtistic work.

The early chapters of this book deal with the development of thinking among those interviewed, and the ways in which these men and women, while young, were driven by their need to know and to ima-

have changed; institutionalization of instruction is one of the most important of these transformations. Still, parental interests and parental work are seen by creative men and women of our century as being influential in their development.

However, instead of directly teaching their children, as did Leopold Mozart, parents today are more likely to create settings and opportunities which affect the intellectual development of their offspring. Frequently neither parent nor child is aware at the time of the consequences of these kinds of opportunities.

The childhood experiences evoked by Noam Chomsky and by Margaret Drabble are representative of what psychologists found in more systematic studies of scientists and artists. Whether they were born into wealthy families or poor ones, their early lives were frequently nourished by lively conversations at home. Mothers of talented individuals were particularly helpful in encouraging and cultivating these early interests.[5]

Learning, playful learning, the chance to absorb at a young age specific stimulation, as was the case of Mozart, or more typically, an interest in learning and exploration that characterizes so many gifted individuals, may contribute to the *fluency* and ease in the work of some creative individuals. The flow of words, of visual associations, of musical themes, of scientific ideas, which are first experienced in the context of childhood wonder and games, may be part of the *informal apprenticeship* that gives strength and support to mature individuals when struggling with the more complex aspects of their craft. Drabble's discussion of her way of writing lends credence to such speculation:

> I do write terribly easily, and I write quickly, by which I
> don't mean a facile outpouring. The difficulties are all
> with the construction. But once I get the scene
> beforehand, then it does come very easily. The word is
> there, the word is always there.

Although many natural scientists do not settle on their chosen profession until college, or even graduate school, their recollections also reveal the impact of experiences in their homes. In his *Memories*, the biologist Julian Huxley wrote of "his embracing inquisitiveness and widespread curiosity." He recalled his mother, who died relatively young, as a person with a great love for literature, who read to her children frequently, and who, despite her responsibilities to a girls' school she founded and headed, found time to join her son and husband on walks: "and the two of them," Sir Julian recalled, "did a great deal to instill a love of nature into me, partly Wordsworthian, partly scientific."[6]

His parents' interests shaped some of his own explorations as a child, said Huxley. Most of all, his curiosity about birds, flowers, and even frogs:

> By the time I was eight I began to be interested in birds.
> We had a bird-table and there I learned to differentiate
> the tits. . . . And one day down Charterhouse Hill, I
> saw a queer little bird, blue-grey above and russet
> below: it was just a common nuthatch, but to me it was
> a revelation.[7]

This interest in birds continued through his college years:

> All through my Eton and Oxford days, I kept an elabo-
> rate bird diary, noting which species of birds I saw each
> day, their approximate number, whether they were
> singing, the nests I found (with the number of eggs or
> young) and notes on their peculiar behavior.[8]

The pleasure Sir Julian gained from his walks and his careful observations (a skill so basic to good scientific work) remained with him all his life. He speaks of his "enjoyment of nature and natural beauty," coupled with a sense of poetic wonder, "providing him with a refuge from his restlessness" and his bouts with depression.

It would be a mistake to see only a charming and childish curiosity in the early activities reported by these scientists and artists. They depict for us the ways in which they were filling up, in their youth, some invisible notebooks of their minds. Their wonder is mixed with lasting impressions; their play is pursued with intensity and determination. The shape of their more conscious efforts cannot be determined at such an early stage, but in their youth they collect some of the raw material they will draw on later. The discipline that will transform such material into novel and useful work will come later in their lives. Formal education helps some individuals to add sharper focus and understanding to their early observations, as recalled by Julian Huxley: "I was early initiated in the mystery of two kinds of flower, pin and thrub . . . but did not understand the mechanism until at Oxford I read Darwin's book on cross-fertization of plants."[9] The continuity of learning is illustrated by this xample.

A somewhat harder aspect to explain of the early experiences of intellectually productive individuals is the source of their intensity and absorption in their activities. In her book on *The Making of a Scientist*, Anne Roe reports on this quality among the sixty-four individuals she worked with. All revealed this singular purposefulness in their adult lives as well as in what is known of their youth.

Many of the people she interviewed had suffered personal loss in their childhood or had been ill for a long time while growing up. Certainly these traumatic events may have contributed to a singleness of mind that is important in the building of talent. In some biographies, more subtle conditions of life emerged as possible bases for the development of intensity, a quality that is an essential source of strength for intellectually productive individuals but which can also contribute to pain and friction in their relationship with colleagues and loved ones.

One such painful life was that of the neglected female member of the famous *Double Helix* team of researchers, Rosalind Franklin, whose life has recently attracted attention. She was born into a family of wealth and varied accomplishments, the child of loving and able parents. Her biographer, Ann Sayre, describes her family as follows: "The intensity of personal involvement was very great and it did not stop with the men in the family; the Franklin women worked beside the men, when they were not running ahead into causes and projects of their own."[10]

Rosalind was the first girl born to her parents; she had three brothers with whom she shared a rather free and active existence. She liked to work with her hands, and she was good at more abstract learning as well. As did many other scientists, she suffered from a prolonged illness as a child. Her strong need for independence and her longing to see the world may have been the result of this painful period of confinement and loneliness as a sick child.

As with many young women born into well-to-do families between the two world wars, she was subjected to conflicting pressures about her future. She was encouraged to use and develop her abilities to the fullest as a child and adolescent, but once she reached adulthood she was pressured to choose an avocation in the service professions befitting a rich young woman. However, Rosalind Franklin did not want to spend her life as a volunteer in social work—she was determined to be a scientist. While she learned from her family's tradition of intense determination, and from their skills at expressing their will, it was unfortunately her own father whom she had to first oppose in her drive toward her career. It was thus at an early age that she had to defend what she wanted and believed, and as a professional she continued to be confronted by opposition or neglect in the highly competitive and masculine settings of physical chemistry and biophysics. Rosalind Franklin's intense commitment to her work and her independence of mind were not viewed with favor by her colleagues, although she made a few friends during her brief career who were supportive of this singularly purposive woman scientist.

The early years of a number of intellectually talented individuals show a mixture of the rich wonder and challenges of childhood combined with the strains of illness and parental opposition. Consequently, the intense, talented child often has an ambivalent relationship with the adult world, which is in part the basis of the child's strength and range of experiences, but at the same time contributes to the child's disappointments and frustrations.

The playwright Lillian Hellman unravels such a skein of emotions in writing of her young self in *An Unfinished Woman*:

> It was in that tree that I learned to read, filled with the passion that can only come to the bookish, grasping, very young. . . . bewildered by almost all of what I read, sweating in the attempt to understand a world of adults I fled from in real life but desperately wanted to join in books.[11]

The biographical accounts and studies of creative individuals show many varieties in these complex patterns. Many traumatic events are recorded: early death of one parent; prolonged illnesses on the part of the child; transient childhood, as was the case of Lillian Hellman, who refers to her schooling as "a frantic tennis game"; or poverty, as in the lives of Maxim Gorky and Charles Dickens. And yet, one also encounters many recollections from richly stimulated, happy, and loved children who responded with intensity and fullness to early years free of any notably traumatic events. The work of all these individuals, whether their childhood was relatively carefree or not, is partly fueled by the drama, as well as the pleasures of their young years.

Of course, the view that the roots of creativity lie in childhood was presented in its strongest form by Sigmund Freud. He saw in the conflicts and wishes arising from the intricate fabric of family relations the motive force behind artistic and scientific labor. In depicting the way writers work, he wrote:

> A strong experience in the present awakens in the creative writer a memory of an earlier experience (usually belonging to his childhood) from which there now proceeds a wish which finds its fulfillment in the

creative work. The work itself exhibits elements of the
recent provoking occasion as well as of old memory.[12]

Undoubtedly, the fusion of the present and the past is an important
aspect of the creative process. But, to my mind, Freud's emphasis upon
the primarily wish-fulfilling aspects of scientific and artistic work and
his assumption that artists are basically neurotic over-simplify one of
the most powerful and healing thrusts of human efforts. Creative and
productive thought occur through many cycles and bursts; they are nourished by encouragement and fueled by both wonder and tension. The
man or woman who pursues solitary endeavors needs a personality capable of renewal and self-confidence.

New work is born out of the playfulness of the young, and the freshness of perception that does not wilt after childhood. But the process of
growth from exploration to the actual construction of a body of work is
prolonged, and it entails manifold links between the childish and the
most disciplined and purposeful efforts of which human beings are
capable.

"The potential of every human being of becoming an artist," asserts
the great French photographer Henri Cartier-Bresson, "remains unfulfilled without the individual's acquaintanceship and immersion into the
artistic traditions of the past, and the distinctiveness of his culture."
The depths of experience represented by the collective past of a civili-
zation must first be refined through the disciplines of human knowledge and then slowly internalized by the truly creative individual before
one can return with confidence, with a deepened vision and a mature
skill, to the intriguing questions of childhood.

Memories of Schools and Teachers

The evocations of childhood years, of friends and parents, of places where
the curious child had a chance to make discoveries, or the bookish
child to forget the world, are done in vivid detail. The descriptions of
schools on the other hand tend to be sparse and lifeless. Nevertheless,
many individuals who engage in such recollections either imply or ex-
plicitly recognize their assistance in expanding the scope of their youthful
interests.

Modern institutions designed to serve the purpose of transmitting
past knowledge, and sharpening the skills of young learners—our private
and public schools—have had mixed success in meeting their functions.
The assessments of schooling made by men and women of diverse

achievements vary from the severely critical to the mildly accepting. Some scientists and artists did enjoy school, particularly as they found there the setting in which they could start engaging in independent projects; others, however, tried to escape from classrooms and teachers as frequently as possible. For these latter individuals, schools were a boring and drab place; they sought an escape, as did Lillian Hellman in a fig tree, where she tried to satisfy intense wondering in reading, in solitary pursuits. But even she had to be taught to read by somebody!

The experiences of artists and scientists can contribute to the recurrent discussions about the nature of a central feature of contemporary societies—education. Some of the issues that emerge from their recollections deal with the nature of schooling. The self-knowledge necessary for sustained mental labor was gained by some in school at the same time that they were acquiring information about the subject matter of their specialized discipline; others, however, needed the personal touch inherent in tutorial relationships.

The English biologist Julian Huxley was one of those who progressed well in school. In the course of his carefully planned education, he found the right combination of hard work and enjoyment to carry him into his career. But even he reported that he responded with some "nervous mannerisms" to his parents' anxious concerns, for they wanted him to excel at Eton. While at school, Huxley was helped by the encouragement of his teachers, and particularly by opportunities offered to him—while still an adolescent—to engage in scientific projects in laboratory settings.

The decision to become a scientist is usually made by an individual once he or she has had the chance to engage in independent work. Biologists, physicists, and some of the social scientists studied by Anne Roe reported this work as crucial to their career. The men (her study was limited to male subjects) were past their teens when they were able to specify career choices. As children, some of them shared the pastime that so intrigued Sir Julian Huxley: they, too, kept field records of flowers and birds. Most of them were not, however, the offspring of families with distinguished histories in scientific accomplishments, like the Huxleys. They were not aware in their youths of the possibility of a scientific career. In her study of the styles of thought, the backgrounds, and the interests of these sixty-four men, Ann Roe found that "in the stories of the social scientists and biologists, it becomes clear that the most important factor in the final decision to become a scientist is the discovery of the joys of research."[13] To most of these men, this discovery could not be made until they were seniors in college.[13]

Once young people engage in an independent project, they have the opportunity to focus upon the structure of the problem, to crystallize the query and eliminate superfluous information. The role that such an experience plays is important. Albert Einstein found fault with traditional education, particularly as it was practiced in the European gymnasiums, because it flooded the student with details and submerged the wondering and inventive young mind. He complained that "it is, in fact, nothing short of a miracle that the modern techniques of instruction have not yet entirely strangled the holy curiosity of inquiry." In his own education, Einstein's need to focus on critical questions was hampered by the many examinations required and by the cramming for these. However, in his chosen discipline of physics, he discovered early "how to scent out that which was able to lead to fundamentals and to turn aside everything else, from the multitude of things which clutter the mind and divert it from the essential."[14]

Similarly, the early years of learning in school were troubled ones for the great French physicist Pierre Curie, who was later, along with his wife Marie Curie, to become the recipient of the Nobel prize for the discovery of radium. His parents decided that he would gain more from instruction at home with the help of tutors than from lessons in a classroom. When writing her husband's biography, Marie Curie interpreted this decision in the light of her knowledge of the physicist's way of working and thinking: "It seems to me, that already from his early youth it was necessary for him to concentrate his thought with great intensity upon a certain definite object, in order to obtain precise results, and that it was impossible for him to interrupt or modify the course of his reflections to suit exterior circumstances."[15] Such a focused attention, necessary for outstanding scientific work, has rarely been encouraged in the context of a classroom.

The childhood and schooling of Marie Sklodovska Curie were quite different from those of her husband. She attended the schools of her native Poland and worked hard, receiving medals and recognition for her scholastic excellence. She spent a number of years giving private lessons to the children of the aristocracy, the usual means by which poor and talented young intellectuals survived. By saving money earned during those early years, she eventually reached Paris, where she continued a penurious existence but finally had the chance to work in scientific laboratories.

In Europe during the nineteenth century, private tutoring of gifted individuals, as well as those born into wealth, was frequent. Count Leo

Tolstoy, whose writings on education are now being rediscovered, spent his childhood in a home where eleven tutors were employed—"not counting the dancing master," writes Tolstoy's biographer, Henry Troyat.[16] The personality, appearance, and habits of these tutors are well remembered in the autobiographies of gifted individuals, as Count Tolstoy vividly evoked his teachers in his book *Childhood*. But children who attend public schools often do not recall those who have taught them. In part, the vividness of recall that characterizes the memories of tutors derives from the familiarity and emotional impact of the environment where the teaching takes place. School children, in contrast, who attend public institutions have to learn in an environment that usually lacks in color and distinctive sounds, and they have to share the attention of one teacher with thirty or more other pupils. In such a drab and difficult setting, when the child does develop a personalized relationship with one teacher among the many encountered through his or her schooling, it may make an impression of unique and lasting significance.

Growing up in a provincial town near the Jura mountains, Louis Pasteur had an undistinguished career as a young student in the country schools of rural France. His friends prized most his skills in drawing. His portraits revealed a keen sense of observation. But during this period no great talent of his was discovered. It was not until he attended a regional college, at Arbois, that his headmaster noticed that his observational skills were of significance beyond his interests in art. The relationship between Pasteur and this master sparked a new development in his life. His enthusiasm for scientific work increased as a result of this attention, and an important career was launched.

In most schools, where the attentions of a teacher are shared among many children, the opportunities to see an experienced individual at work in his or her profession are limited. But though the traditions of learning by apprenticeship are hard to realize, occasionally conditions resembling them do occur. In exclusive private schools, tutors still give personalized care to their pupils, and the facilities for independent work in the sciences and in the arts are available. Such were the settings in which Sir Julian Huxley was educated. But many other students of promise who are driven by their will and their poverty have learned to gain something from their more impersonal public schooling and, if fortunate, they may attract the attention of an imaginative and powerful teacher.

Though born into poverty, the young person who is raised in an intellectually stimulating environment and who has the benefit of personalized and exciting teaching, like Mozart, may have a rich and varied life of learning even at an early age. The comparison between Mozart and Beethoven suggested by Robert Craft has some interesting implications for the development of scientists as well. Many individuals mold their identity slowly without the benefit of much early stimulation either at home or in their schools. These creative persons test their talent over a long period of time, and they tend to labor over their creations as well. Such was the image Craft presented of Beethoven and of his methods of composing. Mozart, on the other hand, composed with ease. In one of his letters, Mozart depicts his method: "When I proceed to write down my ideas, I take out of the bag of my memories, if I may use that phrase, what has been previously collected into it the way I have mentioned. For this reason the committing to paper is done quickly enough, for everything is, as I have said before, already finished; and it rarely differs in paper from what it was in my imagination."[17] Of particular interest in this account is Mozart's emphasis upon his "bag of memories," which dates back to the playful period of his youth. Those in the sciences and in the arts who do not have quite the same fluency and ease in shaping their ideas, may resemble Beethoven. They construct their individual apprenticeships through years of formal schooling and through the many versions of their own work in self-schooling. At times, they may encounter good teachers, whose loving attention helps them to develop their talents and strengthen their self-respect. Such was the rare experience of Louis Pasteur.

There seems little doubt about the contributions to a scientist's development through inspired teaching and access to a laboratory for independent work. The contribution of teaching to the careers of artists presents a more complex issue, as so many of them see their lives as solitary and self-made. But some writers do recall the impact of a teacher.

A most moving tribute is written by James Baldwin, in his recent book *The Devil Finds Work*, to a young white woman who taught him, and encouraged him, when he was ten or eleven years old: "She had directed my first play and endured my first theatrical tantrums and had then decided to escort me into the world," he wrote. Bill Miller, as they called her then, encouraged his reading, discussed with him the movies he saw, shared with him some of her views on such world issues as fascism and revolution, and demonstrated to him that even a white person can act with courage in the face of white racism:

Bill took us on a picnic downtown once, and there was supposed to be ice cream waiting for us at a police station. The cops did not like Bill, didn't like the fact that we were colored kids, and did not want to give up the ice cream. I don't remember anything Bill said. I just remember her face as she stared at the cop, clearly intending to stand there until the ice cream all over the world melted or until the earth's surface froze, and she got us our ice cream, saying, "Thank you," I remember as we left.

In a different setting, Marta Weigle, a folklorist, speaks of her experience with a lovely, older Englishman who taught her in a boarding school in Northfield, Massachusetts:

He started out with Greek drama, and he just made it appear, that there is something you should know, because there is something that good people, *good* people in the fine sense of that word, would enthuse about, enjoy, find magnificent. . . . If you were to like or write good poetry, criticism, literature, you'd share that with them.

Once a week he would invite us to his cottage where he lived with his sisters. We would have tea. And he spent 15 minutes sitting next to each of us, talking. He set a standard, and if it were in you to meet this standard in some way, you would.

In the life of the adolescent the need to reach somebody by words, written words, is important, as the young person frequently feels too tentative for self-expression in the presence of those he or she respects and loves. Or, as in the case of Anaïs Nin, it may be the loved father who has left and whose presence she recalls by her writing: "The diary began as a diary of a journey, to record everything for my father. It was really a letter, so he could follow us into a strange land, know about us." For young persons in search of self-expression, a distant parent or a particularly caring and gifted teacher may become their cherished audience as well as their source of guidance.

The traditions of apprenticeship have changed since those of ancient Greece, where Plato immortalized the dialogues between Socrates and his young disciples of Athens, or since those in Renaissance Italy. There the great painters of Florence—for instance, Leonardo da Vinci, Raphael, and Michelangelo—learned their craft as apprentices in the workshops of master painters. During their apprenticeships, learning took place by observing the master's work and by heeding their occasional comments. The strong bonds established between two generations engaged in a shared task have always characterized the apprenticeship experience, and the impact of personalized teaching is frequently recalled by those who have benefited from it.

The great Mexican mural painter Diego Rivera remembered how he was singled out of a large group of art students when barely thirteen years old. He was then attending the Art Institute of San Carlos, Mexico. One of his early masters at the school was a man named Rubell, who had been a pupil of Ingres. Rivera wrote of the incident:

> One day, when a class of about fifty students was paint-
> ing a model, he singled me out. He found fault with my
> drawing, but he said, "Just the same, what you are
> doing interests me. First thing tomorrow morning come
> to my studio." The other students flocked around to see
> what had interested old Rubell to extract an invitation to
> his studio, to which he had admitted no student for
> twenty years. They could see nothing, and ascribed his
> enthusiasm to a senile whim. But the next day the old
> man told me what he discovered in my work was an
> interest in life and movement. Such an interest, he said,
> is the mark of a genuine artist. "These objects we call
> paintings" he went on "are attempts to transcribe to a
> plane surface essential movements of life."[19]

Diego Rivera was a rebellious young fellow, and he did not last long in the academy. He had other teachers as well, such as a man who worked in a shop as an engraver, who taught him "that nothing can be expressed except through the force of feeling, that the soul of every masterpiece is powerful emotion."[20] But the lessons taught him did not affect him immediately. In his autobiography he realizes, as do many others who write of their life in their maturity, that intellectual and artistic development is slow, and that it does not take place as a straight and continuous process: "Of course the import of this teaching was lost upon me—and for many years afterward. Finding myself in art was to be a long and painful process."[21]

In art as well as science, learning that leads to creative work requires an individual to work at it. Creativity lies in the capacity to see more sharply and with greater insight that which one already knows or that which is buried at the margin of one's awareness.

Teachers from the Past

The great cellist Pablo Casals knew the importance of the bond of musical tradition with his personal creativity; he started his day by playing, first thing in the morning, the Fugues and Preludes of Bach. He explained the role of this ritual in his life to his friend J. Ma. Corredor, author of *Conversations with Casals*. "This music is the perfect elixir of youth. It refreshes the spirit and induces a calm and cheerful frame of mind for the day's activities."[22] In the course of these talks, Casals described many steps in his learning, and the help he received during his long life from his parents, his teachers, and his friends.

Pablo Casals was born in Vendrell, a small Catalan village. He was the son of a church organist, who taught him his first lessons in music. As a child he was intrigued by the sounds of different instruments and by the wandering musicians, dressed in clown costumes, who visited small villages. As soon as the boy's feet touched the pedals of the organ he joined his father in playing; he also sang and wrote music at a very young age. Although his father was delighted by his son's musical talents, he nevertheless wanted him to apprentice himself to a local carpenter. He did not believe that any musician could make a living by music alone. But Casals did receive professional instruction in music in both his home town and in Barcelona. In the midst of a demanding and frequently lonely preparation for his career, the discovery of Bach's music was a source of wonder and joy:

> This was the great event of my life: my father, who had already bought me a full-size 'cello, came to see me once a week. We used to go to the different music shops in Barcelona in search of scores of serious music for the weekly concerts of classical music, given at the Café Tost where I played solos. One day, quite by chance, I came across the *Six Suites* of Bach in one of these musical shops. I was thirteen then. I wondered what could be hidden there, what mystery lay behind the words: *Six Suites for 'Cello Solo*. I did not even know they existed, neither did my teacher, and no one had ever spoken to me about them. It was the great revelation of my life. I felt immediately that it was something of exceptional

importance. On the way home I hugged my treasures: I
started playing them in a wonderful state of excitement,
and it was only after twelve years' practice of them
that I made up my mind to play them in public.[23]

Painters likewise eagerly study the work of their predecessors during
their apprenticeships. When still a young man, Michelangelo would
spend many hours in this way, copying the work of various fourteenth
and fifteenth century painters. It was after his friends urged him to expand the scope of his interests that Michelangelo became interested in
ancient sculpture—the exposure to which later helped him to develop
his own distinctive style.

In many aspects of their education, artists tend to fashion their own
approaches to their work. They are largely self-taught. But their search
for meaningful models from the past is not always successful. While
both Michelangelo and Casals discovered important sources for their
work at an early age, others are detoured in their creative growth. The
prevalent fashions of the times may mislead them and hinder their development. When a style is merely imitated, no fusion between the
artist's temperament and the direction in which the person is moving
takes place. Such a mismatch was described by the British novelist Somerset Maugham, whose training was in medicine, and who taught himself, at times by the recognition of his mistakes, how to write. He described one such period in his book, *The Summing Up*:

At that time a florid prose was admired. Richness of texture was sought by means of a jewelled phrase and
sentences stiff with exotic epithets: the ideal was a
brocade so heavy with gold that it stood up by
itself. . . . I was young, lusty, and energetic; I wanted
fresh air, action, violence, and I found it hard to breathe
in that dead heavily scented atmosphere. . . . But I would
not listen to my common sense. . . . I was intoxicated by
the colour and rareness of the fantastic words that
thickly stud the pages of *Salome*. Shocked by the poverty
of my own vocabulary, I went to the British Museum
with pencil and paper and noted down the names of
curious jewels, the Byzantine hues of old enamels, the
sensual feel of textiles, and made elaborate sentences to
bring them in. Fortunately I could never find an

opportunity to use them and they lie there yet in an old
notebook ready for anyone who has a mind to write
nonsense.[24]

Even those artists and scientists who have learned their discipline in schools and academies, and who were exposed to the classics in their respective fields, do not always gain from these experiences. The survey approach in education offers both too much and too little for the individual who intends to become a writer, painter, or physicist. In their need to discover their own teachers from the past, there is recognition of the importance of an intense and personal kinship that results when the work of another evokes a special resonance in them. Once such a bond is established, the learner explores those valued works with an absorption which is the hallmark of creative individuals. In this way, they stretch, deepen, and refresh their craft and nourish their intelligence, not only during their early years of apprenticeship, but repeatedly, throughout the many cycles of their work-lives.

The British art critic John Berger in *Toward Reality* has engaged in an interesting discussion of the veneration of the classics in modern times. In the chapter entitled "Lessons from the Past," he contends that we see "too easy a confirmation of the continuity of human culture."[25] To him, true learning and creative insight based on study of the art of the past requires a consciousness that goes beyond formalism of imitation; it requires grappling with the realities captured in the works of art.

> Only if we recognize the mortality of art shall we cease to
> stand in such superstitious awe of it; only then shall we
> consider art expendable and so have the courage to risk
> using it for our own immediate, urgent, only important
> purposes.[26]

The veneration and imitation Berger writes about are familiar concerns of many contemporary women in the arts. In our talks, Anaïs Nin spoke of the ambivalence felt by the female writer in her choice of models and preceptors. She criticized those women writers who merely imitated men: "I can think of a lot of women who have written but who have not added to woman's knowledge of herself." But while she considers the task of exploring the complexity of female existence central to her intentions, she does not feel that such an effort can be achieved in a cultural and psychological vacuum. She described her own solution to this challenge in her work with the psychiatrist Otto Rank:

> Everything that Rank and others said to me I converted
> at the deepest level, where differences between men and
> women disappear. The unwillingness to learn from men
> is a pity—I have learned history, philosophy,
> psychology, and then converted it to my own use.

The fear that one may be dwarfed by the accomplishment of past masters is particularly vivid for many women, who are well aware that men dominate in the history of our Western culture. But, Nin sees the female imagination as powerful enough to transform knowledge and in so doing sustain and expand the creative artist as she develops a new articulateness.

Margaret Drabble, the English novelist, has taken a different view than Anaïs Nin's on issues confronting women writers. She feels that in England a strong feminine literary tradition exists, and this sense of continuity has helped her greatly:

> Being a novelist seemed to me, and I still feel this, some
> thing one could do to the utmost, to the last degree of
> seriousness without outside interference, without
> anyone putting any limits on me. I think one feels that
> because Jane Austen did it, the Brontës, George Eliot,
> Virginia Woolf—all did it. *There is a completely
> unquestioned tradition.*

Some of these nineteenth-century women viewed writing as a profession where they could reach the top. This was the way George Eliot felt. Her determination, as well as the meticulousness of this great writer's approach to her plots and settings, has intrigued Drabble. Eliot researched with great care the scenes of her works, such as the flooding of the river where the heroine of the *Mill on the Floss* drowns. A similar sense of place emerges from Drabble's work, in her evocation of cramped row-houses of London and of her native Midlands.

Yet the line between those early writers who can enrich and refresh later ones and those whose work may be detrimental to their admirers is difficult to draw. So that, although Drabble admires the work of Henry James, she avoids rereading him while at work on her own books. She finds his style alien to her own, and is concerned about the possibility of picking up his mannerisms. She said to me: "I have used a great deal of the spirit, but I don't think I want the detail." For somewhat similar reasons she avoids reading some of the contemporary female writers while working. Her preference is poetry. And she returns to the work of earlier novelists, such as Virginia Woolf, of whom she said: "I always find Woolf very nourishing to read because she is such a serious writer, she writes beautifully." The power to select useful models from the past in one's discipline grows as an individual's own talent develops. It takes time and it takes experience.

Performing artists have a particularly difficult time avoiding being unduly influenced by the work of their contemporaries. They need to find their own models and to develop their own style. In his reminiscences in *Actors Talk About Acting*, John Gielgud recalled how he imitated all the actors he admired when he was young. But, eventually, the major influence upon his acting was the understanding he derived from a study of Shakespeare:

> I think most young actors don't understand what Shakespeare gives you—the ideas that even in the most colloquial modern speech there is a pattern which must be found by the actor and which, if he finds his individual approach, will have much more significance than if he allows monotony to take over. . . . In Shakespeare the verse sustains you. . . . The phrasing and rhythm and pace should support one, as water does a swimmer, and should be handled with the same skill and pace.[27]

It is a cliché that acting is a profession in which the specifics of craft—the development of one's voice and movements—are particularly important. But many of the actors interviewed by Lewis Funke and John Booth in *Actors Talk About Acting* emphasized that craftsmanship was not enough. Helen Hayes spoke of the actor's need to enrich his or her talent by the study of "all" the arts and the exploration of life among distant people and their countries. To José Ferrer, the power of acting came from the way in which it ignited the imagination; the actor built upon all the various strains of his experience—"the creative artist is a restless person"—and almost everything such a person did added to the richness of his or her work, said Ferrer. The fabled Shakespearian Morris Carnovsky compared actors to other artists, who he felt have in common a certain consciousness, a capacity to use "crystallized experience." In this, Carnovsky did not consider technique as superficial or external: "the word technique involves one's whole life," he said, for it expressed "the inner history and sensibilities the actor possesses."[28]

A surprising number of the performers have spoken of Shakespeare's profound influence upon their development. He has been the greatest of distant teachers.

In the sciences, influences of these distant teachers who shape the talents of a researcher or a theoretician are harder to distinguish. The different scientific disciplines change at a rapid pace. And the individual scientist is not as directly and immediately affected by the traditions of the past as is the artist. Rather, scientists pay closer attention to the work of their colleagues and even to the efforts of their students. They learn from all of them.

In his book *Darwin on Man: A Psychological Study of Scientific Creativity*, the psychologist Howard Gruber reconstructed the intellectual development of the author of *The Origin of Species*. Of particular interest is the way in which this shy evolutionist was influenced by members of his own family, particularly his grandfather Erasmus Darwin. Their impact was not only intellectual but ethical; they helped shape Darwin's view of the world. According to Gruber, "Darwin came from a tradition which equipped him to express *consistently* an egalitarian and evolutionary point of view."[29] The influence of his family helped Charles Darwin, who was a rather cautious man, to communicate his revolutionary findings and to defend them against his opponents. His teachers from the past gave him an emotional and ideological foothold.

In seeking to understand the ways in which a creative individual's talents are nurtured, I have chosen to look at childhood and the years of learning and apprenticeships. Such a framework may be somewhat misleading. The influences affecting the growth of creative thinkers are not arranged in a neat, chronological order: it is the totality of their experiences that musicians, actors, painters, and scientists bring to bear on their work.

The past and the present, the historical and existential, are not easily separated in the mind. In most instances, what is learned from others becomes part of a dimly conscious awareness, to be summoned in those moments when an individual is trying to push beyond the edge of his or her talent.

Still, the conceptual and communicative means I possess to depict the fabric of the human mind are inadequate. The synthesis of thought is unraveled and ordered into a sequential representation by the use of words. But the flow of events and ideas presented in this way reflects only one important aspect of the processes to be explored. The role of visual memory-images, or the integration of sights with sounds and movements, which takes place in the inner stage of the brain, is hard to capture in words or scientific symbols. And thus we try to symbolize these simultaneous and overlapping processes as an orderly, flowing sequence, to be integrated once more by the active and imaginative powers of the reader.

3 / The Invisible Tools

During their diverse apprenticeships, creative adolescents immerse themselves in the work of their elders. This is also a time in their lives when they first explore their inner resources, those varied invisible tools that help transform a gifted young person into a productive artist or scientist.

The paths which lead to such transformations are varied. Some individuals first approach their task externally, by exploring forms rather than their own personal sources. The writer Lawrence Durrell described such a process in commenting on a young friend of his: "She is still playing with forms in order to learn the job of bookmaking from the outside until she hears her own voice."[1] Others struggle with their inner experience, which drives them toward exploring their artistic world. Herman Hesse in his autobiography evoked his stages of immersion:

> At first, swimming in modern, indeed the most modern
> literature, and in fact being overwhelmed by it was an
> almost intoxicating joy. . . . after that first joy was
> exhausted, it became a necessity to me to return from
> my submersion in novelties to what is old.[2]

Hesse also described the difficulty of finding ways to shape one's poetic intent:

> The thing was this: from my thirteenth year on, it was
> clear to me that I wanted to be either a poet or nothing
> at all. To this realization, however, was gradually added
> a further, painful insight . . . there was a path to every
> profession in the world, there were prerequisites, a
> school, a course of instruction for the beginner. Only for

the poet there was nothing of the sort. It was
permissible and even considered an honor to be a poet;
that is to be successful and famous as a poet—
unfortunately, by that time one was dead. But to become a
poet was impossible, and to want to become one,
was ridiculous.[3]

Part of the despair and the excitement that characterizes the early
years of creative individuals is linked to their efforts to bridge the gap
between their sense of purpose and its fulfillment. The first and most
powerful sign that an individual is committed to a life of creative endeavors is his or her sense of intensity: the need to see, explore, understand, experience, and to go beyond what is already known. All of this
is part of the development of invisible tools. The intellectual and artistic means necessary to transform such intensity into creative endeavors
is the topic of this chapter.

Creative Intensity

The universal and the unique are entwined aspects of existence. In the
course of growth, children are powerfully influenced by the living patterns of their family and community while also being subject to a common, species-specific trajectory of development. Individuals whose goals
encompass creative work frequently exhibit sensitivity to the contradictory pulls of necessity and choice. According to the clinical psychologist Donald MacKinnon, whose research on creativity includes the study
of architects, writers, and research scientists: "Much of experience which
less courageous persons would repress or deny is accepted by creative
persons."[4]

What are some of the sources of such courage? It is hard to answer
such a question because the early lives of artists and scientists do not
form a single arrangement. Many of those whom I interviewed described
an intense and joyful intellectual life that characterized their parents'
homes: frequently recalled were family activities focused on nature or
the writing of magazines and staging of plays. They also remembered
the intense discussions around their dinner tables and that their parents encouraged their own participation and their independence of
thought.

In a study comparing high-IQ and highly creative adolescents, Jacob
W. Getzels and Philip W. Jackson found that the parents of the latter
group valued their offsprings' "openness to experience" and their "in-

terest and enthusiasm for life."[5] The home atmosphere supported the adventurous spirit of those young people who were considering a creative career. It was the parents' enthusiasm rather than specific instruction in art and science that first helped their development. Once these young students' interests became more focused upon a particular art form or scientific discipline, they started to learn how to combine skill and discipline with their earlier sense of wonder and exuberance.

The opportunity to learn from the work of people whose approach is of heightened interest to a beginner contributes to the learner's capacity to make career choices; the music of Bach affected the young Casals in this way. The work of Jane Austen and Virginia Woolf similarly supports the creative intent of many beginning women writers. The influence of these distant teachers helps to shape the craft of a beginner, and the example of their lives enriches the young person's understanding of the challenges inherent in a creative career.

The intensity required to go beyond the known is replenished by such encounters with distant teachers. The young person is enriched by the exposure to the lively wrought works of their mentors. When claiming their experience—through their artistic effort in dealing with the richness as well as the disturbing complexity of their existence—young artists are frequently beset by anxiety. They are confronted by self-doubt. In addition to the encouragement derived from studying the lives of their artistic models, these individuals also need support from those around them, from their parents, teachers, and friends.

The influence of a live mentor frequently serves to validate a young person's own discoveries. The painter Michele Zackheim, whose work on the origins of Jewish female tradition has received much recent praise, recalled such an encounter during our talk:

> My mother was a painter. I grew up with art, doing art
> was like a kid riding a tractor on a farm. It was like
> second nature, and thus it never occurred to me that it
> would be part of my life. I always thought I was just
> going to write. . . .
>
> But while in college in Santa Barbara I had a course in
> still life. The class was full of these wonderful,
> wonderful crafts-people. They really could draw those
> bottles. When their drawings and mine were tacked on
> the walls, I was embarrassed. But it is frequently the
> same story. When the teacher started to walk around the

room, he liked my work best because it was still natural.
I had not yet learned all the tricks. *And that was all I
needed* [emphasis added]. At the end of the semester I
was in New York studying art.

The unexpected recognition of her visual talents contributed to
Zackheim's development, to her ability to synthesize both graphic and
verbal means of expression, which characterizes her work at present.
Praise and recognition can help young artists to define their own objectives. But most creative careers are full of new beginnings as well as
periods of discouragement. In *The Courage to Create,* Rollo May quoted
a friend of the great sculptor-painter Giacometti describing the artist's
recurrent struggles:

> In order to go on, to hope, to believe that there is some
> chance of his actually creating what he ideally visualizes,
> he is obliged to feel that it is necessary to start his entire
> career over again, every day, as it were, from
> scratch.[6]

One aspect of the creative intensity of artists is linked to their
feelings that it is impossible to ever fully realize their intent. The very
artistic conceptions that give rise to their work will also defeat them.
And thus many individuals who are engaged in creative work present
a troubled and troubling personality; their sense of intensity—a combination of great hope and doubt—frequently disturbs and frightens those
around them.

It is not surprising, then, that an interpretation of artistic temperament
as neurotic has appealed to some who have studied the sources of human creativity. In the Freudian framework, art is seen as the transformation of unconscious conflicts into artistic products. Daniel E. Schneider
developed this approach in his book, *The Psychoanalyst and the Artist:*

> Every dream expresses an impermissible impulse and an
> impossible idea. . . . Every dream, like every work of art
> stimulates and discharges psychic tensions . . . . and every
> dream and every work of art is the result of processes
> making for powerful symbolic economy.[7]

According to this analysis, the power of a work of art is that it draws
the audience into the artist's own interpretation of these psychic forces

thus producing a "mass dream." In a more recent analysis, Albert Rothenberg, the author of *The Emerging Goddess,* also compares dreams and artistic work: "Dreams keep the dreamer asleep but creative processes and resulting creations arouse both creators and recipients."[8] Rothenberg views creativity as the "mirror-image" of dreaming, and he stresses the intensity involved in some of the stages of artistic production:

> Every facet of a visual scene, every nuance of a musical
> tone or of a word or phrase, and every aspect of a
> scientific theory or experiment is explored and kept in
> focus at several particular stages of the creative
> process. . . . The heightened state of consciousness is
> highly pleasurable and it is both similar and opposite in
> form and function to dreaming, a reflection or a
> mirror-image state.[9]

Rothenberg's position, while historically connected to Freud's analysis, is also contemporary in its emphasis on active, deliberate, conscious processes in addition to unconscious ones. Creativity involves a high degree of anxiety on the part of the artist in the unearthing of some unconscious material. But it is also distinguished by activity: the creative individual engages in demanding work to prepare him or herself for the future.

Some of the sources of creativity have their origins in childhood traumas: loss of a parent, prolonged illness, economic pressures, or social isolation. The novelist Anne Tyler recalled a friend's comment in this regard: "In order to be a writer, you have to have had rheumatic fever in your childhood. I have never had rheumatic fever," Tyler explains, "But I believe any kind of setting apart situation will do as well."[10] For individuals who had suffered isolation or loss during their early years, creative work is frequently nourished by their wish to construct an imagined world less flawed than the one they had experienced as children.

But creative intensity is not always the outcome of childhood suffering. Many of those whom I interviewed depicted their childhoods as serene and their work fueled by the stimulation of their early years. For some these joyous years contrasted with later difficulties in their lives. The well-known children's author Judy Blume depicted a childhood that nurtured creativity during our talk in Santa Fe:

> As a child I very much enjoyed my fantasy world. I loved
> the long summers when I could "mess around,"

sometimes by myself, sometimes with my friends. . . . I could not wait to get up in the morning and stayed out until it was dark. And it was just wonderful. . . . I did a lot of things: I worked with my hands, helped my father and brother, who were very imaginative, constructed a playhouse in our yard. And I danced. . . . I made up melodramatic stories and when I was home and sick in bed I listened to the soap operas, then made my own paper dolls, with which I acted out the stories from the radio. I loved movies, too. . . .

I discovered adult literature in junior high school, and then I started to enjoy reading. But earlier I liked to make up things as much as to read. . . . When I was ten I organized a huge dance with costumes, scenery, choreography. . . .

I got married at the end of my junior year in college, and when I had babies, there were no longer any creative outlets. I could neither admit nor see how limited my life was. I saw my adult life as an end, not as a beginning. It was all written out; I never dreamt that it could be better. I know I wrote because I felt life was over. I did not see any other role but that of being a wife and mother . . . and while it was thrilling to have babies to care for, to watch them grow and develop, it wasn't enough.

Life was much more exciting at 12 than at 28, so writing about children of that age was right, it was what I knew best then.

This pensive exploration of the sources of Blume's writing highlights the fact that no single set of circumstances gives rise to creative work. For some, the will, courage, intensity, and imagination required to produce is rooted in the stimulating world of their childhoods, in the joys of sharing word-plays, or in observing the changing face of nature with their families. Others are moved to engage in creative work as their means to overcome loss or isolation suffered during their early years.

Some artists deal in their work with the impact of troubling social events. The Midwestern writer Nelson Algren depicted his own development and the great effect the Depression had upon him in his conversations with H. E. F. Donahue:

> I was always trying to write. Even in grammar school I think I was trying to write. It was something that I never thought of not doing. . . .
>
> It was just something you did, you know, just like a race horse runs. But I never thought really it came to anything. I thought you could write if you had a trade or if you were a teacher or newspaper man. Then you could write. . . .
>
> I wanted to write in this sense all through the University. When we did themes, I wanted to write good themes. I wanted to be a writer in the literary sense. . . . But the experience on the road gave me something to write *about*. . . .

His wandering in search of a job during the Depression furnished Algren with a different view of his world and pushed him past the usual adolescent need for self-expression:

> All these scenes, one after another, piled into something that made me not just want to write, but to really say it, to find out that this thing was all upside down.[11]

Throughout history the impact of war, poverty, and political persecution has motivated many artists to produce their best works. In the biography of the folksinger Pete Seeger, David Dunaway writes:

> A dark period had again produced one of Seeger's universal songs. The musician who thrives on poverty and despair has become a cliché; yet in Seeger's case, when everything tipped against him, when his liberty, career, and safety were in jeopardy, a spark inside ignited a song.[12]

The creation of art and the construction of new knowledge requires artists and scientists to take risks. In the early stages of the development of quantum mechanics and nuclear physics, the men and women who were freeing themselves from older paradigms found themselves in a state of doubt and painful confusion. Werner Heisenberg in *Physics and Beyond* describes this change in the 1920s by using a mountain-climbing metaphor:

> In the valley the weather was poor, and the mountains
> were veiled in clouds. During the climb, the mist has
> begun to climb in upon us, and, after a time, we found
> ourselves in a confused jumble of rocks and
> undergrowth with no sign of a track. . . . At the same
> time it grew brighter overhead, and the light suddenly
> changed color. We were obviously under a patch of
> moving fog. Then, quite suddenly, we could see the
> edge of a steep rock face, straight ahead of us, bathed in
> bright sunlight. The next moment the fog had closed up
> again, but we had seen enough to take our bearings
> from the map. After a further ten minutes of hard
> climbing we were standing in the sun—at saddle height
> above the sea of fog. . . . In atomic physics likewise, the
> winter of 1924–25 had obviously brought us to a realm
> where the fog was thick but where some light had
> begun to filter through and held out the promise of
> exciting new vistas.[13]

In exploring this image Heisenberg evokes the insecurity many of the scientists experienced during these crucial years. He recalled how difficult it was "to give up an attitude on which one's entire scientific approach and career have been based."[14] An even more demanding conflict is faced by those individuals whose scientific work contradicts powerfully held religious beliefs.

Howard Gruber described Darwin's long struggle with himself over the likely public reaction to his discovery concerning the evolutionary continuity of animals and human beings. Darwin remembered well the humiliating fate of some of his scientific predecessors who faced similar conflicts, including the tragic events of Galileo's trial and the ensuing requirement that he denounce, in his old age, his great discovery in front of the Church fathers. Darwin could not admit his own fears to many; he wrote in a letter to his friend Joseph Hooker that telling the secret of his evolutionary ideas was "like confessing murder."[15]

Eventually, Darwin did publish his book on *The Descent of Man*. He was helped in facing the inevitable attacks upon him by the examples of his own liberal family and by the support of some of his teachers. The most important among the latter was the geologist Charles Lyell, who first introduced Darwin to the naturalist's method of research. He also learned from Lyell—who held many unconventional ideas—how "to avoid unnecessary public bitterness in scientific controversies."[16]

The strength required to face opposition and to tolerate anxiety is sustained by support from mentors and peers. In addition, many sources of nourishment are linked to creative work itself.

Thomas Mann wrote in one of his letters of the passion for one's task; the Hungarian biologist Szent-Györgyi spoke of intellectual hunger as a lasting characteristic among those committed to a life of discoveries. Physicists who knew Einstein well saw in him these qualities of enjoyment and passion for intellectual work. "No one has ever enjoyed science as much as Einstein," remarked the Nobel prize-winning inventor of holography, Dennis Gabor.

> Scientific problems, you might say, simply melted in his mouth. . . . When he spoke of relativity, you could see it. The formulae were no longer abstract, they came to life through Einstein's gestures. One could almost say he did gymnastics while lecturing.[17]

In their personal accounts, creative individuals describe not only their fears but also the sustaining joys of their endeavors. Aaron Copland spoke during our talk of the day "when all different musical materials run to their proper places." The film director Henry Jaglom described his flow of cinematic ideas while we spoke in his garden in Beverly Hills "as being on a bicycle going down hill." Similar feelings of delight were voiced by both artists and scientists in the interviews collected by Rosner and Abt for their volume *The Creative Experience*. The Canadian neurologist Wilder Penfield spoke of the exhilaration that accompanies creative thinking. The sustaining powers of one's craft are sometimes sensuous; this aspect of the artist's work was described by the abstract expressionist painter Eugene Newmann. He spoke to me of his gratitude for the medium: "It is the material that informs the world, and it is soothing to me that it does."

Thus, many sources sustain creative intensity in the lives of artists and scientists. Some of these are internal and may reach back to the person's childhood; others are more clearly linked to the challenges of social existence. Creative individuals' openness to all their feelings and reactions distinguish them—according to psychologists who have studied them—from others less able to confront their emotions. The skill and effort needed to give form to one's experience and insight requires commitment, a "passion for one's task," and the life-long compulsion to probe the troubling, joyous flow of life.

The Bag of Memories

Among the invisible tools of creative individuals is their ability to hold on to the specific texture of their past. Their skill is akin to that of a rural family who lives through the winter on food stored in their root cellar. This ability was described in fine detail by Stephen Spender in his well-known essay on creativity. He suggested that poets do not forget their sense-impressions; they know how to record, both mentally as well as in notebooks, the facts and shapes of their existence.[18]

To some, the birth of a creative idea is linked to memories reaching back into childhood. Ingmar Bergman wrote that "to make films is also to plunge again by its deepest roots down to the *world of childhood*."[19] The creative use of one's past, however, requires a memory that is both powerful and selective. Judy Blume spoke of these processes when she compared herself to some of her intellectual friends who do not recall precise, sensory impressions as she does: "I remember smells, feelings. I will walk in a house and say, this is B. N.'s home. This is the way his house smelled on a winter morning. All the sensations are there to be brought back." Stephen Spender wrote of his difficulty in recalling phone numbers or the placing of objects around his home, but he commented: "I have a perfect memory for the sensations and experiences which are crystallized for me around associations."[20]

The film-maker Henry Jaglom made a similar comment in the course of his interview:

> I don't remember people's faces, I never remember addresses. Colors, smells, feelings, associations that are emotionally important I do remember. . . . I really think I have two places in my mind somehow. One is a receptacle for everything that is productively, creatively useful to me, the other is for everything else that has no place creatively.

There are professions where total recall is necessary. Igor Stravinsky in *Expositions and Developments* wrote of "the performer's memory" as follows:

> I could not have made a career as a pianist however— abil-

ity apart—because of the lack of what I call "the
performer's memory." I believe that composers (and
painters) memorize selectively, whereas performers
must be able to take in "the whole thing as it is," like a
camera; I believe, in fact, that a composer's first memory
impression is already a composition.[21]

Some of the specificity of memory among artists, the way in which
they match the needs of their profession to their powers of recall, grow
as they exercise their talents. These individuals embrace their perceptions and work with them. Stephen Spender wrote:

Memory is not exactly memory. It is more like a prong,
upon which a calendar of similar experiences happening
throughout the years, collect. A memory once clearly
stated ceases to be a memory, it becomes perpetually
present, because every time we experience something
which recalls it, the clear and lucid original experience
imposes its formal beauty on the new experiences. It is
thus no longer memory but an experience lived through
again and again.[22]

The distinction drawn by Stravinsky between two different kinds of
recall is supported by recent research illustrating diverse memory processes. The performer's processes may be akin to what the psychologist
Ulric Neisser called "echoic memory"[23]—that is, a manner of remembering auditory material precisely, without extensive analysis— while
the composer's processes imply a more analytic approach.

Memory also plays an important role in scientific work. The researchers' raw materials are facts in unordered array: findings which no longer
fit into an existing paradigm, but which need to be transformed through
experimental and intellectual inquiry into a new, more adequate explanatory theory. In order to meet this demanding task, researchers have to
both accumulate and organize large amounts of information. Charles
Darwin was well aware of this need. In *Life and Letters* he described his
organizational system: he had carefully indexed all the books he had
read and organized the material into portfolios that he consulted at the
beginning of each new project. In the twentieth century, scientists are
assisted by specialized libraries and information retrieval systems when
they initiate a new research endeavor. Nevertheless, a powerful and

personally developed structuring of information—an active and selective memory—is as necessary for scientists as it is for poets.

The Polish-born mathematician Stan Ulam described in his autobiography the importance he attributes to memory in research:

> It seems to me that good memory—at least for mathematicians and physicists—forms a large part of their talent. And what we call talent or perhaps genius itself depends to a large extent on the ability to use one's memory properly to find analogies, past, present and future, which as [Stefan] Banach said are essential to the development of new ideas.[24]

The suggestion that richness of associations and concepts are important to scientific work has been made by a number of individuals. Linus Pauling spoke of having many good ideas as part of his success as a Nobel-prize winning chemist. The author of *The Art of Scientific Investigation*, W. I. Beveridge, remarked that it is easy to abandon a faulty notion if the investigator has a fertile mind.[25] The use of remembered ideas and the connections made between them and new insights may occur both consciously and unconsciously. Stan Ulam thinks of these cognitive processes as operating along multiple channels; his notions, based on introspection, are quite compatible with recent psychological analyses. He asks: "How is memory gradually built during one's conscious or even unconscious life and thought?"

> My guess is that everything we experience is classified and registered on very many parallel channels in different locations, much as the visual impressions that are the result of many impulses on different cones and rods. All these pictures are transmitted together with connected impressions from other senses. Each such group is stored independently.[26]

The cognitive psychologist Colin Martindale hypothesizes that what human beings perceive is parsed according to sensory, perceptual, semantic, and episodic "analyzers." An experience is processed in multiple ways, as each type of memory "storage" has its own special characteristic. The stories of one's life are recorded in episodic memory, and these are tagged according to the time and place of their occurrence. More abstract knowledge lacks such coding; instead it is recorded in a more formal structure such as biological taxonomies or other facts, which are organized according to heirarchical concepts.

In addition to these categorizations of remembered knowledge, the self-reports of experienced thinkers highlight the role of different modalities in thought and memory. The centrality of the visual modality is emphasized by painters and photographers. Paul Gauguin wrote in his *Intimate Journal:*

> I have a remarkable memory, and I recall this time in my life [his early childhood], our house and ever so many things that happened [Gauguin described the story of his running away from home.] . . . It was a picture that had beguiled me, a picture representing a traveler with a stick and bundle over his shoulder.[27]

Gauguin's powerful episodic memory (his ability to evoke specific experiences) was linked to some of his other visual talents; he could recall and claim for his work much that he had learned from other artists. When he moved to Tahiti where no museums or galleries were available to him, he relied on his memory. The paintings he made in the South Pacific reflected his broad exposure to the varied styles of the visual arts. While his canvases interpreted his surroundings—the strong island colors, the graceful Tahitian people, his new-found sense of silence and peace—they also revealed complex artistic influences, that of the Impressionists, the varied Italian schools of painting, and even Egyptian approaches to composition. Gauguin had fully assimilated these sources into his own style; they were part of his powerful and selective memory, part of his invisible tools. In one of his infrequent letters to his wife, Gauguin wrote: "My artistic center is in my head."[28]

Mental images are an important resource for the working artist's talent. The San Francisco painter and photographer Barry Brukoff spoke of his reliance upon his visual recall during a quiet November afternoon in my house: "I have a movie camera in here," he said pointing to his forehead, "I can go back to a town in Europe that I had visited ten years ago, and go to the hotel I had stayed in, or to the restaurant I had eaten in during a short, two-day visit. I just run the movie again."

The vividness of Brukoff's visual memory is part of a precise visual imagination that activates the exceptional abilities of this artist-designer. For instance, he can mentally walk through an environment and reconstruct it, and he remembers numbers by projecting them on a screen that only he can see. To him, these are gifts that he was born with; how-

ever, I see the use of a specific modality—or language of the mind—as
the outcome of both a genetic predisposition and the honing of one's
mind, which results from the sustained work of the creative individual.

The development of self-knowledge—the realization of one's special
talents and the best way to use them—does not necessarily follow a
simple linear progression. Students of creativity have identified cycles
in the lives of productive individuals. At times a person spends years
absorbing new experiences, styles, or theoretical ideas without making
his or her own contributions to a field, only to be followed by a period
of intense bursts of productivity.

An apparently fallow few years in the life of the great French novelist
Marcel Proust were described as part of such a cycle by his biographer
André Maurois:

> Superficially considered, the four or five years that fol-
> lowed Marcel's military service were lost years. The
> truth is that he was absorbing his honey and filling the
> pigeonholes of his mind with characters and
> impressions.[29]

At the end of his lengthy years of apprenticeship after the death of his
parents, Marcel Proust "had developed a prodigious memory peopled
with scenes and conversations. He had not frittered away the harvest
of his childhood and his adolescence. . . . He had reached the age of
great undertakings with his granaries filled to bursting."[30]

The live, active use of memory reported by artists and scientists forces
us to use some caution in our language describing this central mode of
thought. In the professional literature of psychology, we often use terms
such as memory *storage*, a word which implies that humans file their
experiences, the yields of their lives, into a dark and dusty back-chamber
of the mind. A different process emerges from the accounts of poets
such as Stephen Spender, who have described the many ways in which
they attempt to maintain the freshness of their perceptions throughout
long periods of time. In a similar vein, Stan Ulam has commented on
the importance of keeping one's knowledge current by linking the known
to new ideas and insights. Memory, then, is an ever present resource,
a potential source of raw materials that are reworked in art and science.

The transformation that characterizes the creative process can bring
forth great changes when a gifted person starts claiming his or her experience. May Sarton described such a metamorphosis in *Writings on
Writing*:

I was bowled over recently when a letter from Willa Cather
came by a happy chance into my possession: in it she
states categorically that she never wrote anything that
did not come out of a direct and rather shattering
experience. These cool and classic novels sprang from
her blood.[31]

In the course of creative endeavors, artists and scientists join fragments of knowledge into a new unity of understanding. This process is
demanding; it calls upon all the inner resources of the individual—
active memory, openness to experience, creative intensity, and emotional courage. It demands self-knowledge in the use of expansion of
one's talents.

Discipline in the Shadow of Failure

"We must always work," wrote the composer Peter Ilich Tchaikovsky
in a letter to a friend, "a self-respecting artist must not fold his hands
on the pretext that he is not in the mood."[32] One of the most neglected
areas of the study of creativity is that of discipline, the structure that
the individual who works outside of institutions imposes upon him or
herself. Discipline has many functions among these creative individuals. For Tchaikovsky it contributed to his sense of self-confidence:

I have learnt to master myself, and I am glad I have not
followed in the steps of some of my Russian colleagues,
who have no self-confidence and are so impatient that at
the least difficulty they are ready to throw up the
sponge. This is why, in spite of great gifts, they
accomplish so little, and that in an amateur way.[33]

The great Russian musician believed that patience was an essential
aspect of his sustained creativity. While he treasured his intense moments of musical inspiration, he also knew that the music he created
during these short bursts of time needed expansion and re-working.
He carried a pencil and paper with him during his daily walks, the setting for most of his new ideas or "germs" of compositions; later in the
day he transcribed these, using his technical knowledge and "cool
headwork."
Sustained, productive work requires more than the mind for shelter-

ing thought. It requires a well-organized and well-selected work space. In the long journey of the apprentice who is on his or her way to becoming a professional, the moment when such a person can assert a claim for the right space in which to work is an important one. Tchaikovsky liked to live in simple, country houses at a distance from Moscow, where he could protect his daytime concentration and solitude. (At night he liked to be with a few close friends.)

The British novelist Margaret Drabble described during our talk in London how her work space had changed during her career as a writer. While her children were small, she worked at home. Her early novels capture powerfully the sense of confinement, the closed-in feelings from which young mothers suffer. In more recent years, Drabble has been able to move to a hotel room for several days at a time. There, no one interrupts her; her characters expand in that empty space and take possession of the room. She explained: "I usually go someplace that is vaguely appropriate. It is extraordinary how one can work in a situation like that."

The choice of a quiet work place is particularly important when a novelist is engaged in writing a large work with many characters. When Katherine Anne Porter first began as a writer, she worked wherever and whenever she had a chance. But once she was well-known and possessed the means to create a more suitable setting for her writing, she plunged with joy into what Yeats has called "the solitary, sedentary trade." She wrote *Ship of Fools*—her most complex novel—in rural Connecticut where she lived for more than three years without a telephone and with few visitors.[34]

Porter worked best in the morning, as did Hemingway and scores of writers whose work habits are recorded in the successive volumes of *Writers at Work*. In answering questions about his work life, Thomas Mann wrote:

> For many years I have done my serious writing, that intended for publication, almost exclusively during morning hours, from nine to noon or half past twelve. . . . About one and a half manuscript pages constitute my daily stint. This slow method of working springs from severe self-criticism and high requirements in matters of form.[35]

The structuring of time and space according to one's needs and values is part of the invisible tools of creativity. Thomas Mann, Katherine Porter, and Ernest Hemingway knew how to build a "house for their thoughts." Their self-knowledge contributed to a life-long record of productivity and their high degree of self-criticism was responsible for the continued shaping of each author's excellent style. This striving toward a consciously developed form was described by Thomas Mann when he characterized the "symbolic content" of his writing as follows: "Every word and every phrase counts, for one never knows what part one's present phraseology may have to play as a motif within the total work."[36]

One of the most demanding aspects of creative discipline is the revision process: artists and scientists clarify their condensed thoughts through the successive drafts (or versions) of their work. Such efforts require the same active intelligence as generating novel ideas does. The process is like a dialogue between the artist and his or her product. May Sarton described this willingness to learn from one's work in her essay "The Writing of a Poem." She wrote:

> There are pages and pages more of this battle to find the
> right words, the right form. Probably most of you,
> plagued by such notes, would have decided to give up.
> But I was stubborn; I was interested; and finally I did
> manage to fashion the poem "Truth" out of these
> fumbles. . . . The poem teaches us something while we
> make it . . . the poem requires all your capacities of
> thought, feeling, analysis and synthesis. I hope this
> might suggest that there is nothing dull about revision.[37]

The children's author, Judy Blume, also finds the reworking of her material an important, even joyous process. She explained her feelings concerning revisions during our talk: "I love to rewrite. You take something that has a little promise, that is unfinished, and you make it come right. . . . It is really like putting together a puzzle and watching the progress and feeling excited as it begins to form a picture."

Blume works on several cycles of composing and rewriting. Each time she begins a new novel she also starts a handwritten notebook in which she keeps material that does not fit into the section she is working on. She showed these notebooks to me: they include several names for her characters, descriptive details (for instance, for her book written about a Florida childhood she described the 1940 Packards), bits of dialogue. "I keep things I don't want to lose," Blume explained. "I might write a page of a manuscript, and feel that it is not quite relevant in this part of the book, so I'll tape it into the notebook. I'll want to get back to it . . . my mind will race ahead to this or to that, but I am still only on page 30."

This method of writing illustrates once more that the human mind is multi-channeled not only in the way in which we record experience, as described by Ulam's insightful analysis of memory, but also in the way in which writers, poets, and composers think while engaged in a new work. While Blume composes her narrative in a focused forward movement on her typewriter, she is also aware of the more diffuse associations that accompany her writing.

A disciplined approach to creative work requires that the individual structure his or her time well, so that it supports one's working habits, the building of "the houses of thought." The writer, poet, or composer must become skilled in keeping track of both focused and evanescent lines of thought. Thomas Mann described how he had arranged these invisible tools while he was working:

> For writing I must have a roof over my head, and since I
> enjoy working by the sea better than anywhere else, I
> need a tent or a wicker beach chair. Much of my
> composition, as I have said, has been conceived on walks;
> I also regard movement in the open air as the best means
> of reviving my energy for work. For a longer book I
> usually have a heap of preliminary papers close at hand
> during the writing; scribbled notes, memory props, in
> part purely objective—external details, colorful odds and
> ends—or else psychological formulations, fragmentary
> inspirations, which I use in their proper place.[38]

A sense of balance or certainty is evident in Mann's description of his methods of work; a more anguished tone is present in the reports of some other writers. Van Wyck Brooks wrote in *Opinions of Oliver Allston* about the writer's life:

> No work this morning. My brain feels like an old sponge,
> battered by the waves and rocks of dozens of winters.
>
> In thirty years of writing, I have not gained an ounce
> of confidence. I begin each new book (as I have probably
> always begun, although I never remember it) with a
> sense of impotence, chaos and desperation that cannot be
> overstated. I always feel that I am foredoomed to failure.

> Everyday I begin my work with the same old feeling,
> that I am on trial for my life and will probably not be
> acquitted.[39]

A similar passage from Iris Murdoch has been quoted by Gail
Godwin in her essay on "Becoming a Writer."

> I live, I *live*, with an absolutely continuous sense of failure.
> I am always defeated, always. Every book is the wreck
> of a perfect idea. The years pass and one has only one
> life. If one has a thing at all one must do it and keep on
> and on and on trying to do it better.[40]

Godwin writes that she loves this quote, as it expresses her own feelings about her work. It captures the notion of discipline, which is
not only a joyous self-confident exercise of one's craft, but also the emotions involved in working while being nagged by doubts and fear. "I
work continuously in the shadow of failure," Godwin explained.

> For every novel that makes it to my publisher's desk,
> there are at least five or six that died on the way. And
> even with the ones I do finish, I think of all the ways they
> might have been better. . . . But I believe that with
> enough practice and skill and good faith, you can learn to
> recognize when the work is achieved. There is such a
> thing as fussing too much; it can deaden the work. There
> is also such a thing as stopping too soon; this gives the
> work a kind of incompleteness that is more annoying
> than it is mysterious. Learning when "enough is enough"
> *is the discipline of a lifetime.*[41] [Emphasis added.]

The Mind at Work

In attempting to answer the question *what is creative thought?* one aspect of the answer—the notion of synthesis—emerges from the accounts
of creative individuals and from the analyses of research studies. Of
greatest importance in the thought activity of artists and scientists is
their pulling together of ideas, images, disarrayed facts and fragments
of experience, which have previously been apprehended by them as
separated in time and space, into an integrated work. It is this synthe-

sis that most concerns me in this discussion: the joining of rapid bursts of thought with a regime of disciplined work.

Generally speaking, the germ of a future composition comes suddenly and unexpectedly, Tchaikovsky wrote. The success of working with such "thought-trains"—in Hannah Arendt's expression—depends on a fully prepared mind. But the mental powers necessary to extend one's understanding and to transform one's thoughts into creative works mature slowly. The nurturance and expansion of the talents of the gifted individual requires not only the mastery of his or her craft, but also a strong and enduring sense of self.

Howard Gruber described the creative individual's life as a "self-regenerating system":

> A creative moment is part of a longer creative process,
> which in its turn is part of a creative life. How are such
> lives lived? How can I express this peculiar idea that
> such an individual must be a self-generating system?
> Not a system that comes to rest when it has done good
> work, but one that urges itself onward. And yet, not a
> run-away system that accelerates its activity to the point
> where it burns itself out in one great flash. The system
> regulates the activity and the creative acts regenerate the
> system. The creative life happens in a being who can
> continue to work.[42]

Many aspects of a creative life contribute to its regenerative possibilities. Some of these are inherent in the activities themselves: the pleasure that artists derive from working with stone, wood, or paints; the poets' enchantment with powerful images; or the satisfaction drawn by scientists after identifying an elegant model of hidden realities. These are among the sensuous, playful and aesthetic rewards of creative work. Men and women who are renowned for their life-long productivity (Picasso, Einstein, Sarton, Copland among them) have voiced their enjoyment of the sensual and tactile nature of their work even while struggling with relentless intellectual demands. Thomas Mann quoted the great German Goethe in this regard: "In the making of art there can be no question of suffering."[43]

Concerning the darker side of artistic work, Goethe has characterized writing as "eternally rolling a stone that forever had to be raised anew."[44] Each time an individual completes a novel, a research project or a composition, he/she discovers new, unresolved issues that have to be addressed. In creative work, a single product is just a temporary resting place in the continuous and demanding process. The psychologist Isidor Chein portrayed the struggle when he wrote: "The essential psychological human quality is . . . one of commitment to a developing and continuing set of unending, interacting, interdependent, and mutually modifying long-range enterprises."[45]

The creative "enterprise," then, is that which gives meaning to experience, and, however demanding such a task may be, it is this sense of purpose that confers dignity to the life of those struggling towards understanding. The contradictory pulls of joy and discouragement, of sudden bursts of insight and tiring efforts of execution, of process and product, are the necessary tensions that fuel creative thought.

Such inner tensions can be consuming. Artists and scientists, while driven by these, also search for a living foundation for their work; they build upon past knowledge and renew their sense of immediacy by recollecting their own beginnings. In addition to their personal powers of drive and regeneration, creative individuals need external supports. "Literature is not created in midair," is an often-quoted line from Virginia Woolf; she reminded us that creative work is rooted in the material conditions of existence, such as space, money, and experience.

The mind at work is engaged in diverse efforts at unification. Energy and commitment are needed in shaping the inner shorthand of ideas into publically available work—the joining of thought and realization—which is sustained in a variety of ways: by "the courage to create," by a well-honed discipline and a fully-prepared mind, by the artist's passion for his or her task. The hope that is essential for regeneration is nourished by the emotional support and intellectual sharing of those "places, people and things," as Santayana has said, upon whose support the creative individual depends.

> When just as the soil tarnishes with weed
> The sturdy seedling with arched body comes
> Shouldering its way and shedding the earth crumbs.
> > Robert Frost, "Putting in the Seed"

These, then, are the many layers of the soil into which the seed is placed.

PART TWO   THE LANGUAGES
OF THE MIND

The diverse processes of expression—the ways in which individuals acquire powerful means to convey their thoughts to others—constitute the central topic of the next few chapters. Are ideas shaped differently when communicated through graphic, musical, or verbal languages? Or is there a uniform relationship between internal representation and external ordering across different modalities of thoughtful expression?

The intense and difficult struggle to give shape to the content of one's thoughts is powerfully evoked by the painter Ben Shahn, the writer Gail Godwin, and the choreographer Martha Graham, among many others. Part of the difficulty of such a process lies with the highly condensed nature of inner thought. While inner representations have this compression in common, there are also important developmental, cognitive, and affective differences present in various modalities of thought.

Many of those interviewed for this book spoke of their early immersion into music or the graphic arts as part of their later ease with a particular expressive modality. These experiences helped to shape a particular kind of internal and external language of thought. At the same time it would be an oversimplification to assume that writers, for instance, are limited to verbal thinking only, or that painters are limited to the visual aspects of their imagination and understanding.

In the pages that follow, the specific features of visual, verbal, musical, choreographic, and scientific languages are examined. Both essays written by experienced thinkers and interviews are used in the exploration of the manifold transformations that characterize the externalization of thought. The skilled and confident use of a particular expressive modality is an important aspect of creativity. Separate chapters are presented to document the development of visual or verbal thinking and the internal and external forms that characterize each of these modalities. At the same time, many overlaps exist between these forms of thinking: scientists, for instance, use verbal, visual, and mathematical approaches to solving problems. Thus, the division of complex, overlapping modalities of thought into separate treatments is to be thought of as an analytical convenience, rather than an absolute division between the languages of the mind.

4 / Visual Thinking

"To draw is to put down your thoughts visually," remarked Fritz Scholder, the well-known Native American painter. A similar comment was made by the photographer Diana Michener: "I have always taken pictures the way other people keep journals and diaries. It is a way of ordering my reactions to the world, of placing my ideas and feelings in a concrete form outside myself, of breaking my isolation."[1]

In describing their approach to thought, these artists highlight an oft-ignored aspect of reflection, the visualization of ideas. The human need to order the flow of experience, to reshape it, or simply to remember it, requires a multiplicity of means, and among these, language and imagery are of particular interest. Both of these processes assist the individual in bridging the personal and social aspects of experience. In comparing the role of words to those of pictures, Michener illustrates this similarity of function.

Language is a highly conventionalized form of expression, but images—the constituent forms of visual thought—are hard to standardize or to define. There is no dictionary of images, or thesaurus of photographs and paintings. Imagery and visual expressions reflect the uniqueness of an individual's life. Nevertheless, images have intrigued the students of the mind since the beginnings of recorded history.

In the philosophical writings of the ancient Greeks, images, or the inner perceptions of the world, were thought of as faint traces or impressions of past experience.[2] The Hellenic scholars were primarily interested in memory images, a concern still shared by contemporary investigators.

In spite of this long-standing interest in imagery, the scientific study of this subjective phenomenon reveals many changes and reversals. During the early years of this century, the exploration of images through introspective reports was an accepted part of scientific inquiry. But as a consequence of the strong criticism leveled by the behaviorist John B. Watson against mentalistic phenomena, research in imagery declined sharply after World War I. An important exception to this trend was the work of those clinicians who continued the study of images in dreams, those produced under hypnosis, and those reported during the therapeutic hour. More recently, as part of the impressive renaissance in the study of thought, students of cognition have once more discovered the importance of imagery as part of the work of the mind. Many phenomena are now being explored; among them are research into images as mnemonic devices, the study of creativity as a visual process, and neurophysiological investigations of verbal and imaginal processes.

The Power of Images

My own interest in visual thinking was awakened by the reports of physicists and mathematicians who have described the role of images in their thinking. Some of these introspective descriptions were gathered by psychologists based on letters and interviews: for example, *The Creative Process* edited by Brewster Ghiselin, and the more recent collection by Stanley Rosner and Lawrence Abt entitled *The Creative Experience*. In the conversations that I have conducted with experienced thinkers, I also have tried to explore the role of visual thinking in the course of scientific discovery.

An evocative description of such abstract visualization was given by John Howarth, a physicist who was engaged in cancer research at the time of our discussion:

> I make abstract pictures. I just realized that the process of
> abstraction in the pictures in my head is similar to the
> abstraction you engage in dealing with physical
> problems analytically. You reduce the number of
> variables, simplify and consider what you hope is the
> essential part of the situation you are dealing with; then
> you apply your analytical techniques. In making a visual
> picture it is possible to choose one which contains
> representations of only the essential elements—a

simplified picture, abstracted from a number of other
pictures and containing their common elements.

In order to facilitate their introspection—because it is not easy to
describe one's processes of thought—I frequently asked these scientists
to reflect on the personal observations of others in their field. In working with physicists, I presented them with a passage by Einstein, written in 1945 in response to Jacques Hadamard's oft-quoted questionnaire,
which he sent to a number of eminent mathematicians:

> The words of the language, as they are written or spo-
> ken, do not seem to play any role in my mechanisms of
> thought. The physical entities which seem to serve as
> elements in thought are certain signs and more or less
> clear images which can be 'voluntarily' reproduced or
> combined.[3]

Most of the individuals he queried stressed a reliance on visual
symbols in their thinking, as had Einstein. Evidence of a life-long pattern of using visual and kinesthetic pictures was found among Einstein's
papers at Princeton; among these was a description of a "thought experiment" he conducted at age sixteen. After Einstein read Maxwell's
theorem which proposed to explain light waves, "he imagined himself
riding through space, so to speak, astride a light wave and looking back
at the wave next to him."[4]

The findings of Hadamard were similar to those of Anne Roe, who in
her study *The Making of a Scientist* found that physicists and biologists
reported a preference for visual modes of thought, while social scientists wrote that they used inner speech as their dominant mode of cognitive representations. In both groups there were, of course, some
individuals who indicated that their thinking could not be described in
terms of any sensory modality.

Just as individuals differ in their preference for visual or verbal thinking, similarly differences exist in psychological theories in regards to
the role of words or images in cognition. The importance of visual
approaches has been most convincingly presented by the Gestalt psychologists. In their writings, thought and sight are dynamically interconnected: the laws of vision serve as the model of the fluctuating
processes of the mind engaged in problem-solving. The strongest contemporary exponent of this tradition is Rudolf Arnheim, the author
of books on perception, art, and thought. He proposes that "concepts

are perceptual images and that thought operations are the handling of these images."[5] In his book, *Visual Thinking*, he characterizes this idea in sweeping terms:

> Visual thinking calls, more broadly, for the ability to see visual shapes as images of the patterns of forces that underlie our existence—the functioning of minds, of bodies or machines, the structure of societies or ideas.[6]

Although Arnheim does not ignore the role of words, he considers them secondary in shaping thought—hence the title of his chapter dealing with language is "Words in their Place." He suggests "that language is essentially stabilizing and conservative" and its power for thinking is in the facilitation of "the mass evocation of images."[7]

Another important, but infrequently observed difference between verbal and visual thinking relates to a contrast in the external, communicative forms of each of these inner processes. While language is a socially constructed and conventionalized mode of expression, no corresponding single visual language exists. There is, consequently, a great diversity of graphic and plastic means used by creative individuals in shaping and communicating their inner visual notions. Some researchers use schematic drawings when exploring a problem; others like fuller, pictorial illustrations. Three-dimensional models are of great importance in the study of the structure of matter, such as the three-dimensional single and double-chained models which Crick, Watson, and Wilkins experimented with before they arrived at the elegant "double helix," which won them a Nobel Prize in 1962.

The absence of a single visual language may assist in the discovery process. Images come rapidly and are changeable—and it is difficult to externalize them fully. However, these very attributes contribute to their effectiveness in the exploratory and playful combination of ideas. In contrast, words may fix a notion: Arthur Koestler recalled the difficulties faced by physicists such as Ernest Rutherford in the early days of atomic physics. The word *atom* meant indivisible in Greek. The hold of such a notion upon the understanding of physicists was a strong one; they had to break away from what Koestler called "the snares of language"[8] to demonstrate that the atom was a divisible unit of matter. In the opinion of Arthur Koestler, Silvano Arieti and Ernest Schachtel, and others who have written about creativity, a reliance on verbal concepts alone may lead the scientist to a certain rigidity of thought which can interfere with the discovery process.

In a recent article the psychologist J. C. Gowan suggested that the continual stream of internal discourse overshadows imagery, an on-going right hemisphere process in the brain. It is necessary, he believes, to allay the work of the dominant left hemisphere—where language is mediated—and to pull or focus the thinker's attention to visual processes which he, too, considers critical in creativity. He further asserts "that in the case of every historic scientific discovery which was researched carefully enough, we find that it was imagery, either in dreams or in a waking state, which produced the breakthrough."[9]

These highly visual theories of thought and creativity have been opposed by behaviorists, who have argued that thinking takes place primarily through a reliance upon internalized language. Even if imagery is seen by some as important in their thinking, it is a difficult phenomenon to study within the framework of experimental studies. Allan Paivio summarized this position in his volume *Imagery and Verbal Processes:* "This is one of the classical behaviorist arguments—imagery is subjective and inferential, words are objective and manageable."[10]

To my mind, neither the behaviorist nor the Gestalt position does justice to the complex and interwoven process of thought. Both of these schools attempt to highlight only a fraction of the experience of consciousness, which includes inner monologues, crystallized concepts, reveries, fleeting as well as generic images, abstract pictures, visualized movements, and subjective feelings. Each psychological theory offers to examine in slow motion the rapid processes of thought, and thus untangle the many-sided, welded, inner flow of ideas; but no single, universal hierarchy exists in the modalities of thought which characterizes all human beings. The dominance of visual, verbal, or movement-linked thinking varies from person to person. Anne Roe's report on the differences between social and physical scientists illustrates this situation, as do the results of many cross-cultural studies that describe certain historically shaped preferences in the modalities of thought. Those theorists who ignore these individual and cultural variations limit their theories and do not reach a much-needed exploration of the full life of the mind.

While the theoretical debates concerning the nature of thought have not been resolved, new approaches to the study of the mind are promising. One such approach was developed by Howard Gruber in his cognitive case studies of Darwin and Piaget. This method has also been applied by Gruber's students to the examination of John Locke's and Mary Wollstonecraft's development as thinkers. These investigators are intent on documenting the way in which intellectually purposeful work develops and changes throughout the span of a lifetime; they refer to a network of enterprises in their description of sustained intellectual labor. The dynamics of a changing system of thought intrigued Martha Moore-Russell in her study of Locke; she identifies this lengthy struggle "to resolve the structural instability of his early philosophical thought"[11] as generative of many of his works.

In his study of Darwin's early notebooks (1837–40), Gruber discovered a frequently occurring image, that of nature as an irregularly branching tree. This image is described in words as well as drawn on the pages of these notebooks:

> The trees captured many aspects of Darwin's thought as he is approaching the formulation of evolutionary change: "the fortuitousness of life, the irregularity of the panorama of nature, the explosiveness of growth and the necessity to bridle it so as to keep the number of species constant." And most important, the fundamental duality that at any one time some must live and others die.[12]

These images of *wide scope* serve many functions for the thinker: as powerful metaphors they pack a lot of meaning in a condensed form; they also have aesthetic and emotional appeal—witness the care with which Darwin drew his trees in his notebooks. Their central role in scientific work is described by Gruber as follows: "the scientist needs them in order to comprehend what is known and to guide the search for what is not yet known."[13]

Many of these images are not hard to produce, nor is it difficult to get individuals to describe what they see in their mind's eye. In contrast with these fleeting phenomena, there are the generative images which are so critical for the process of discovery. These may be quite numerous according to Gruber: "the individual can cope with 4-5 images which serve as *leitmotifs* for an entire life and a somewhat larger number, say 50-100, that are used in the elaboration of these thematic organizers."[14]

Some scientists make sketches of their images similar to the trees Darwin drew in his notebooks. But these individuals are a minority; in most cases people find it easier to translate the visual shapes of their thoughts into words. The use of imagery is less elusive for those who are experienced in giving concrete and communicable expression to their subjective experience through drawings, sculptures, photographs, and paintings.

The Genesis of Visual Expression

Young children play quite spontaneously with visual forms and they enjoy scribbling. These playful activities are similar to their explorations with sounds, gestures, and large movements. But once they had drawn their many suns, mandalas, or stick figures on paper, or in other cultures or communities on sand or snow, they needed a deeper immersion into their visual culture to be able to go beyond these designs.

It is the need for such a deeper acquaintanceship that György Kepes emphasized in his book *The Language of Vision*. He wrote:

> Before one begins to use the visual for the communication of a concrete message, he should learn the greatest variety of spatial sensations inherent in the relationships of these forces acting on the picture surface. The storing up of such varied experience is the most important part of the training for visual expression.[15]

Many future artists search for varied visual stimulation long before they know why it is so important for them to do so. The self-taught Hungarian gypsy painter János Balázs wrote of his childhood forays during the difficult years of World War I:

> I was such an oddball that wherever I went, alone as usual, I would pick up stray newspapers, torn books, discarded notebooks, and most of all, picture magazines, and with great joy would take them home, making sure no one observed me. There, expectant, tense with excitement I would forage through the worthless pile of papers. Later I made the rounds of the city garbage dumps where there was a mass of magazines and newspapers.
>
> What pleasure it gave me to read them, how passionately I pored over the illustrations, whatever they were. I read everything that was printed, gaped in admiration at each picture and drawing. Driven by some kind of instinct I began to copy in pencil those I found the most appealing on a clean sheet of paper.[16]

The art educators and painters Brent and Marjorie Wilson, who have studied the work of artistically gifted children, view these young artists as having "keen kinesthetic and aesthetic sensitivities, an uncommon fascination for all things visual, and an encyclopedic visual memory. . . . They possess an unusual penchant for imagery and fantasy as well as a drive to expand the boundaries of their awareness through their own visual productions." In decades past, young artists searched for visual stimulation in books and magazines; the sources of such stimulation in the drawings of today's children may also include comics and television.

During his own childhood in a small Western town, Brent Wilson developed a voracious visual appetite, which was hard to satisfy in a town lacking museums and galleries. He used to wait eagerly for *Life* magazine, "his window to the world," and pored over the photographs. Unconsciously, he realized at an early age that in addition to drawing from nature, young people need models and schemas to help them in their representational efforts. The Wilsons suggest that the need for the transmission of effective visual schemata from one young artist to another is necessary because of the overwhelming complexity of visual experience in "the raw." To them, visual input is "too numerous, too complex, too general" and at the same time "too vague to provide sharp mental images from which to draw." Their studies illustrate the way in which some young artists may acquire visual conventions as part of their earliest art-making.

A lovely description of the process of learning to draw was given by Raphael Soyer in his *Diary of an Artist*. In the small Russian town of Borisoglebsk, the Soyer children were stimulated by their poet father to read, think, and draw:

> He [Soyer's father] could draw, too. He would make pictures of Cossacks on horses and all the trimmings on both of them, the horses in prancing position showing their horseshoes, the Cossacks brandishing their sabres. Moses and I would copy these pictures, and I still remember how hard it was to draw horseshoes on hoofs. My father would "correct" the drawings and exhibit them . . . .
>
> One evening a young man named Ivan Ivanovich Pozdniakov came to our house and did a drawing of our father from life. That one could draw a living person was a sudden revelation to me. I stopped drawing for several days, then asked my father to pose for me as he

had for Ivan Ivanovich. When the drawing was praised, my elation was boundless.[17]

In the Soyer home, learning to draw was indeed a social process; a life-long, loving competition existed between Raphael Soyer and his twin Moses, whom he repeatedly included in his canvases. But some of their discoveries of visual conventions were made by studying illustrations. Soyer writes:

> As time went on I made other discoveries. There was a wood in the outskirts of town to which our father would take us on Sundays, to picnic and to draw. Even in those days I was fascinated in a childish way by space and perspective. But I was also frustrated by my inability to indicate on paper the differences between the trees close to me and those far from me. One day I saw a picture of a forest in a magazine and I noticed that the nearer trees began at the bottom of the paper and as the trees receded, the farther up the paper they were. How this illusion of distance from tree to tree was effected was another revelation. I made many drawings of our woods according to this guideline, and I never ceased to wonder at the space and distance I was able to create on the flat surface of the paper.[18]

The shaping of a visual language of communication is a slow, developmental process. In some cases considerable time lapses between the early, impressionable years of stimulation—of seeing the world as fresh and wondrous—and linking these sights and images to a mature, personalized form of expression. Paul Gauguin is an example of this. He spent some of his earliest years in Lima, Peru, and he wrote of those times in his journal many decades later. Though he did some carvings as a child, Gauguin did not start to draw and paint until he was in his twenties. But those early impressions of childhood remained powerful:

> I recall this time of our life, our house and ever so many things that happened; the monument at the Presidency; the church, the dome of which was entirely carved wood put on later.[19]

To the pleasures and habits of seeing as well as the keenly

remembered early impressions, many painters discover an interest in the work of past masters early in their life. A well-known representational artist, Eli Levin, recalled in the course of our talk the impact that reproductions of the work of famous painters had on him. He grew up in a very literate New York family. He remembers three of the books on his parents' living room table: "We had Cézanne, Gauguin, and Van Gogh there. As a kid of six or seven, I spent long hours paging through these books and studying them. I particularly loved Van Gogh, the humanist. He is still one of my favorite painters."

The intensity with which artists experience and remember their early years is frequently linked to the help and encouragement they received from their parents and other adults who were engaged in taking care of them. In one study of creative architects, the psychologist D. W. Mac-Kinnon found that the parents of the men who were part of his study "were of artistic temperament and considerable skill."[20] They fostered their children's talents both by example and tuition. The enrichment artists receive throughout their childhood under these circumstances can contribute to their life-long openness to experience, to the intensity of their vision, and to their ability to test the boundaries of the known and the familiar. Several painters who have written of their childhood have mentioned the impact of their parents' attention to their earliest efforts at art: Käthe Kollwitz, in describing how she and her sister played with the large wooden blocks her father had built for them, has written: "We also had many long strips of waste-paper from Father's architectural designs . . . . Father kept an eye on our work and soon began saving the strips of paper we had scribbled on."[21]

And the feminist painter Judy Chicago, who also started to draw at a young age, described her mother's involvement in her work in this way:

> When I was three, I began drawing, and my mother, who
> had wanted to be a dancer, gave me a lot of
> encouragement. She told me many stories about her life
> prior to her marriage, when she went to the Jewish
> People's Institute and mingled with musicians, poets,
> and other creative people. Throughout my childhood,
> she told me colorful tales about the creative life,
> particularly when I was sick in bed, and these stories
> contributed to my developing interest in art, for, from
> the time I was young, I wanted to be an artist.[22]

The help and interest of parents who appreciate their children's talents is particularly important because most public schools fail to encourage or extend their pupils' artistic growth. On the whole, teachers often prefer highly intelligent and studious pupils to those with creative abilities. In a study where two groups of teenagers were compared (a high IQ and a highly creative group), Jacob W. Getzels and Philip W. Jackson found just such a preference among teachers. Their study showed some interesting differences among the parents of the students as well. The mothers of the high IQ adolescents were critical of their children and of their education—the authors characterized their attitude as "vigilant;" on the other hand, "the highly creative family is one in which individual divergence is permitted and risks are accepted."[23]

In a more recent study entitled *The Creative Vision*, Jacob W. Getzels and Mihály Csikszentmihályi worked with students drawn from the School of the Art Institute of Chicago. They found, as did the Wilsons, that as children these art students drew cartoon characters and copied comic book heroes. Once again these young artists remembered that the beginnings of their art-making activities were encouraged by their parents. "Most of the young artists insisted that although their first attempts were not substantially better than those of other children, their drawings were noticed more and praised more."[24] Pleased by the attention, they became more and more interested and dedicated to art. On the whole, these students felt different from their classmates, mostly because they avoided sports. Through drawings, posters, or the building of stage settings, these young people found a useful role for themselves in their classes, and thus they were able to overcome to some extent their feelings of isolation.

Fritz Scholder spoke of his own beginnings during my conversation with him. His ability to make strong personal statements in his paintings, he felt, was the outcome of a lengthy struggle leading toward self-definition. During his childhood, Scholder was plagued by a sense of alienation: he was not athletic and his Indianness was ignored by his family, who were of mixed blood themselves: "As a child, you are supposed to be the same as other children," he explained in his clear, well-modulated voice. "I, too, wished that I was everything that I was not. But, it finally dawned on me, that this is the way it had to be."

Scholder remembered that he always knew what he wanted to become: "All kids draw, but I just continued." To plan to be an artist was not easy. His parents shared the notion "of an artist as somebody in a garret who would never become anything until dead." Nevertheless, they were supportive of him, hoping, he thinks, that he would outgrow his desire to become a painter, or at least choose to go into commercial art. A similar concern was voiced by the young artists in Getzels and Csikszentmihalyi's study, who recalled that during their adolescence, their parents were also quite concerned about their choice of career.

During those years, what sustained Scholder was his recognition that he liked to draw and that he could do it well. As a shy and self-conscious young man, the recognition that he gained through his art work—starting with a poster competition that he won in the fourth grade—gave him a much needed feeling of identity: "It was even more important to me to become someone, to be something."

In their childhood recollections, many artists recall a mixture of encouragement, pride, and a sense of alienation. Though many of them have been helped by their parents, in some studies it was found that fathers tended to be emotionally removed from their creative children, while in school, many teachers seemed unsure of the best way to handle young artists. Because of their unusual interests, they were often separated from their more conforming schoolmates. At the same time, these young people's skills in drawing, painting, and building are needed and praised—while the school offers little help in developing their expertise, many young artists contine to gain visibility and thus slowly shape their sense of self.

Even within public schools, however, a place is occasionally created where artists-in-the-making find a much needed connection with others. Some high school art classes become that place, including, according to Marjorie Wilson, "communitas"—a way of being together in a group in a high school in New York State.

> The art room stands as a sanctuary between the students
> and the demands of the school. They remain free to
> transcend the limitations of the structure, to engage in
> acts which are creative or ludic or subversive, and to
> participate in a kind of communitas, a way of
> experiencing may occur in liminality, in leisure-time, by
> definition—in the world of art and artists.[25]

In her observational study, Wilson described how high school art students found, during the times when they were free from the structural demands of ordinary schooling, a "freedom to experiment and to play with the language and uses of art."[26] The students went to this room to draw: there models were available to them who posed in their leotards, and occasionally, they were exposed to an artist-in-residence. In spite of these resources, they were never under any coercion to produce. It was their own involvement in the activities—their shared enthusiasm for drawing—that strengthened the bonds among the students themselves. It was they who made this art room their sanctuary.

To those fortunate adolescents who experienced such an atmosphere, in which they learned to prepare for the art world, entering art school can be like a homecoming. Getzels and Csikszentmihályi have described some of the continuing pleasures of the young who were learning to become artists:

> It is impossible to overemphasize the intrinsic rewards
> that art work provides. The complete control over each
> action, the immediate results of each movement, the
> concreteness of the products are powerful rewards.
> Squeezing a tube of paint becomes a pleasurable sen-
> sation, the smell of the pigments is exhilarating, and so is
> the yielding feel of the clay in one's hands.[27]

The sensuous appeal of the arts and how they had influenced his eventual choice of career was described in the course of a long and thoughtful discussion by Gene Newmann, a Santa Fe abstract painter. Newmann was raised in a religious environment; he saw little art around him. His first interest was mathematics, but after several years at the University of Chicago he started to frequent a studio on campus and to paint. And yet he ruefully states "that there is no fundamental reason why anybody should become an artist. Nowadays to become an artist you have to be part of a seduction. Society, at present, does not provide a function for the artist, and any man who is reasonable would not become one."

Nonetheless, the magic of the arts continued to delight Newmann. While young, he grew up next to Ebbetts Field in Brooklyn, where his very first drawings depicted his heroes, the Dodgers. Once he started to work more seriously on his paintings, Newmann experimented with a variety of derived styles (that of Gauguin, the Fauves, and the Cubists). "When I first really tried to settle down, I thought I was tapping myself for a kind of imagery, but in fact, I was tapping whatever was available," he recalled.

The motivation for growth for the artist-in-the-making is of interest to Newmann; he is thoughtful in his opinions and hard on himself as he reconstructs his development.

Newmann spent some time in New York during the period when de Kooning, Reinhardt, and others of the New York abstractionist school were first acquiring disciples. Though at the time he did not fully understand their work, Newmann is now aware that his approaches have been deeply affected by their concerns. Among these is the need to resolve the long-standing conflict between expressionism and formalism. His description of some of the major issues in twentieth-century painting is interesting:

> I think the realization came that the structure of traditional painting was hiding too much, and although it enabled the painter to give an incredible amount of information, it was the kind of information that did not take into account a new twentieth century awareness about time. It fixed everything in static places and gave you insight into the appearance of something at a particular time. But it did not give you any room to talk about the essential attributes of a thing. That is the central discovery in Cubism, that is what I think it is about.

While he sees painting as a joyous and sensuous enterprise, Newmann also demands a stringent sense of truth from his own work:

> If you cannot get corroboration for your sense of life from any place else, you tend to bring it back, reduce it to absolutes that you can stand by.

A similar search for a true source of one's work has preoccupied other contemporary artists who do not want to repeat that which is already known or fully explored. The end of their long apprenticeship, during which they have immersed themselves in the visual concepts and cultures of their time, comes when they have found a strong and novel personal form of expression.

The noted American painter Ben Shahn wrote of this long trajectory as follows:

> Painting . . . . is not a spoken idea alone, nor a legend, nor a simple use or intention that forms what I have called the biography of a painting. It is rather the wholeness of thinking and feeling within an individual; it is partly his time and place; it is partly his childhood or even his adult fears and pleasures, and it is very greatly his thinking what he wants to think.[28]

To Make An Image That Signifies the Self

How to achieve a memorable image, how to find a contemporary and authentic subject, preoccupies most contemporary artists. There are too many styles and genres to choose from for the young artist, and "almost all [these] subjects constitute a visual cliché" remarked Fritz Scholder as he explained the challenge facing the contemporary painter:

> With the bombardment of billboards, television, and movies, we have seen everything. It is not like it was in the past, when the painter returned from North Africa, for instance, and his depiction of camels was interesting for his viewers, because they themselves had never seen such an animal. Through pictures, or through travel, we are familiar with everything.

In the response to the continuing pressure "for finding a new idiom, a new subject," Scholder seeks to maintain a profound sensitivity to all that happens to him, particularly to the interplay of color. "Painting, in twentieth century art," he explains, "has to be paint, besides being an illusion. This emphasis upon the reality of paint evolved as a recognition of the camera as a strong and competing visual force." He sees his immediate environment as profoundly affecting his work; he recalls his first walk in Paris a couple of years ago; the greys and the russets, which are so different from the clear and strong colors of the Southwest, and which are revealed in his beautiful lithograph "Indian in Paris."

"Color has to be experienced," he says. "It is a tremendous force. Once you start analyzing it, you kill it. Because it is just there to use."

Painting represents many things to Scholder. It is his catharsis, his source of sanity, and it is also a continuous and fascinating paradox. He was raised in a family where being Indian was neglected and denied. Though his father worked for the Bureau of Indian Affairs and was himself part American Indian, he was determined to be fully accepted by mainstream society. Only when Fritz Scholder took a job as an instructor at the Institute of American Indian Arts, where he has taught some of the most gifted students, did the young painter have much contact with Indians. Their conflicts, their beauty, and the changing pace of life that faced these young people at the Institute affected the young instructor deeply. Through them Scholder developed an interest in the ways in which Indians have been painted in the past:

Here is a subject which has been depicted in a romantic
vein in history books, in Hollywood, by the Taos
[Anglo] painters. Everybody has done "The Noble
Savage" sharpening his arrows and looking into the
bonfire . . . and of course, this role is usually played by
an Italian in the movies.

I became interested in doing it in a different way as so
much is to be said!

In his own work Scholder has rejected all easy stereotypes about
Indians. Some of his canvases are the expression of pain, such as the
"Massacre at Wounded Knee." In others, he displays a joyous, at times
satirical, style in his contemporary depiction of cowboys, film Indians,
and others in his series of "Indians in Transition." He is convinced that
such a new and less romantic view is necessary as "it had never been
painted honestly before, and nobody, certainly, had painted the Indian
the way he is today." His work, Scholder stresses, has the objective of
painting strong visual images. These are exciting and memorable for
the viewer, and they furnish the artist with surprises, while he or she
is in the process of fashioning them.

My own way of thinking is primarily verbal, so I asked a number of
graphic artists to clarify what they meant by a "strong image." Martine
Franck, the Belgian photographer, spoke of it "as a structure which enhances the content." In a more personal vein, Scholder spoke of it as
the source of effective imagery in his own work:

I truly believe that a strong image, or any kind of strong
statement, must come from the person who has found out
who he is, and who has accepted it. . . . And then the
artist takes his strength and develops it.

We all can gain from a certain amount of knowledge
and training, but it has to be digested into "one's own
thing." It is all from oneself, that is where these energies
come from.

Gene Newmann also spoke of meaningful sources of painting in his
comment about the English artist Francis Bacon:

It is very sad, that a painter as phenomenally gifted as
Francis Bacon, who has all the attributes required to

create great paintings—in the sense of the old
masters—cannot do it because he is too honest. He feels
his honesty obligates him to deal strictly with his
own life.

The need for honesty in painting is something of an obsession for
Newmann: "It is one of the tragedies of our time, as far as painting is concerned, that in order for us to have any authenticity, we have to become rudimentary: to get to a most fundamental vision about a figure,
an environment, a landscape."

The journey involved in finding one's own place in the course of "continual creation" (Newmann's phrase) is expressed with great power by
several women painters. Judy Chicago wrote of her search in her autobiography *Through the Flower*. She had examined various sources, including women's self-portraits in women's literature of the past and
present, in an effort to find her own resolution:

> Studying women's art and literature made it clear that
> most female creators had *not* had a mode of expression
> that was essentially different from men's. Rather, they,
> as I, had embedded a different *content*, in the prevailing
> aesthetic mode of their time, and in so doing, had
> rendered their point of view invisible to mainstream
> culture.[29]

She wanted to go farther in her own work; she wanted to throw off
the massive male content of her early paintings, and develop a form of
art that expressed and communicated a female point of view. She turned
to the writings of Virginia Woolf and Anaïs Nin, who in their writing
had articulated some of the issues of greatest concern to her:

> I had discovered a quality of transparency, both in the
> writing and in the imagery. I asked Anaïs about it and
> she spoke about the "transparency of the psyche"—the
> sense of being able to see through successive layers to
> the very core of reality. . . . This realization helped me
> affirm one of my own impulses as an artist—to make my
> work openly subject-matter oriented (while still being
> abstract) and to try to reveal intimate emotional material
> through my forms.[30]

Recently, Judy Chicago completed a major project aimed at the development of a female visual language, celebrating women's culture and history. *The Dinner Party* consists of a room-size sculpture, in the middle of which is a table with thirty-nine plates representing the most outstanding women throughout the ages. Chicago chose ceramics and embroidery to celebrate these women. While she worked alone to plan the project, she chose a group of collaborators for its final execution. This was not the first time that she was working with a collective. At the California Institute of Art, Chicago started a feminist program with the help of the well-known painter Miriam Shapiro. Together, they created "Womanhouse," which became "both an environment that housed the work of women artists working out of their experiences and the 'house' of female reality into which one entered to experience the real facts of women's lives, feelings, and concerns."[31]

In New York, where she was born, Miriam Shapiro had worked closely with the then dominant group of abstract expressionist painters. After moving to California, and collaborating with other women artists, her work changed. She abandoned her previous style of large "architectural visions of space," and a new and exciting imagery developed—one that reflected her involvement in women's lives—and where she used different materials.

Still, she was prone to self-doubts. In an interview published in *Working It Out*, Shapiro gave voice to these doubts, and tensions confronting women throughout their careers:

> When I look back on the years of excessive self-doubt, I
> wonder how I was able to make my paintings. In part, I
> managed to paint because I had a desire, as strong as
> the desire for food and sex, to push through, *to make an
> image that signified.*[32][Emphasis added.]

The painters I talked to seem to thrive on the challenge of overcoming both the self-doubt and the cliches of which Shapiro spoke, and in so doing making art with an elation. They are committed to creating images "that signify." The sources of their "strong images" include the artistic and social demands of their times: their pleasure in nature, in color, in remembered sights. And they view painting with the utmost of seriousness, and with the utmost of pleasure, while giving form to their understanding, a form which enhances and extends the known contents of the languages of vision.

The Moving Images of Thought

At the turn of the century, the great American psychologist William James compared the stream of consciousness to a bird's life:

> As we take, in fact, a general view of the wonderful stream
> of consciousness, what strikes us first is this different
> pace of its parts. Like a bird's life, it seems to be made of
> an alternation of flights and perchings.[33]

In one of the slower phases of thought, images appear in consciousness and are inspected like paintings in a gallery. One kind of a view that appears in front of the mind's eye are the recollections of childhood. While these images are not always available to our consciousness, once some of them are effectively lifted from some inner layer of the mind, they become accessible to us with increasing clarity. Raphael Soyer mused about this phenomenon in his *Diary of An Artist:* "Now that I am engaged in writing this, I find some early memories appear more vivid, in the literal sense of the word [they] appear. They come out of the deep recesses of the mind."[34]

The way in which images call forth one another may characterize not only the course of our recollections, but some of the aspects of artistic creation. Ben Shahn has described such a clustering of images that gave form to one of his paintings in *The Shape of Content,* his Norton lectures at Harvard on the nature of art. Shahn wrote of how the report of a tragic fire in Chicago served as the beginning of the painting, which he named "Allegory." It was Shahn's goal to capture on canvas an "immense idea" which "asks for a full orchestration of color, depth, texture, and form."[35] At first he could only sketch the diverse images and associations that came immediately to mind. As he thought about the event, trying to give form to his somewhat inchoate notions, he relived the fires he had witnessed as a child: one such fire had injured his father and destroyed his family's home and possessions. And he then began experimenting with a variety of mythical figures, symbols of the dreaded, fire-wrought destruction. In the finished painting, the allegorical beast which fills the canvas combines a flame-crowned lion head, some features of the Roman wolf of antiquity, as well as others drawn from an oversized family cat. The large red creature towers over its small, dead victims, which lie heaped upon each other under the animal's legs.

In reconstructing the experiences tapped for this painting—the sources of his images—Shahn identified several distinct influences. Some of them were drawn from his childhood, some were based upon artistic works, while others were derived from his daily life. As with shavings drawn by a magnet, these diverse images were pulled together by Shahn's "immense idea" and in the course of the long artistic "tug of war between idea and image" the "Allegory" was completed.[36]

As is clear from Shahn's account, the final work of the artist is the outcome of a visual grammar of composition. In linking separate elements into an integrated whole, visual composition is a relational process that is akin to the grammar of verbal sentences. The picture on the surface of the canvas is constructed from varied flights of the artist's thought; but for the viewer, only the strong and stable image is visible. Once completed, a painting becomes a Jamesian "perching," a framed moment in the shared visual culture of time. A variety of these visual grammars are evident in the arts, and the compositional process in painting belongs to this category.

The visual grammar governing the construction of cinematic narratives is another. Film is orchestrated movement; many intriguing parallels exist between the manifold itineraries of the human mind at work and the ways in which images, memories, associations, and stories are combined on celluloid. The great Italian maestro of movies Federico Fellini spoke of the connection between these two processes in the course of an interview with Eugene Walter:

> Human beings have been staring into the clouds and imagining "ifs" since time began. Now they have the cinema screen with some "ifs" already set up to trigger their own. Think what a bale of memories and associations and all we carry about with us. It's like seeing a dozen films simultaneously. There's memory, there's memory that has been sorted and filed, what they call subconscious. There's also the cellar of the subconscious, a subconscious subconscious. There is a kind of idealized set of sketches of the dinner party we'll go to tomorrow night. And there's also what is happening around us, visible and invisible. Fiction imposes order and invents a manner to contain life, but cinema just picks up her muddy skirts and chooses a path through chaos. She just wants to give pleasure. She solicits memory or association as easily as she does daily reality.[37]

Film-makers select from human experience the images that illustrate this approach to truth. In this pursuit, a great number of younger film-makers now reject careful advanced planning in filming; instead, as in *cinema verité*, they wish to record life as it is.

The limitations and problems of such an approach were pointed out to me by George Stoney, a New York documentary film-maker. At the time of our talk in 1976, he was working on a reconstruction of the filming of *Man of Aran*. The original Flaherty film was made in the early thirties on a rugged island off Scotland to which Stoney had returned. In preparation for his film, he had taped many of the daily activities of the fishermen and their families on Aran. The notion of time was central to his work, and it was while playing back his footage to an audience who was not familiar with the setting that he had some interesting new ideas about juxtaposition and time: To be simply faithful to the unidirectional flow of time is not always the preferred way to make a movie. He said:

> Some very fine film-makers of the realistic school say that
> they cannot intercut things from out of time, they
> cannot cut through the time sequence. But, my God, we
> do this in our mind all the time. I mean, we are haunted
> by this fracturing of time.

The cinematic possibilities of representing on film the complex chain of mental images, the rapid and slowed visions of the mind's eye, also intrigued Henry Jaglom, a Hollywood director of art films. During a long and leisurely talk in his wonderfully overgrown garden, Jaglom spoke of his training as an actor, of the first time he used a camera during the Six Day War in Israel, and of his editing work on *Easy Rider*, which established his reputation in films. Movies make it possible, he said, "to make something live from the past."

Even while asleep, Jaglom had the desire to construct moving images from his dreams:

> I have some photographs of my father's father and mother
> in Russia. . . . I never knew them. But by putting my
> grandfather's hand in a certain way and his head back, I
> could get him to move, to walk. And finally to create a
> few frames.

His interest in exploring what he called the "undermind" dated back to his childhood. "From the age of twelve, it was clear to me that I wanted to create these images; if I could grasp what is going on in my brain successfully, I could do it by putting it up on the screen." When I asked Jaglom about his own memory—film-makers need to have exceptional recall, particularly when editing—he said that he was absent-minded in daily life, but not when working on a movie. He thinks that his mind, by itself, selects those things he needs for his art: colors, smells, feelings, and associations. These perceptions and experiences are grouped together, and he seems to be able to call upon this commonly stored resource; moreover, events that are artistically less valuable to him are stored elsewhere, as it were.

The subject of memory formed the basis of *A Safe Place*, the movie that is his favorite among his work to date. Orson Welles plays a kind of wonder rabbi in the film; he is a magical figure who tells the film's main character, Susan, played by Tuesday Weld: "Last night in my sleep I dreamt that I was sleeping, and dreaming in that sleep that I had awakened, I fell asleep."

A Safe Place was made in 1971 and reflected themes common to several films made at that time: the sense of insecurity and sudden loss in America and people's isolation from each other. But Jaglom wished to go beyond some of these shared themes and deal with deeper, emotional truths as well. He cherishes Anaïs Nin's comments about the film, which the great diarist reviewed and praised: "For the first time a description of the mixture we live by, this interweaving of dream, childhood wishes for magic power, fantasy interfering with experience, the constant transformation of reality by illusion."[38]

To achieve these ends, Jaglom worked with actors whom he had cast very carefully, and whose movements and insights jointly helped shape his directorial work:

> I can write a superstructure, but the film is expressed in the actors: I know what I want to explore, and I cast *very* carefully—I cast actors very close to the characters. Basically if Tuesday Weld makes a turn of her head, it is film, it will be more moving to me, than if I write four pages of dialogue to show the mood she is in when she turns her head. . . .
>
> I just have to encourage the actors to break all inhibitions between themselves and their expressiveness and to get their emotions out on the screen, to get the

fullness of their own expression. They do the scene and
then I tell them at the end of the scene, "those are my
words, now just continue the scene in your own
words." And frequently, in the editing, I cut out all my
words and just use the dialogue they gave me.

It is in the process of editing that Jaglom makes a movie into his own.
He compares his film editing to painting, and recalls that as a child he
spent a lot of time drawing, working repeatedly with the same design,
which he would not abandon until he was completely satisfied. He brings
the same obstinacy and need for excellence to his editing. But he has a
joyous sense of play as well; editing is "like adding a little blue to the
sky, and then seeing the trees as too green, and changing the tree to
red; and then distorting the shape of the tree," he says.

There are many similarities in the ways in which film-makers shape
the common cinematic language. Each of them also strives to express—
both in content and in form—a specific view of the power of the cinema, of its marvelous possibilities. To Jaglom, this is a medium in which
emotional truth can be captured:

I want to be moved by every piece of film of mine that I
see. I want it not to lie and I want it to reflect the
confusion and chaos of our existence rather than try to
dishonestly create an illusion, that there is a purpose, a
clarity, a structure; and that somehow if you follow the
structure, everything is going to be all right.

Luis Buñuel, the Spanish director, saw his films less as a conscious
than a subconscious montage of images, not reflecting, but creating chaos:

The screen is a dangerous and wonderful instrument, if
a free spirit uses it. It is the superior way of expressing
the world of dreams, emotions and instincts. The
cinema seems to have been invented for the expression
of the subconscious, so profoundly is it rooted in poetry.
Nevertheless, it almost never pursues these ends. . . .

The particular story, the private drama of an
individual cannot interest—I believe—anyone worthy of
living in our time. If a man in the audience shares the
joys and sorrows of a character on the screen, it should

be because the character reflects the joys and sorrows of
all society and so the personal feelings of the man in the
audience.[39]

Although these film-makers differ in their emphases upon the social
or personal truths of their work, they share the view that the cinema
differs from other art forms in the way it uses visual grammar to represent internal and external reality.

The film idiom is still a rapidly changing one. Its technical innova-
tions such as color, stereoscopic cinema, hand-held cameras, techniques
of montage, and new editing devices are still historically quite young
and contribute to a constantly shifting cinematic language of expression. The director can create filmic time and space that is different from
that of daily experience and difficult to achieve in other, more slowly
evolving, artistic media. In part, the great excitement and popularity of
cinema in our time is due to its ability to represent the moving images
of thought on many levels—conscious and subconscious. It is through
these languages of cinema that viewers may experience the previously
hidden links between the past and the present, the observer and the
observed, and the mind and the "undermind."

The Visual Networks of Thought

In the course of the twentieth century, both the arts and the sciences
have explored the complex and contradictory processes of nature and
human nature. No longer are the objects of study represented as isolated substances; it is relationships that we seek in our new, post-
Einsteinian era of understanding. The power of visual thinking is that
it illuminates and makes manifest this ability to conceptualize our experiences as structures in motion, as relationships.

But this is a most difficult task. It was Cézanne who brought forth a
new visual consciousness of the multiplicity of relationships inherent
in viewing the world. His exploration started with a rather simple fact:
if one approached a visual surface first with one eye open and then closed
that eye and looked at the same area with the other eye, the view
changed. Similarly, if one changed position in relationship to what was
observed, the view was altered again. Though most people prefer to
inhibit the results of these shifts in favor of a stabilized view of the world,
Cézanne was both troubled and intrigued by the aesthetic possibilities
these differences of perception offered the artist. His approach to a res-

olution of these and other visual paradoxes was described by John Berger, the British art critic:

> The order in a painting like *Trees by Water* has been established *between* the possibilities suggested by the different viewpoints. A new kind of certainty has been called into being—a certainty based on the acceptance of doubt. Nature in a picture is no longer something laid out in front of the spectator for him to examine. It now includes him and the evidence of his senses and his constantly changing relationships to what he is seeing.
>
> Before Cézanne, every painting was to some extent like a view seen through a window. Courbet had tried to open the window and climb out. Cézanne broke the glass. The room became part of the landscape, the viewer part of the view.[40]

Many of the artistic conventions developed in the wake of Cézanne's trailbreaking work deal with the dynamics of the picture surface. As György Kepes has said, "The representational image is never identical with spatial reality, but approximates it according to the prevalent standards of interest and knowledge.[41]" And so, to give form to their visual insights, contemporary artists not only study each other's work, they acquaint themselves with photography, with work in optics and color research, and with the findings of the psychological investigations of perception.

It is not surprising, therefore, to find a similar emphasis upon the dynamics of visual phenomena among scientists and artists. Such an approach has replaced the earlier view. No longer do we believe that sensations and images were simply presented to the mind's eye. Rudolf Arnheim has written that the necessary activity of construction inherent in perception comes from "the wrestling with the work of visual art (until it) reveals how active shape-building is."[42]

The construction of stable precepts is needed for effective human adaptation, but the perceivers also have to pay attention to rapidly shifting information in the course of their activities. The dynamics of perception are formed by the interplay of these two modes: one mode yielding a stable world by shaping forms into more enduring concepts; and the other mode, consisting of the "jump-cuts" of vision, in which the perceiver monitors the staccato changes of light, movements, and events that give new meaning to his or her experience. It was such a dynamic view that dazzled Cézanne, who at one time was worried about some possible deformity in his vision.

In her book *The Mind and the Eye*, the biologist Agnes Arber wrote of "the visual and conceptual interpretation of the perceived."[43] She described how even the simplest acts of seeing require the work of an integrated nervous system—capable of a sensory division of labor and of synthesis—or what the British psychologist R. L. Gregory has called the work of "the intelligent eye." In the more complex construction of concepts, the individual is engaged in streamlining, accentuating, and categorizing impressions that are then crystallized into larger entities. These acts of knowing are both individual and social in nature because categorizing is rooted in and influenced by the cultural framework of experience.

However, no single theory of perception and thought can embrace all of these various processes of adaptation and knowing. Both scientists and artists, therefore, tend to focus upon some singular, salient, and simplified aspect of the totality. In the search for theories, the influence of the British empiricists, those philosophers and psychologists who emphasized a rather passive flow of sensations and associations, held sway for a long time. Their efforts at simplifying the constructive work of the mind were sympathetically followed by the American behaviorists, whose efforts had a similar reductionist objective.

In this century, European psychologists on the continent, whether of the Gestalt school, as students of Freud, or of Piaget's Geneva school of epistemologists, have not favored the reductionist approach. The analysis of cognitive processes into isolated elements was rejected by these thinkers, who have developed various approaches to the dynamics of perception and thought. While their work is justly influential in perceptual, clinical, and developmental inquiries, these European scholars have tended to ignore the social and historical roots of thought.

Artists and critics, rather than psychologists, have stressed the necessity of examining the historical shifts in our visual preferences and conceptualizations. Painters, film-makers, and photographers, by relying upon the visual construction of thought, have given form to the volatile and stable features of our world. Their work expresses the relativity of observations. And it emphasizes the importance of material and technological developments and their effects on the inquiring mind of the perceiver. In these ways they accentuate some of the shared sources of imagery that individuals born into the same culture have in common. The shapes of dwellings, the styles of clothes, the nature of tools, and the recurrent images on television and in the movies contribute to our habits of seeing. The very power of these influences creates visual clichés, which visual artists are constantly struggling against, to break through, to overcome, and to recreate in new forms of perceived life.

What, then, is visual thinking? It is the representation of knowledge in the form of structures in motion; it is the study of relationships of these forms and structures; it is the flow of images as pictures, diagrams, explanatory models, orchestrated paintings of immense ideas, and simple gestures; it is work with schemes and structures of the mind.

In this study of visual thinking, I have relied in particular on the insights of those who have linked the internal forms of visualization to a mastery of graphic, plastic, or cinematic language because no direct observation of inner visualization can be done. The easy availability of images was frequently mentioned both by artists and scientists whom I had talked with, or whose written works I had searched for a description of their thought processes. These individuals share with others outside their professions a reliance upon mental pictures as a record of their past, and the reliance upon more generic images as kernels of their understanding of biological and physical processes. But productive thinkers use their stubborn patience to work with these images to go beyond the representational function of visual thought. They find new thoughts hidden as metaphors in their reflections, as did the young Einstein while riding on his wave; these images lead them to new generative syntheses.

The internal and external forms of visualization are fluid and flexible means of representation that respond well to the personal imprint of the artist. Visual thought and visual languages have in the twentieth century provided a much needed resource for making relativistic statements about reality. In contrast with verbal language, where it is sometimes difficult to soften or to qualify a statement, visual expression is ready-made for a myriad of nuances. And it is in cinema, particularly, that the rapidly changing, questing, uncertain, doubting times in which we live have found their most memorable reflection.

5 / Verbal Thinking

A thought may be compared to a cloud shedding a shower of words.

L. S. Vygotsky

It is by means of language that poets, writers, and philosophers, who are driven by the need to think beyond the limits of the known, have attempted to share with others their personal inquiries. While film and the graphic media lend themselves well to the fluidity of experience, words are frequently used to explore some of the more universal aspects of existence.

Language is a bridge between individuals who wish to overcome divisions born of the diversity of human experience. It is also a bridge between inner thought and shared understanding: the past and the present, the world of the senses and the realm of thought.

The differing forms of language reveal these different uses. Writing is an explicit and expanded form usually addressed to distant or unknown audiences. Inner speech, on the other hand, is directed inward, toward the self. It is a highly condensed language of thought where each word may stand for manifold ideas.

A psychological description of the processes of separation and unification of the diverse aspects of language is shallow without a reliance upon the insights of writers, they who have charted the varied ways in which ideas are woven into text.

The Telegrams of Thought

In the notebooks and journals of writers, one occasionally reads entries which, while intriguing, are rather hard to interpret. When writers are at the edge of new work, their thoughts may occur in quick bursts. When their ideas are jotted down, they lack the usual polish of well-crafted prose found in most other passages in these journals.

On a late September day in 1938, Virginia Woolf wrote in her diary that she was too tired to proceed with her work in the usual manner. Instead she chose to sketch the next chapter of her biography of Roger Fry. Her ideas were jotted down in a staccato, thinking-aloud manner as follows:

> Suppose I make a break after H's death (madness).
> A separate paragraph quoting what R. himself said.
> Then a break.
> Then begin definitely with the first meeting.
> That is the first impression: a man of the world, not a professor or Bohemian. Then give facts in his letters to his mother.
> Then back to the second meeting.
> Pictures: talk about art. I look out of window.
> His persuasiveness—a certain density—wished to persuade you to like what he liked.
> Give the pre-war atmosphere. Ott. Duncan. France
> Letter to Bridges about beauty and sensuality.
> His exactingness. Logic.[1]

Little of communicative value is found in these transcriptions of Woolf's thoughts unless the reader examines the finished biography to reconstruct the direction and meaning of her thoughts. It then becomes clear that when Woolf wrote of a "first meeting" she was referring to her first encounter with Fry, or that H. stands for Helen Fry, the critic's wife who suffered from an incurable disease and was hospitalized for the last three decades of her life. These notes are jottings to the self; they assist the writer remembering an organization of important details and concepts that emerge in the sequence of her work. Use of a telegraphic style makes it possible to gallop ahead, exploring new connections, a task that is much harder when the writer's intention is to shape connected and readable prose. Often when there is some transcribed record of the way in which writers plan their work, it takes the form of these very condensed thoughts.

In recalling an early period in his life as a writer, Henry Miller described an incident to George Wickes, his interviewer for *The Paris Review*. Miller, who had just quit a full-time job, was having a hard time in getting anything written. Rather than producing works on paper, he would talk a great deal about his ideas. But one day, when his wife had left town,

> Instead of going home, I was seized by this idea of plan-
> ning the book of my life and I stayed up all night doing
> it. I planned everything that I have written to date in
> about forty or fifty typewritten pages. I wrote it in notes,
> in a telegraphic style.[2]

These telegraphic notes through which the writer explores the first outlines of a plot resemble inner speech, as it was characterized by the Russian psychologist L. S. Vygotsky. One aspect of inner speech, which he described in *Thought and Language*, was that "a single word is so saturated with sense that many words would be required to explain it in external speech." In this way inner speech is given to "heavy predi-cation" and "semantic shorthand."[3]

A wonderful example of this is provided by Dostoevsky's notebooks. In the first entry in the notebook on *A Raw Youth*, the great novelist sketches some of his still very vague ideas about characters and settings:

> A school teacher, a novel (description of the effect of
> Gogol's work, . . . *Taras Bul'ba*, has on him).
> Enemies, the village clerk (a correspondence leads to
> their approval).
> A Christian Hamlet.
> A tale about a humble Russian peasant, Ivan Matveevich
> Prokhodimor.
> An apocryphal gospel (N.B. Temptation by the Devil, a
> clay bird before those poor in spirit. Socialists and
> nationalists in Jerusalem. Women. Children.)[4]

Edward Wasiolek, as editor of the notebooks, did extensive research on Dostoevsky's life and on succeeding versions of his plots in order to offer a key to the notebooks. Regarding the phrase "Temptation by the Devil," for example, Wasiolek informs us,

> The theme of the temptation by the devil will figure im-
> portantly in "The Legend of the Grand Inquisitor" and
> is apparently on Dostoevsky's mind at this early date. A
> short time later, in January, 1876, in *The Diary of a Writer*,
> Dostoevsky will address himself to the question of what

is meant by one of the devil's temptations, "turning stones into bread."[5]

Some of the notations in journals perform what is basically a planning function. There are others that represent a first attempt to express a new and complex idea. The task of translating inner speech into effective language is the task of communication. The challenge is particularly great when one attempts to express an innovative idea in a manner that will be clear and which will hold the reader's attention. And such new concepts are especially likely to possess "the extreme, elliptical economy of inner speech, changing the speech pattern almost beyond recognition"[6]—a characterization of generative inner speech given by Vygotsky.

In the course of developing effective forms for the externalization of thought, the writer produces successive approximations of texts through expansion, rephrasing, and editing. This process can be observed in the early pages of Dostoevsky's notebooks for *The Possessed*. The following notation is found in the early pages:

1) Lizaveta (illegible word) Shchurov
2) Kartuzov . . . "An Attempt of an Idea"
3) Three People, etc.

Later in the notebook he begins to develop the character Kartouzov in the following way:

Kartouzov is a poor conversationalist; he never finishes his sentences. He is never embarrassed, apparently he does not suspect that he is funny. He can be quite businesslike when necessary. He conducts himself well, strictly according to etiquette. But only to a certain point, so long as he can remain silent and is not obliged to do anything.[8]

In the next entry the novelist shapes his work with an eye to the point of view of the reader:

N.B. Begin by drawing a picture of how Kartouzov becomes interested (in the Amazon, E.W.), and intrigue the reader by a description of his early moves: he is critical of the Amazon, he dresses himself up; he is with his

> friends, the jeweler, the governess; he gets to the point
> of hating; he raises his finger to the peak of his cap.
> And suddenly he is in love—everything becomes clear.[7]

These notes illustrate a move from single-word jottings to quick character sketch and then the beginnings of plot, a method of work that Wasiolek views as characteristic of Dostoevsky who, he believes, proceeds in his creative movement from the logic of his characters, to action. Even so, these early entries are not used in the final novel; much of what the writer does in his notebooks is, according to his editor, "the purging of old ideas, old situations, and worn-out intentions."

One aspect of the writer's work that is illustrated in Dostoevsky's notebooks is the way in which he gained a critical distance from his own words. The many cycles of writing facilitate the development of the inner critic in the writer, as well as the polishing of his or her craft. It is this latter function of diary writing that is illustrated by the published journals of H. D. Thoreau, André Gide, Anaïs Nin and many others who explored their reactions to the day's events by putting their observations into words. The private nature of these journals contributes to a relaxed shaping of their style. While thinking frequently erupts in bursts of connected ideas, in writing it is sometimes important to develop fully a single thought. In reading Thoreau's journals, one encounters many entries that illustrate the careful unfolding of an observation into a thoughtful paragraph:

> Nov. 8 [1858] Each phase of nature, while not invisible,
> is yet not too distinctive and obtrusive. It is there to be
> found when we look for it, but not demanding our
> attention. It is like a silent but sympathizing companion,
> in whose company we retain most of the advantages of
> solitude, with whom we can walk and talk, or be silent,
> naturally, without the necessity of talking in a strain
> foreign to the place.[8]

Thoreau paid close attention to nature and sought to adapt its rhythms to his style, while Anaïs Nin was particularly interested in capturing the fluidity of character in words. She saw her life-long habit of diary writing as a way to break out of the prison of inarticulateness, a thought Thoreau might have agreed with.

Many writers have a need to make life more understandable and memorable by the use of words. Margaret Drabble spoke to me of language as a way "to find order and sense in experience." Saul Bellow, in speaking of the "primitive commentator in all of us," recalled the strong tendency to observe and put observations into words that dated back to childhood years.

The function of writing as a means of reaching out to others through words—friends or relatives who are removed from the writer—was frequently discussed by Anaïs Nin, who started her *Diaries* after she had immigrated to America. She came to this country as a young girl with her mother and brothers. Her father chose to remain in Spain, and the young Anaïs was deeply troubled by his absence. She wished to include him in all that they did, in all that happened to them, and thus she started to write daily in a journal. Eventually, the writing itself became an important part of her own life, and she frequently addressed the diary, in a somewhat childish manner, as "friend."

For many writers, the need to verbalize experience, to express in language some of the more tangled and difficult aspects of living, begins at an early age. Margaret Drabble told me that she started to write at age six or seven and Jessica Mitford wrote continuously: "if one was away from home, one would write one's sisters two or three times a week, and the parents and such." Since part of verbal fluency consists of the skill of translating inner, telegraphic speech into an effective written text, this activity may well be made easier for those who have started to organize their thinking through written language at an early age through the keeping of a diary, correspondence with family members, the construction of plays and skits in childhood—all of which may assist the future writer in acquiring his or her craft.

Future writers are not the only ones who rely upon words as a way to overcome personal isolation. It is with the aid of language that we bridge different aspects of our existence: the past, the present, and the future. From the very beginnings of life, the infant is surrounded by language, which he or she acquires through the daily exchanges of play and mutually articulated need. The genesis of verbal thinking is linked to these dialogues, which strengthen the bonds between children and those who take care of them.

From Verbal Dialogues to Verbal Thinking

Infants are deeply dependent beings: they discover the smell, shape, and feel of their world with the help of their caretakers, who guarantee their survival. Just as the mother accommodates her body to support her child physically at a time when it cannot as yet stand alone, she also alters her language to make it clearer and more vivid to the child who has not yet mastered speaking. The profound reciprocity that characterizes the early years of human living is illustrated by the joint attention paid to interesting objects and happenings by the child and the caretaker: by their games, such as peek-a-boo; by looking at books together; and by the finely-tuned language of the adult who both follows and leads the child in their mutual dialogues.

During the short absences of caretaking adults, some theorists have maintained that children practice language in order to fill the void they experience so keenly.[9] Their own voices and those they hear originating at a distance help them to feel part of those family activities which are still beyond their strengths and skills for direct participation.

Much as Anaïs Nin used her diary as a way to feel connected with the absent parent, very young children use vocal and verbal play as part of their efforts at building human connections. Thus, the communicative and emotive functions of language are rooted in the young child's dependence, in the unceasing needs of the very young to be sustained by others. During the lengthy process of acquiring speech, the child discovers that objects have names, and starts asking for them. By substituting the more precise words for communicative gestures, the child is not only more successful in having his or her needs satisfied, but is also starting to embark on a cognitive path of learning about referential meaning.

In their intellectually momentous preschool years, children experiment with words and sounds in addition to imitating some aspects of the language that is addressed to them. At the beginning of the acquisition of their native tongue, they have a short production span; at the age of two, they can string only two words together into an utterance, for instance "airplane bye" or "Adam write." These early, abbreviated or telegraphic phrases are usually understood by those who share with the child the context in which the words were uttered. When adults expand these utterances into fully formed sentences, they are helped in making their guesses by their participation in the child's activities and by their personal knowledge of the child. An interesting parallel might be drawn between these early exchanges between two generations during which the adult adds to the child's utterances, and the very different expansion of inner speech into communicable language done by the adult speaker or thinker.

Some developmental scholars underestimate the great variety of forms and functions of language. They see this cognitive and communicative process as socially constructed and lacking in the flexibility of imagery.

Jean Piaget is among those who limit the theoretical importance of language as a means of thought.[10] But the closer study of language reveals an extraordinary flexibility in the manifold transformations from external to inner speech. The fine tuning of dialogue between more and less experienced speakers are examples of this structural and semantic variety; for, although the varied functions of language are embedded in a social context, in the course of language development, particularly through the internalization of speech, new intrapersonal functions emerge in the individual's need to construct a verbal model of reality.

Nevertheless, the development of the cognitive function of language is a slow one. This may be linked to the plenitude of discoveries made by young children during the first years of their active explorations. They discover varied aspects of their world directly and indirectly, through touch and taste as well as through words and pictures. To ascribe meaning to these encounters, these young scientists of life advance many hypotheses: they test the edibility of objects placed before them and discover that some are neither soft nor digestible; they encounter physical barriers and learn to circle around them; they ask the questions "What is this?" or "Why do things happen this way?" and they use the answers they receive to join their own discoveries to the knowledge they are given by the older generation.

Children are both taught and they teach themselves. Their self-education is through play during these early years. The solitary practice of language is described in *Language in the Crib* by Ruth Weir, who taped her son Anthony's presleep monologues unbeknownst to him. The child seemed to be rehearsing his newly fashioned sentences while lying in his crib: "Bobo is not throwing. Bobo can throw it."[11] In addition to the bedroom, it has been found that children speak to themselves in the bath tub, the sandbox, the doll and block corner, and so forth.

The children's monologues become more complex with age as they shift from playful rehearsals to the commentary about their activities. One of the first of these "thinking-aloud" monologues recorded in the psychological literature appeared in Piaget's classic *The Language and Thought of the Child*. At the Institut Rousseau's nursery a six-year-old boy, "Lev," was sitting at his table talking to himself:

> *I want to do that drawing, there . . . . I want to draw*
> *something, I do. I shall need a big piece of paper to do*
> *that.*
> Lev knocks over a game: *There! Everything's*
> *fallen down.*

Lev has just finished his drawing: *Now I want to do something else.*[12]

In this segment, "Lev" is planning his future activities, as well as musing about what he is engaged in at the moment. The directive, or planning function, of these monologues is of particular interest to me, as it is one of the precursors of inner speech. In the course of the acquisition of language, children move at times in a zig-zag fashion, between the public and private uses of words. The communicative pressure for clarity is demanding even for experienced, adult speakers; for the young learner it is exhausting. Thus, talking to oneself is helpful to preschool children, for it allows them to privately rehearse difficult words and complex grammatical structures. Under the pressure of school, these overt rehearsals and commentaries are internalized: they form the subvocal speeches of thought and become the basis of the much condensed inner speech.

The Magic of Words

In playing with language, children discover the charm of the rhymes and rhythms with which they sing, tease, argue, and enchant. Preschool children have a particularly fine flair for figurative language, as was shown by the psychologist Howard Gardner, who collected many examples of these in his study of the development of figures of speech: "sad as a pimple" or "quiet as a magic marker" are examples.[13]

Some nursery school teachers are gifted in encouraging this sort of experimentation with words. They frequently take the time to write down children's early poems. My son was fortunate in having such a teacher who transcribed many of his spoken "poems":

> Painting is fun,
> Painting is done
>   with yellow
>   and jello
>   and brown
>   and hown (?)
>   S.J. age 4

These lines have the quality of short songs, moving like the toddler does when listening to the same music again and again. The words and rhythm of nursery rhymes, lullabies, the much treasured lines of books, such as *The House at Pooh Corner,* add to the treasury from which more structured and knowing poetry writing is later born.

In the Southwest, young Indian children hear traditional tales at bedtime, especially during the long winter months, from the grandfather, who is the cherished storyteller. These quiet times together create a very special bond across generations, and are frequently recalled in interviews and in poems by American Indians. One teacher told me that she used to run to fetch very cold water from the pump for her tired grandfather when he came into the house after working in the fields. She would do this even if a friend had asked her to come and play together: "But, then he is my Grandpa, and he is the source of my Indian stories. Whenever I come to him, no matter how tired he is, if I need an Indian story, he never tells me to go out and play with your friend."

Grandfather and I

Grandfather and I talk
Grandfather sings, I dance
Grandfather teaches, I learn
Grandfather dies, I cry.

I wait patiently to see Grandfather in the work of
darkness,
I miss my Grandfather, patient waiting is greeted by
loneliness,
I cry, and cry, and cry, when will I see him?[14]

This poem was written by Joseph Concha, a young man from the Taos Indian Pueblo. In the day school he attended, his teacher Constantine Ailello had introduced creative writing, and found that the students were as imaginative with their words as they were in their drawings. Concha at first read and copied poems from published collections. Then his teacher suggested to him some possible themes for poems of his own, but he quickly outgrew these and discovered his own poetic domain.

Concha's writing in part concerns the visual power of Taos. This mountain village has been celebrated by many painters and writers, including D. H. Lawrence, and the young poet is aware of its hold on him and the difficulty of capturing all of it in verse.

"Sometimes when I see things I just admire them," he told me during our talk at the outskirts of the Pueblo: "So I think there is my poem out there, I want to catch it, but I am lazy. I cannot run, so I just watch it run away. I enjoy seeing it leave, like a bird flying away." Actually,

Concha writes quite a lot. Often, when he finds himself without a pencil, he scratches his words into the red-clay earth.

On graduating from the Taos day school, Concha enrolled at the Institute of American Indian Arts in Santa Fe. There, he responded with enthusiasm when his new teachers helped him to pay attention to the new sounds he heard, like those of the highway next to the school, and in this way he expanded the sources of his imagery. When he was only fifteen-years old, Concha published his first small volume of poetry, *Lonely Deer*. During our talk the young poet mentioned that when he is too busy to write—meeting his responsibilities to his family, or school—the poems and unwritten stories well up in him. His mind is full of them, for this form of self-expression has become an important part of his life.

In urban as well as many rural schools, experienced poets have been placed in classrooms to work with children. The best known among them is Kenneth Koch, who in *Wishes, Lies, and Dreams* published a large variety of poems written by the children whom he had taught.

In this book he has described the way he went about poetry writing sessions with children between the ages of six and twelve. He felt a program should help children to overcome unnecessary barriers, such as the belief that all poems have to rhyme, or that they have to be spelled correctly. "Good poetry ideas often come as fast as one can write; in the rush to get them down there may be no time for commas or for respecting a margin."[15] That description of course, is suggestive of some processes of inner speech.

The recognition that these short bursts of poetic ideas may lead to useful future work has led some poets, such as Stephen Spender, to keep careful notebooks.

> The best way of explaining how I develop the rough ideas
> which I use, is to take an example. Here is a notebook
> begun in 1944. About a hundred pages of it are covered
> with writing, and from this have emerged about six
> poems. Each idea, when it first occurs is given a number.
> Sometimes the ideas do not get beyond one line. For
> example No. 3 (never developed) is the one line:
> A language of flesh and roses.[16]

This line was based on a specific experience in Spender's life, but it brought back such a wealth of associations that he was unable to shape a poem from the varied feelings and sensory impressions. Thus he wrote:

> How easy it is to explain here the poem I would have liked
> to write! How difficult it would be to write it. For writing
> it would imply living my way through the images and
> experience of all these ideas, which here are mere
> abstractions, and such an effort of imaginative
> experience requires a life-time of patience and
> watching.[17]

Children write more playfully, and as Koch reminds us, they may
not conceive of the creation of poems as work. The magic of words is
not discovered in a solitary way; they feel most alive in sounds and
rhythms in the midst of noisy movements, and they share lines with
each other. There is an immediacy to this approach, as there is to most
of their play, that the poet-teacher Kenneth Koch knew how to encourage. In part his success lay in the way in which he prepared children
for poetry by suggesting varied themes, such as colors or wishes, for
starting points.

Koch struggled with the issue of models. He read to the children he
worked with some of the poems of Dylan Thomas, Walt Whitman, and
D. H. Lawrence. But he found that what stimulated his pupils most
was what other children had written:

> Images, lines, and ideas in one poem, if they were good
> ones, carried by my voice across the room, would
> instantly begin to blossom in a new place, changed by
> the personality of the writer.[18]

He found that the times children were most attentive to the work
of others was when they were getting ready to start a new poem of
their own.

I was interested in finding out what children had to say about writing
poetry. Several students in a Santa Fe, New Mexico, elementary school
talked to me about their feelings, and the difficulty of starting to write
a poem. A tall, intense, young student named Alex expressed it in
this way:

> You get a feeling of proudness after you write your first
> line and you are writing. A lot of my poems never mean
> anything to me or anybody else, but it makes you feel

like you had taken a tranquilizer or something. *It is like
untangling a string.* It just pours everything out.

Alex P.

Her friend Suki agreed that it was often hard to start a poem. Their
teacher used music at times to help them be in a mood for poetry writing.
In Taos, Mr. Ailello (Joseph Concha's teacher) relied on placing pictures in front of his pupils when they needed some assistance in finding a theme. He realized that even adults have a hard time when faced
with a blank piece of paper. Suki's approach was to start with a single
word.

> Sometimes when I start a poem I just put down a word.
> And I want to keep that word. Then I put down one line
> and I might be thinking about that line, and perhaps I
> make a few adjustments. Then it just comes out; it just
> *flows* out.

Other children spoke of images and feelings that gave rise to their
inspiration to write. A young girl from Taos Pueblo told me that one
especially warm spring day she was craving moisture. She pictured a
waterfall and nearby a village of Indians living in teepees. She remembers how she saw the people in this story in her imagination; later, she
wrote it all down in Mr. Ailello's classroom.

One of the Chicano students I interviewed in Santa Fe also relied on
strong visual images while writing:

> I think of a candle. You light a candle, and you know it
> just starts the wax, and it just burns down. And as the
> candle drips the wax, you sort of watch it, and as you
> watch it, ideas start coming into your head . . . (To the
> question, "Do you know what the candle may mean to
> you?" he answered:) "I don't know . . . to me it means
> growing, an idea is growing in my head. And as the
> drips are growing the ideas are getting bigger.

At the beginning of their efforts at writing poetry, these young students in New Mexico and New York profitted from external props,
such as pictures, the teacher's suggestions, hearing the poems written
by other children or the sounds of music. Eventually, they became more
attuned to their internal changes in mood. Alex recalled how she started
a poem the day before we talked to each other:

I had a feeling . . . I knew I wanted to write about something and because I was feeling sort of glum . . . there
were not any words, nothing telling me, nothing put
into words. It was just sort of black.

She realized as she was talking that she is often surrounded, even
engulfed, in a sensation of color when first starting to write.

Years after I had spoken to these children I was reading the memoirs
of the great Chilean poet Pablo Neruda. He had been frequently asked
to recall when he wrote his first poem. Remembering the occasion, he
evoked the power of a deep emotion, which precipitated his first efforts as a poet:

Once, far back in my childhood, when I had barely
learned to read, I felt an intense emotion and set down a
few words, half rhymed but strange to me, different
from everyday language. Overcome by a deep
anxiety, something I had not experienced before, a kind
of anguish and sadness, I wrote them neatly on a piece
of paper.[19]

Neruda found himself writing in a style that differed from everyday
language. Through prosody, rhythmic chants, and the use of alliterations and metaphors, he discovered more effective ways to realize his
communicative intent, and this is part of the special power or magic of
words. In grappling with strong and even overwhelming emotions,
young poets discover this function of heightened language. Herman
Hesse recalled that as a child many occupations attracted him, but of all
of these that of the magician had the greatest hold upon him:

This desire, as for all magical powers, has accompanied
me all my life in many forms, which often I did not
immediately recognize. Thus it happened later, long
after I had grown and was practicing the calling of
writer, that I frequently tried to disappear behind my
creations, to rechristen myself and hide behind playfully
contrived names.[20]

And to be able to use fully the playful magic of words, and thus transcend reality, the growing writer frequently becomes a voracious reader.
Again and again in the autobiographies of men and women of letters,

the discovery of reading is recalled: once such people have made this discovery, their appetite for books becomes enormous. Neruda wrote, "I gobbled up everything, indiscriminately, like an ostrich."[21]

For some young children even the appearance of books holds an awesome promise. The British novelist Jean Rhys wrote in her short autobiography *Smile Please*, "before I could read, almost a baby, I imagined that God, this strange thing or person I heard about, was a book."[22] And as reverently, though less religiously, Jean-Paul Sartre devoted a considerable part of his recollections, entitled *The Words*, to the role of reading in his childhood:

> I began my life as I shall no doubt end it: amidst books.
> In my grandfather's study there were books
> everywhere. It was forbidden to dust them, except once
> a year, before the beginning of the October term.
> Though I did not yet know how to read, I already
> revered those standing stones: upright or leaning
> over. . . . I disported myself in a tiny sanctuary,
> surrounded by ancient, heavy-set monuments which
> had seen me into the world, which would see me out of
> it, and whose permanence guaranteed me a future as
> calm as the past.[23]

The rich promise of books as adventure, wisdom, or sanctuary is evoked in many of the personal writings of novelists, poets, and philosophers. Neruda wrote of "moving in the world of knowing, on the turbulent river of books, like a solitary navigator."[24] Lillian Hellman found refuge from a confusing adult world in her fig tree with her books; Nikos Kazantzakis in *Report to Greco* wrote that after he had learned to form words he started to read the legendary lives of saints:

> Selling all my toys to my friends, I purchased the lives of
> the saints in popular, pamphlet-sized editions. Each
> evening I sat on my little stool amid the basil and
> marigolds of our courtyard and read out loud all the
> various ordeals the saints had endured in order to save
> their souls. . . . In my imagination the saints now
> merged with the vehement knights who set out to save the
> world. . . . When I read Cervantes, still later, his hero Don
> Quixote seemed to me a great saint and martyr who had
> left amidst jeering and laughter to discover, beyond our

humble everyday life, the essence which hides in back of
appearances.[25]

The search for going beneath the appearance of things, of which
Kazantzakis wrote, is shared by those who unconsciously yet purpose-
fully prepare for a life of the mind, whether in the sciences or the arts.
But at the beginning, all that the young reader seems to be aware of is a
great love of the uncommon and of a devouring need for the written
word. During childhood and adolescence, most young people read with
little discrimination; it is the intoxication of an imagined world which
pulls them back, again and again, into the abundance of books. It is an
image evoked by Lillian Hellman's description of herself as one of "the
bookish, grasping, very young" who spent hours in a New Orleans fig
tree, where she did her first, hungry reading.

Of course, as writers mature, their choice of written material becomes
more selective. Margaret Drabble explained to me the importance of deliberate judgment, especially when the novelist is engaged in daily
writing: "I try to avoid contemporary writers, particularly women who,
at times, sound like echoes of me, or I wonder if I am an echo of them?"
As she was talking, I looked at her bookshelves which filled the warm,
comfortable living room in which the interview took place. When Drabble noticed my attempt to decipher the titles on her shelves, she added,
"There are some writers I re-read frequently during the long span of
time it takes to write a novel. George Eliot and Jane Austen are among
them. I find them constantly useful." The choice of reading matter by
experienced writers may indicate a new direction of their thought, which
might harbinger a new project as well.

In his remarkable *The Story of a Novel*, Thomas Mann described how
he came to write *Dr. Faustus*, an important work written in his physically waning years. The novelist and his family lived in the United States
during the Second World War, and as an important anti-Fascist figure
Mann was asked to travel quite a bit. During one such trip the writer,
while still engaged with his major work *Joseph and His Brothers*, found
himself attracted to books on music and some by Nietzsche. He wrote:

> What strikes me and impresses me as something myste-
> rious is the kind of reading that I did on this trip during
> train journeys, evening hours, and brief rests. Contrary to
> my usual habit on lecture tours, it bore no relation to my
> present occupation, nor to the next work I had in view.[26]

As a writer who dealt with a large sweep of ideas in his work, Mann usually relied heavily upon scholarly books while preparing for a new project. Indeed, he once wrote to his friend Erich Auerbach that certain books appeared on his desk precisely at the right moment. The collection of reading material that accumulated as he progressed fit into what he called "a magic circle." But even during the winter of 1942, he was not aware that his mind was forging ahead to a new project, until, in retrospect, he discovered from his diary entries that his reading was starting to fit a certain pattern.

Then, the day after he packed up all the books dealing with his great opus about Joseph, his journal simply read: "Dr. Faustus."

The Woven Fabric of Writing

Diverse records exist of the beginnings of a new work in the writer's life. Some of these can be found in the journals and diaries of authors. Many others are noted in letters or in interviews with celebrated playwrights, poets, and novelists.

In the widely read series *Writers at Work,* questions dealing with the germ of a new project were frequently asked. Malcolm Cowley summarizes some of the responses in his introduction to the first volume of these interviews sponsored by *The Paris Review:* "Almost always it is a new and simple element introduced into an existing situation or mood. . . . Henry James described it as 'the precious particle'."[27] To illustrate his point, Cowley outlined the beginning of one of Joyce Cary's stories. The British writer was on a visit to Manhattan and, while circling the island on a boat, he noticed a young girl with a nice expression who had a wrinkled forehead. Weeks later the author woke in the middle of the night with a story in his head: it was set in England, and its heroine had a wrinkled forehead similar to the young woman on the boat.

Remembering such carefully observed details, writers choose a starting point for their intricate task of weaving together resonant language with the themes of their intellectual and emotional concerns. To achieve such unification of ideas with artistic form requires a lengthy process of development. The early sources of the writers' craft can be linked to their playful explorations in childhood, to their feverish, all-encompassing reading, to their immersion in the work of a favorite master, or to the work of "the primitive commentator" in noticing, clarifying, and recording impressions in words.

The lengthy apprenticeships needed to develop a personal and memorable style are the continuation of some of these first experiences of play, reading, and immersion into the work of others. They are followed by the experimental writing in childhood and adolescence—the first poems and short stories and the novels destroyed before they are shown to anybody. In these early creations, young writers rehearse the integration of feeling, thought, and text that informs powerful writing. In emphasizing these telegrams of thought—the condensed idioms of inner speech—I have attempted to illustrate the broader issues confronting all artists and thinkers; namely, the way in which one transforms thought into a communicable form.

I believe that this process of transformation and expansion is intimately related to the issues of style. Jorge Luis Borges, the Nobel prize-winning Argentinean writer, in a *Paris Review* interview evoked some of the difficulties he, together with most young writers, faced in developing a seemingly simple and effective style. At the beginning of their career many have a need to overwrite. They choose carefully turned-out phrases; they want to impress their readers with their large vocabulary. But by the excesses of their language, these young men and women try to hide their sense of inexperience. Borges went on to say that with maturity, the writer becomes more secure in his ideas, and "he finds his real tone. . . . I think what I write nowadays is always on a certain level and that I can't better it very much, nor can I spoil it very much either."[28] Borges did not mean that he doesn't edit his writing; he was referring to the achievement of a certain style akin to that of a musician whose playing style most experts recognize.

In undertaking a major work, writers may require many favorable internal and external conditions: a sense of pervasive curiosity about the details of existence; a certain control of tone and style; or nurturance and support from others. Of particular importance in crafting a big book is what Harvard psychologist David Perkins has called "the lively interplay between developing work and the mind of the artist."[29] In a study of artists and of aesthetic development, Perkins and his co-workers at Project Zero used the "thinking-aloud" technique (asking participants to verbalize their thoughts in the midst of writing or editing a poem) as a means of getting information concerning the cognitive processes involved in writing. They were interested in eliciting detailed commentary from poets and painters about their work in progress in order to monitor what the investigators described as the "moment-to-moment process of making in the arts." The data gathered in this study revealed that "the creator spontaneously detects problems and opportunities most often achieving a rather focused and explicit understanding of them."[30]

The description offered by Perkins of the lively interplay between completed work and the next stages in writing is confirmed by writers themselves. In one interview Anthony Burgess was asked whether he charts each of his books in advance. "I chart a little first," he answered, "list of names, rough synopses of chapters, and so on. But one doesn't overplan; so many things are generated by the sheer act of writing."[31] A similar comment was made by Nelson Algren, who spoke of a book finding its own shape in the process of its creation.[32]

One of the underlying reasons these novelists can trust the emerging book as a source of development for their writing is that their work is set within the framework of large and unifying themes. The recognition of these governing intentions emerges at different stages of a writer's career. Thornton Wilder described how some of his ideas promoted his work before he was conscious of them. The vastness of the past plays a critical role in his thinking, he said. He first recognized the frightening range of the human past while a young man on an archeological expedition in Rome:

> I see myself making an effort to find the dignity in the
> trivia of our daily life, against these preposterous
> stretches which seem to rob it of any such dignity: and
> the validity of each individual's emotion.[33]

The author of *Our Town* could not tell in advance whether a particular drama or novel would meet his criteria, and he found that a number of things that he had worked on failed to engross him. If a deep absorption was missing while he worked, he took that as an indication that that particular piece might be a false one.

Somewhat similarly, the day Thomas Mann began *Dr. Faustus* he had but scanty notes and no written outline. But his inner conception of the book was a clear one, and he felt himself driven to undertake *Dr. Faustus* by his vivid and painful feelings about his native Germany. Actually he had first made a reference to the Faustian theme in 1901, but at that time he did not pursue the project. Forty-two years later, when he re-read the nucleus of a plot dealing with an artist's pact with the devil, Mann experienced great inner tumult. "This one time I knew what I was setting out to do," he wrote in *The Story of a Novel*, "and what task I was imposing upon myself: to write nothing less than the novel of my era."[34]

In spite of his determination, Mann experienced cycles of productivity followed by periods of discouragement—at times protracted ones—and of terrible weariness. He has described days and weeks of questioning and dissatisfaction. But in the evenings he would gather a circle of friends and read to them a newly finished chapter. The enthusiasm of his intimates, and even more importantly the various contributions they made in deepening his understanding of music, one of the central themes in *Dr. Faustus,* usually gave Mann a renewed sense of confidence in the demanding work of progress.[35]

Another important record of the construction of a novel emerged in John Steinbeck's daily letters to his friend and editor Pascal Covici. Published after Steinbeck's death in a collection entitled *Journal of a Novel,* these letters described his plans for the book as well as the development of his ideas. These morning entries were like finger or voice exercises with which musicians start their day, and the result constituted a remarkable documentation of what Perkins has called "art-making." Delineated in detail are Steinbeck's somewhat biblical theme, the development of his plot, the varying aspects of his style, and his feelings about his characters and about his tools (both external and internal) upon which he relied during the long months of writing.

In his very first letter, Steinbeck's theme in *East of Eden* was stated: it was, he wrote, "the story of my country and the story of me."[36] The early version of the novel was addressed to his young sons, whom he considered his primary audience. Steinbeck wanted to share his recollections of the Salinas valley with them, his feelings about his magnificent Irish grandfather, and the whole large family whom he called the Hamiltons in the novel.

Similarly personal was the motivation guiding Katherine Mansfield in the writing of "Prelude." In the winter of 1916, after her beloved only brother lost his life in World War I, this young ailing writer from New Zealand wrote of her work:

> Now—now I want to write recollections of my own country. Yes, I want to write about my own country till I simply exhaust my store. Not only because it is "a sacred debt" that I pay to my country because my brother and I were born there, but also because in my thoughts I range with him over all the remembered places. I am never far away from them. I long to renew them in writing.[37]

Although Mansfield knew clearly why she wanted to write of her home, she did not have the well-honed discipline of more mature writers, such as Mann, who were able to bar outside impressions during their steady working hours each day. "Even during this time," Thomas Mann wrote in May 1945, "[I] reserv[ed] these hours wholly, as a matter of principle, for solitude and work. Had it not been for this habit, I should scarcely have brought myself to continue, in spite of so many pressures from outside."[38] But Mansfield repeatedly had to ask herself, in her journal, whether she could finish her New Zealand material, which was "pressing against the swollen gate" of her mind. Did she have a right "to 'a table in my own room?' " Could she consider herself a writer when the writing came so slowly?[39] Eventually she broke her silence, and found her powerful metaphor for her childhood reveries—the aloe tree—a tree which flowers but once a century.

Some writers find the beginning of a new novel is not easy. At the end of his first week of working on *East of Eden*, after he had finished but a page and a half, Steinbeck ruefully wrote "that it is always that way. I must sit a certain length of time before it happens."[40] It was by addressing his editor Covici, and thinking of him as an immediate and caring audience, that Steinbeck found a way to "come out of the cold."

Each Friday the editor would come to collect the finished pages of the manuscript written in Steinbeck's small and dense handwriting. His deep involvement with the work was both a blessing and a burden to the writer, who feared that a chance remark by Covici might derail him or interfere with his own conceptions. The delicate balance needed by artists—between their desire for loving attention and support from friends and family and the necessity to maintain a certain protective aloofness from these very same people—is touchingly related by Steinbeck in his daily letters. Some writers share Nelson Algren's belief that it is impossible to write a book in which the novelist "goes all out" and still have a personal life. But Steinbeck found in his third marriage a protective "house for his thought"; his wife Elaine understood his contradictory needs very well.

The construction of a large, personal book creates some particularly serious problems. Steinbeck wrote that every facet of the book "leads down a long road of character and its effect. . . . I hope I can keep all the reins in my hands at the same time, make it sound as though the book was almost accidental."[41] And yet the autobiographical features of the book served him well: he was helped in his writing by his memories, by his recall of his grandfather's speech, by reading the Salinas papers, and by recalling more and more of the family stories as he worked.

At the same time Steinbeck worried that the book might be getting too long. In self-defense he wrote, in his letters to Covici, why he valued a large work of the kind he was constructing as a deeply felt form of communication between writer and reader.

> Now—we must think of a book as a wedge driven into a man's personal life. A short book would be in and out quickly. . . . A long book, on the other hand, drives in slowly and if only in point of time remains for a while. Instead of cutting and leaving, it allows the mind to rearrange itself to fit around the wedge.[42]

Both theoretical and personal considerations therefore may govern the decisions writers make about their novels' plots. In talking with Margaret Drabble just after her book *The Realms of Gold* was published, she described why she had introduced a new kind of heroine for her book. The book she wrote before *Realms* was *The Needle's Eye*, "a very low key book in which people had to put up with very little in life," she said. Now she was ready for a change:

> Let us suppose a book in which somebody gets everything. I wanted her [the heroine of the new novel] to lead a less claustrophobic life and indeed expand the cosmos a little rather than centering it in a restrictive domestic sphere. So she had to move around a bit. Also there was an element of pure enjoyment . . . she had a great deal of freedom of movement. And that was fun, also a way of embracing a lot of different scenes with people.

Their involvement with a major character is one of the sources of sustained motivation for the writer of novels. In *Dr. Faustus*, Thomas Mann wrote of Leverkuhn that he was "a person who bore the suffering of our epoch." He found it difficult to invent him, but confessed to one of his friends that

> I never loved a creature of my imagination—neither Thomas Buddenbrook, not Hans Castorp, nor Aschenbach, nor Joseph, nor the Goethe of The Beloved Returns—as I did Adrian [Leverkuhn]. . . . Quite literally I shared good Serenus' feelings for him, was painfully in love with him from his days as an arrogant

> schoolboy, was infatuated with his "coldness", his
> remoteness . . . with his conviction that he was
> damned. At the same time, oddly enough, I scarcely
> gave him any appearance, any physical body.[43]

Mann's love for his creations equalled that of Flaubert, who also wrote with passion about his imaginary characters, complaining that they pursued him, that he found himself in them.[44]

Portrayal of a deeply flawed personality creates a more troubling but equally motivating challenge for writers, aiding them in maintaining an involvement with the work during the long and arduous labor of writing. The exploration of the complexities of a character may motivate the writer toward a sustained effort in the completion of a work. In an essay on *Death of a Salesman*, Arthur Miller described this process in the genesis of the central figure Willy Loman, and some of the ways that as a writer he tried to understand the man he had created.

> For myself it has never been possible to generate the energy to write and complete a play if I know in advance everything it signifies and all it will contain. The very impulse to write, I think, springs from an inner chaos crying for order, for meaning, and that meaning must be discovered in the process of writing or the work lies dead as it is finished.[45]

The Ever-Varied Words of the Theater

The well-shaped drama comes to full life on stage through resonant and vivid language. In a plea to free the theater of "bedridden" language, W. B. Yeats wrote "what the ever-moving, delicately molded flesh is to beauty, vivid musical words are to passion."[46]

Playwrights have always deepened their sense of the rhythms and cadences of speech by listening to the varied dialogues around them, from Shakespeare to *Up the Down Staircase*. Rosemary Sisson, a scriptwriter for that television series, is the daughter of a Shakespearean scholar. She has always been immersed in language, and as a television writer has become particularly sensitive to everyday speech. All that she overhears "goes into the computer" she told me during our conversation in London.

The musical, auditory quality of language is more crucial to drama than it is to the construction of novels. Conscious of this need, playwrights search for different devices to ensure the authenticity of their theatrical language: the reading aloud of what they write, the use of acting experience by playwrights to help them imagine the different possibilities of the stage, and a commitment to a constant search for vivid words and gestures.

The English playwright Harold Pinter, who is well known for his carefully crafted, sparse dialogues, wrote his first play while acting with a travelling repertory theater. His acting past had helped him, but when asked whether he had rather clear-cut notions concerning the way a part should be played, Pinter told *The Paris Review,* "Quite often I have a compelling sense of how a role should be played. And I am proved—equally as often—quite wrong."[47]

The ways in which acting and playwriting are mutually enriching was described to me by Douglas Turner Ward, the director of the Negro Ensemble Theater in New York. I visited with him in his summer home on Martha's Vineyard, the house set on a small lane and surrounded by children's toys and bicycles. Ward is a strongly built man, whose love of words was apparent with the first sentence, in which he described his growing up years in the South. A child of working-class parents, his self-styled apprenticeship resulted in his becoming an avid, passionate reader. "My love for reading meant that I gloried in reading aloud," Ward said. "When most boys in my class wanted to scrooch under the seats, afraid that the teacher will call upon them, I was always ready to read aloud. I did it in Sunday school, too." To this day, the flow and rhythmic qualities of speech are critical to Ward's craft: "I like assonance and alliteration," he stressed. "Even some of the realistic speeches I write are heavily weighted with inner rhythms."

Like many other writers, Ward did not care for mathematics and science. "It was obvious," he commented, laughing, "that if I was to become someone, it will have to be through writing." To seek such a career was not easy for a young boy whose family had no experience with the literary world. As he was an athlete in school, Ward was first interested in sports writing. And the only time he acted in high school was when he appeared in an operetta, "because I could not play football that year."

Ward became a political activist during his university years and decided to move to New York so that he could participate fully in the political life of New York and of Harlem. As part of his interest in the issues of the day, he started to write short topical skits, and also wrote a narration for a choral work based on the life of the slave leader Nat Turner. "The impact of this piece upon the audience made me convinced that if I wanted to write, I should do dramatic writing."

And that was the real beginning of Ward's apprenticeship. Instead of taking classes in playwriting, Ward immersed himself in world literature. But in his early twenties, after his first success in New York, the young writer had to return to his home town in the South. There, removed from the stimulation and support for his writing of the big city, Ward wrote his first full length play. He was spending much time with his childhood friends, and their language influenced his writing: "I used everything I knew, and it was a rough, beginner's work. Like most young writers, I was trying to say everything about the world in the play. The best thing . . . what worked about the play, was the strong and live language of some of the characters."

After returning to New York, Ward enrolled in an acting school. I had always thought that the beginnings of his career were in acting, but he corrected me: "No, the very opposite happened. I had *willed* myself to become a playwright, but I was first known as an actor." He considers his acting studies, however, as central to his development: "My decision to study acting was the best decision I made about writing. The relationship that acting has to the form and structure of drama is a crucial one. Studying with Paul Mann [his acting teacher, whom he praised for teaching him more than narrow technique] taught me more about drama than any lessons, books or courses in drama-writing could have done."

Since those beginnings, Douglas Ward's career has been a very rich one: he has acted in many plays, produced and directed others, and has organized the Negro Ensemble Theater, which he directs. In the theater he collaborated with many younger playwrights, some of whom had sought and received his advice for sharpening their work. At the time of our talk, Ward was writing "The Haitian Chronicles," a trilogy about the Haitian revolution. As the playwright became familiar with the complex story of that revolution and discovered some of its ironies—for instance, that at the beginning of the revolt, Toussaint L'Ouverture was actually opposed to the uprising—an idea began to intrigue him. Instead of a psychological drama, Ward wanted to write an epic work; a form which requires many theatrical devices different from those he had used for his more contemporary plays. Once he generated some of these—a Greek-type chorus, a versified style, the role of a commentator who was a voodooist leader of the revolution—Ward felt ready to start writing. His thinking is in "total theater terms. . . . I visualize all the people, the terrain, the voices and movements of the actors." In writing the speeches he also reads them and listens for vocal shapes of irony, or passion.

When I asked whether he needed to become familiar with the locale of this trilogy, he answered with some passion, "The Haiti of my imagination is more real to me than the Haiti of today!"

Often in the course of our long talk, Douglas Ward referred to the many qualities of drama that distinguish it from other art forms. He spoke of the importance of a rhythmic and poetic language, and his comments echoed some of Yeats' concern for resonance, and the use of a living, vivid speech in the theater. He described how he is planning a sweeping, historical play which goes beyond the psychological conflicts of individuals, and his comments are similar to some of the issues Bertold Brecht had raised. He spoke of the necessity to find "theatrical metaphors" and his search for these is akin to those of Miller, Hellman, Wilder and others, who are constantly looking for devices which are specific to the stage. His working methods as well have parallels to these other authors, who had emphasized the need to hear what they write. They used their sensitivity to language to help them correct some of their own mistakes. Arthur Miller once spoke of the excellent training he received in this regard—his discovery of the power of a good sentence—when he was writing radio plays.

The living theater combines passion and poetry, wrote John Gassner.[48] I think Ward would agree. He might have added irony as another essential component of drama in contemporary society.

Towards the Integration of Thought with Words

In examining the way writers work, we can identify some new insights into the nature of sustained intellectual labor. These are of particular interest because they expand our current, limited knowledge of the human mind. Psychologists have found it hard to depict the continuousness of thought, and instead they have traditionally looked at short spans of cognitive activities under controlled conditions. But in some of these laboratory studies, they have addressed "art-making"; in one such inquiry, Catherine Patrick asked poets and lay persons to write a poem about a picture she showed them, and to describe what they were thinking as they were working on the construction of the poem.[49] In a more recent study, David Perkins also used this "thinking-aloud" method and found an interesting interplay between the developing work and the way in which the artist responds to the emerging qualities of his or her product.[50]

This kind of a dialogue plays a significant role in sustaining creative work—labor "as hard as quarrying rocks" in Hemingway's phrase. The diaries of Thomas Mann and Virginia Woolf and the letters John Steinbeck wrote his editor are excellent sources for examining the ways in which writers maintain their momentum past the initial, enthusiastic phases of a new project. Few novels and plays are planned in advance in their entirety, but in the course of sustained activities writers draw upon previously hidden inner resources. They start using new techniques; facts and ideas that may have been carelessly stored in "the notebooks of the mind" are introduced through the interplay of the growing work and the writer's ability to identify new themes. There is an organizing power in major creative efforts that can best be identified by following the successive stages of a work in progress. In this way students of creativity can identify the way unused techniques, new insights, and interesting themes clothe the raw bones of a writer's early drafts.

Some writers on creativity have suggested that art-making is characterized by an organic growth process. A germinal idea often is at the start of a new project. John Steinbeck described such a beginning for *East of Eden* as the story of the Salinas Valley that is also the story of his life. But work does not proceed in a single line. The longer Steinbeck worked on this novel, the more he recognized a complex web of themes that governed his efforts.

The contradictory movements by which creative work might progress was noted by the psychologist Rudolf Arnheim. He studied Picasso's sketches and photographs of the developing painting *Guernica* and found that the painter proceeded through many erratic leaps as well as modifications and compensations before he achieved the desired unity of composition that distinguishes the finished painting.

The philosopher Hofstadter proposed a dialectical approach to creativity, one that incorporates the process described by Rudolf Arnheim.

> The essence of dialectical thinking is to find in each case
> what are the oppositions, conflicts, contrasts,
> contradictions, the otherness, estrangement, alienation
> that are possible in the context and to find the notion
> that unites them by incorporating and using rather than
> destroying their tension.[51]

The most basic tension that fuels creativity, according to Hofstadter, is that of opposing nothingness, negation. Through the efforts at appropriation, human beings strive toward mutual belonging, "the urge to be with other as with own." The examples he uses to illustrate these creative struggles are chosen primarily from the visual arts.

He is not alone in such a choice. A number of well-known critics and philosophers neglect literary creativity and favor, instead, the work of modern painters as the best illustrations of their analyses.

This neglect is revealing of a larger issue in contemporary discussions of creativity, namely, the differing assessments of the role of language. While critics use language to organize and communicate their understanding of creativity, some individuals among them view the function of words as minimal in productive thought and discovery. This is the position of Rudolf Arnheim, who wrote of the scope of language in thought "as essentially conservative and stabilizing."[51] To Arnheim, creativity is best represented as a visionary process, and the primary vehicles of such thought are percepts and images. In a similar rejection of the role of language in thought, Jean Piaget emphasizes physical and mental operations as the basis of the development of symbolic functions in human beings.

Is language, then, an after-thought in thinking? I do not think so. The centrality of language is simply but powerfully expressed by the philosopher Hannah Arendt, who wrote that "thinking beings have an urge to speak, speaking beings have an urge to think."[52] Arendt sees the role of language as essential in "disalienating the world into which, after all, each of us is born as a newcomer and a stranger."[53] I have quoted Arendt because I agree with her emphasis upon language as crucial to the human quest for meaning, and to give account of experience. However, she also views thought as a form of soundless speech, which leads to the assumption that the language of thought and the language of communication are but mirror images of each other. A more careful analysis reveals that inner speech is not simply the interior counterpart of external speech.

One needs only to compare the rapidity of certain flights of thought— or what Arendt calls "thought trains"—to the slowness of translating these into a verbal form understandable to others to realize the difference between these two processes. We have all had the impression that an idea could be communicated in a few words, only to discover that extensive elaboration was required for communication success. Nonetheless, some scientific studies of thought have challenged those who trust personal, subjective reports as useful in trying to determine differences between internal and external psychological phenomena. Is it possible, then, to know what the inner language of thought may be like? What are thoughts turned inward?

Aware of the ease with which rapid, planning-ahead thought can get erased in the midst of diverse activities, some individuals take note of them. These, then, are written thoughts that have not been reshaped into effective forms of communication. The best examples of these lines of inner speech can be found in the notebooks of poets and writers.

An example of written thought was offered by Stephen Spender in his essay on "The Making of a Poem." In the essay, Spender quotes from one of his notebooks the line "A language of flesh and roses." He has multiple associations and memories attached to this highly condensed thought; they deal with a man-made world, and a language of sorts, which has gotten outside of our control. Similar condensed phrases and descriptions were found in some of Dostoevsky's notebooks, in Virginia Woolf's diary, and in Henry Miller's description of planning "the book of his life."

The inner language of thought differs from language used for communicative exchanges in its rapidity, in its condensed form, and in its functions. In the maintenance of human contact, language may indeed be "stabilizing" in Arnheim's sense. But language has multiple functions and forms, some of which are more suited for discovery and others more suited for the construction and maintenance of shared experiences, beliefs, and knowledge. These differences are frequently ignored by philosophers and psychologists. The latter's use of the "thinking-aloud" method—the description of internal processes in the midst of problem-solving or poetry writing—has contributed to the mistaken notion of the identity of language and thought. Language and thought are neither identical nor totally independent processes. Verbal thinking is often condensed and metaphorical, akin, in some ways, to poetry. Hannah Arendt was interested in this commonality when she wrote that "all philosophical terms are metaphors, frozen analogies, as it were, whose true meaning discloses itself when we dissolve the term into the original context, which must have been vividly in the mind of the first philosopher to use it."

Such a process of dissolving, of placing a thought into its verbal and social context, is required in turning thoughts outward. It is through making explicit not only what is new inside one's mind, but also what is the implicit background of ideas, knowledge, and beliefs that novelty and insight arises.

6 / The Languages of Emotion

Music

In examining the nature of creative thought, many psychologists and psychiatrists have chosen music as their focus. One such analysis is provided by Albert Rothenberg, whose description of the ways in which composers contrast tonal and rhythmical elements exemplifies his Janusian (or oppositional) view of creativity.[1] A reliance upon the concepts of generative grammar characterizes Leonard Bernstein's approach to composition, described in his Norton lectures at Harvard University. In these lectures, entitled *The Unanswered Question,* Bernstein examined the various levels of music—elements, strings, deep and surface structures—and how they combine into "idioms [that] can all merge into a speech universal enough to be accessible to all mankind."[2] The subject of a musical grammar also engaged the psycholinguist Ray Jackendorff, who was interested in the roles of musical groupings and metrical structures in examining "what the listener hears."[3]

Are all human beings equally sensitive to the musical experience? Or are there differences in the analytical and representational resources brought to music based on exposure and expertise? These are questions that have interested neuroscientists. In their studies of hemispheric specialization, they have found that professional musicians process sounds in both their right and left hemispheres, while those less sophisticated in this domain rely only upon their right hemisphere.[4]

A somewhat different question is asked by Howard Gardner, a student of creativity and cognition. He has challenged the usual concept of intelligence and argued instead for the existence of core abilities in *Frames of Mind.* He considered music to be one of these abilities, describing it as "an autonomous intellectual realm."[5] This realm unites affective and cognitive competencies, living up to Aaron Copland's characterization of music as the language of emotion.

In view of the great richness of the treatment of music in the literature of thought and creativity, the analysis provided in this volume will be quite short. I will highlight only those themes which have been explored throughout this book in other contexts; of particular importance to the study of the musically talented is the nature of their early development and their varied apprenticeship. In addition, the transformation of germinal musical ideas into fully elaborated, publicly available works will also be discussed in this chapter. I owe a special debt to Aaron Copland and his life-long friend Harold Clurman, who talked to me during a hot summer afternoon in Santa Fe in 1977 about these issues.

Musical apprenticeships: The biographies and memoirs of musicians and composers frequently refer to their immersion into music while very young. Stravinsky's father was an opera singer; both Mozart and Beethoven were born into musical families; the family of the Hungarian composer Zoltan Kodály played chamber music; and, while Aaron Copland's parents knew little of music, they provided lessons in instruments to his brother and sister when the future composer was a small child.

The impact of these early experiences is variously described: the violinist Joseph Szigeti wrote in his autobiography of "the inexplicable wonder of the first croaking, cylinder-playing phonograph, set up in our courtyard by the itinerant marketplace showman."[6] Others recall praise for their "good ear" when listening to music and reproducing it. Such a memory was shared by Stravinsky with his friend Robert Craft in *Expositions and Development:*

> The countrywomen of Lzy sang an attractive and restful
> song on their way home from the fields in the evening, a
> song I have recalled in the early hours of evening at odd
> times throughout my life. They sang in octaves—
> unharmonized, of course—their high, shrill voices
> sounding like a billion bees. I was never a precocious
> child, and I have never enjoyed extraordinary powers
> of memory, but this song was branded on my ear the
> first time I heard it. My nurse brought me home from
> the village where we have been perambulating one
> afternoon, and my parents, who were trying to coax me
> to talk, asked me what I had seen there. I said I had

> seen the peasants and I had heard them sing, and I sang
> what they had sung: [notes] . . . Everyone was
> astonished and impressed at this recital, and I heard my
> father remark that I had a wonderful ear.[7]

In musical families parents frequently wait for evidence of talent and interest as a sign that they should provide training for an offspring. In Dimitri Shostakovich's memoirs *Testimony*, he recalled pressing his ears to the wall so that he could hear a string quartet performed at his neighbors. His mother, herself a pianist, started lessons only after she noticed his interest in music. One of the stories quoted in the introduction to *Testimony* captures the intensity of belief in one's child's talent in musical families. The young Shostakovich made rapid progress with his mother's teaching, so she decided he was ready for another teacher. When presenting him, she said:

"I've brought you a marvelous pupil."

"All mothers have marvelous children . . . (the teacher replied)."[8]

Jeanne Bamberger, a student of musical prodigies, described in the course of our talk how musicians give strong, and at times conflicting, messages to their children as they try to shape their future careers. She suggested that at least one of the parents of child musicians tends to center his or her life on developing the young person's talent. Bamberger's own growing-up years fitted such a pattern: there was a piano in the house, and at age four, once her parents had realized that she had perfect pitch, they started to give her lessons. As a rule Bamberger finds that "young musicians frequently practice before leaving for school, after their return and during the weekend. They are made to feel special but, at the same time, their parents and their teachers expect them to lead a normal life with their friends and family."

The contradictory pressures that constitute the lives of many young musicians lead some of them to give up playing during their adolescence. Others, like Pablo Casals, remain grateful to the end of their lives for their parents' devotion. In *Joys and Sorrows*, Casals recalled those early years:

> From infancy I was surrounded by music. . . . To hear my
> father play the piano was an ecstasy for me. When I was
> two or three, I would sit on the floor beside him as he

> played, and I would press my head against the piano in
> order to absorb the sound more completely.
>
> I began playing the piano when I was four years
> old. . . . It was my father who taught me to play the
> piano and gave me my first lessons in composition. . . .
> Before long I had learned to play the organ well enough
> so that I sometimes took my father's place when he was
> ill or busy with some other work.
>
> When I was eleven years old, I heard the cello played
> for the first time. . . . When the first composition ended,
> I told my father, "Father, that is the most wonderful
> instrument I have ever heard. That is what I want to
> play."[9]

But there were no cello teachers in the small Spanish village in which Casals was born, and it was only because of his mother's belief in him and her determination that he should receive the necessary schooling (at the School of Music in Barcelona) that Casals was able to realize his potential.

The nurturing of young musical talent is a complex task. Even in a family as devoted to it as the Casals, tensions and conflicts exist. The single-minded commitment to her son's talent that characterized Casals' mother—illustrating the pattern described by Bamberger—created many disagreements between her and her husband. Nevertheless, such dedication and support seem to be a necessary component to the achievement of excellence in music.

Indications of talent among young children include a strong interest in music, a "good ear," and the ability to reproduce musical fragments. While these are important indices, they need to be given support. Gardner wrote "even the most gifted young child will take about ten years to achieve those levels of performance or composition that we associate with mastery of the musical realm."[10]

Aaron Copland first expressed his interest in music by listening to his sister practice the piano and by making up some songs of his own. As a young teenager he arranged for his own piano teacher. The life of a musician appeared to the adolescent Copland as insecure; all the same, "the urge toward spending a life in music was irresistible,"[11] he wrote. Friends with commitments to the arts were important to him during those years; he shared with them his ambitions, his study of classical music, and the treasures of New York City's public libraries: "I can still recall the thrill of coming upon racks of music scores in the dingy up-stairs corner room at the library. And what was equally surprising was the fact that music scores, like the books downstairs, could be borrowed for study at home. I learned to orchestrate by borrowing scores from the library."[12]

These adolescent years in New York were important to Copland; he acquired the classical foundations of music. But it was in the 1920s—which coincided with Copland's own twenties—that he fully mastered the techniques of his art. Copland saw this exciting, glamorous decade as basic to all that has happened in music since that time. He spent part of it in Paris as one of Nadia Boulanger's students. In her description of herself as a teacher, Boulanger said: "I can explain the grammar of music."[13] Copland's own description of those years with Boulanger stresses her enormous musical culture, her interest in and knowledge of contemporary developments, the lively artistic life that characterized the Boulanger salon, but most importantly: "She knew that unerring musi-cianship had to become a reflex so that the mind could be free for the art of composition. 'To study music, we must learn the rules,' she used to say. 'To create music, we must forget them.' "[14]

The work with a highly disciplined, masterful, and original teacher is central to musical apprenticeships. Shostakovich evoked such an expe-rience when he described studying with Glazunov at the Leningrad Conservatory:

> Glazunov spent all his life thinking about music, and
> therefore, when he spoke about it, you remembered it
> for life.... . Each student . . . could see for himself
> Glazunov's marvelous, even unique abilities as a
> musician. . . . First there was his pitch. Glazunov had
> perfect, absolute pitch. . . . Glazunov caught all false
> notes, flawlessly. . . . The other way in which Glazunov
> amazed us was with his memory. Musical memory,
> naturally. . . . Glazunov could also sight-read the most
> complicated score and make it sound as though an
> excellent orchestra was playing it. . . . His practical
> knowledge in the important area of musical instruments
> was invaluable. . . . For instance, he learned to play the
> violin while writing his violin concerto.[15]

The importance of a powerful foundation in music is clearly expressed by Stravinsky in his *An Autobiography:* "No matter what the subject may be, there is only one course for the beginner: he must at first accept a discipline imposed from without, but only as a means of obtaining freedom for, and strengthening himself in, his own method of expression."[16] The foundations include a mastery of instrumental techniques as well as the rudiments of composing, such as counterpoint, harmonization, and invention. During his apprenticeship years, Stravinsky, the son of a highly regarded opera singer, was the beneficiary of excellent instruction, of the chance to meet and work with some of the most outstanding musical figures of his time, and to attend rehearsals and performances of opera, chamber, and symphonic music in St. Petersburg.

Training on an instrument is important for a composer, even if he or she does not engage in public performances. In *Expositions and Developments* Stravinsky spoke to Robert Craft of the role of the piano in his work: "Whether or not I am a pianist, however, the instrument itself is the center of my life and the fulcrum of all my musical discoveries. Each note that I write is tried on it."[17]

The memoirs of composers have provided us with a remarkable record of development, the ways in which individuals master their collective artistic past while preparing for their individuality, for their artistic future. Leonard Bernstein has suggested in his "A Tribute to Teachers"— a New York Philharmonic Young People's Concert—that while there may be self-taught painters or writers, musicians have all been deeply influenced by their teachers. In Bernstein's own life, teachers have played a critical role. He has learned from and with some of the major conductors of the world: Serge Koussevitzky and Fritz Reiner; he has studied with the pianists Heinrich Gebhard and Isabella Vengerova; and as a young man he was befriended by Aaron Copland, who gave him valuable criticism when Bernstein first started composing. Thus it is not surprising that Bernstein chose to celebrate his teachers and the transmission of an art that he describes as "the most natural, inborn aesthetic human experience, the most abstract and exalted of the arts.[18]

Tradition and innovation in music: The extraordinary presence of the past nourishes young composers, but it also presents them with a burden. The prolonged apprenticeships of musicians, their immersion into the work of past masters, haunts them when starting a new work of their own. Leonard Bernstein described in *Findings* how he needed to clear his mind of the echoes of many compositions he had studied and conducted when he started searching for and finding his own notes.[19]

There are many different ways in which composers start on their own work. Even at a very young age, the future composer does not simply play a piece; he or she brings an analytical curiosity to it. Gardner described the process as follows: "For the future composers, like Stravinsky, pleasure comes increasingly . . . from experimenting with pieces that they were performing, rewriting them, changing them—in a word, *de*composing them."[20]

Learning how to compose involves acquiring the principles of composition as well as trying to duplicate the work of someone more highly experienced. The great Russian composer Rimsky-Korsakov taught the young Stravinsky in such a way. In addition to explaining the differing structures of musical pieces, he had the young man orchestrate his own pieces and then compared the novice's efforts with his own work on the same passage:

> Once a week I took my work to him and he criticized and
> corrected it, giving me all the necessary explanations,
> and at the same time he made me analyze the form and
> structure of classical works. A year and a half later I
> began the composition of a symphony. As soon as I
> finished one part of a movement I used to show it to
> him, so that my whole work, including the
> instrumentation, was under his control.[21]

Learning orchestration in this way was also highly thought of by Shostakovich, who had re-orchestrated some of Mussorgsky's works. He wrote: "I would recommend that all young composers make their own versions of the work of those masters from whom they want to learn."[22]

Such a process of re-composing can result in a somewhat imitative phase in a composer's work. Since the early 1970s, Beethoven's creative life has been carefully analyzed, and musicologists have divided his fifty-seven years into three major periods—imitative, heroic, and introspective. Studies of his first works, during the imitative period, provide detailed information of the way in which he had followed Haydn (with whom he studied for a year as a young man) and how deeply he was also influenced by Mozart. One of his biographers, Robert Haven Schauffler, suggested that in Beethoven's first symphony it was easy to detect the influence of these masters. He further wrote: "This procedure held true for his first work in other media, whether piano or duet sonatas, trios, quartets, or masses. While he was feeling his way to easy mastery in an untried field he was reminiscent. Only at the second or third attempt did he become the original thinker we know."[23] Beethoven did express his gratitude to some of his immediate and distant teachers by dedicating some of his works to them and by noting in his Diary: "Portraits of Handel, Bach, Gluck, Mozart in my room—They can promote my capacity for endurance."[24]

The reliance upon the past as well as upon living composers—both as teachers and as friends—emerges as an important theme in the literature on music. In the writings of twentieth-century composers, the role of these connections is drawn particularly vividly. Leonard Bernstein described his first meeting with Aaron Copland in an article celebrating the latter's seventieth birthday. A junior at Harvard, Bernstein met Copland at a dance recital in New York. Later that evening the very young man from Boston played Copland's compositions with fervor at a loft where Copland worked and occasionally partied:

> And thereafter, whenever I came to New York I went to
> Aaron's. . . . All during those years I would bring him
> my own music for criticism. . . . I would show Aaron,
> the bits of pieces, and he would say, "All that has to
> go. . . . This is just pure Scriabin. You've got to get that
> out of your head and start fresh. . . . This is good; these
> two bars are good. Take these two bars and start from
> there." And in these sessions he taught me a tremendous
> amount about taste, style, and consistency in music. . . .
> Through his critical analyses of whatever I happened to
> be working on at the moment, Aaron became the closest
> thing to a composition teacher I ever had.[25]

Copland's own experience with Boulanger and his participation with *Les Six*, a group of composers of diverse talents who spent some crucial years together in the "unique artistic atmosphere" of Paris in the 1920s, convinced him of the importance of exploring and working together. It was during those years that Copland also met Stravinsky, the most influential composer of that time.

> For me there was no doubt that Stravinsky was the most
> exciting musical creator on the scene. He was the hero of
> my student days. . . . Heading the list of Stravinsky's
> gifts was his rhythmic virtuosity. . . . There was also
> much to learn from Stravinsky's bold use of dissonance
> and his unusual instrumental combinations. . . . He
> borrowed freely from folk materials, and *I have no doubt*

that this strongly influenced me to try to find a way to a
distinctively American music. [emphasis added][26]

Thus, composers do indeed transmit from one generation to another much of their art. They influence each other in terms of techniques, and they share a strong musical culture. An experienced musician can support a younger man or woman's sense of direction and worth and provide an expression of faith in the novice's talent that is crucial for artists in the early stages of their careers.

Aaron Copland's first compositions did reveal the strong influence of Stravinsky, Hindemith, and Schoenberg, but his work was also seen to "have bite and power, both rhythmical and harmonic," according to Lawrence Gilman, the New York critic.[27] Those were the years when he started to search for his own varied sources in jazz, in American folk music, and in Jewish traditional music.

> Copland had gone to Europe to learn how to compose,
> and had "found" America while viewing it from abroad.
> He saw European composers take up American jazz and
> thought that if composers like Debussy and Ravel,
> Stravinsky and Milhaud could use ragtime and jazz
> rhythms, the way might be open to American
> composers.[28]

In the *Concerto for Piano and Orchestra*, Copland did use jazz elements: "Two basic jazz moods are incorporated in each section—the slow blues and the snappy numbers. . . . My primary aim was to explore new avenues in the area of polyrhythms."[29] But jazz was just one of Copland's sources, one that was particularly important in the 1920s. During the populist years of the Great Depression, Copland turned more fully toward folk music. His knowledge of the West was limited, but when asked to write a ballet about "Billy the Kid" by Lincoln Kirstein, who tucked several volumes of collected folk tunes under his arm, Copland became interested.

> It is a delicate operation to put fresh and unconventional
> harmonies to well known melodies without spoiling
> their naturalness. Moreover, for an orchestral score, one
> must expand, contract, rearrange, and superimpose the
> bare tunes themselves, giving them something of one's
> own touch.[30]

In our talk in Santa Fe, Copland elaborated further on the challenge of composing with folk tunes:

> You could use the tune and still not do it successfully. You
> might think that by the use of this cowboy tune you're
> going to make a cowboy effect, but that's not true. You
> give the same tune to a European who has never been to
> America and was just using the tune out of a book, I
> don't think you'd get the same effect. So you really have
> to base the music not only on the tune itself, but your
> sense of the kind of people and the kind of country that
> produced the tune.

Copland was not the only young modernist who turned to folk music in a search of new tonal and rhythmic patterns. Stravinsky's reliance on Russian sources was already mentioned; Gershwin and Bernstein have used American jazz as musical motifs in some of their compositions; and the Hungarian composers Bartók and Kodály were deeply committed to a synthesis of folk sources with modern techniques of orchestration and composition.

These Hungarian composers devoted a considerable part of their lives to collecting and recording previously unknown folk music. From the first years of the century until his last years in New York, when Bartók edited a major Yugoslav folk collection at Columbia University, such work was central to this great modernist composer. He was frequently questioned by musicologists, who were familiar with the breadth of his interest and the range of his collecting, whether he saw himself as a nationalist or an internationalist in his musical approach:

> My creative work, just because it arises from three sources
> (Hungarian, Rumanian, Slovakian), might be regarded
> as the embodiment of the very concept of integration so
> much emphasized in Hungary today. . . . My own idea,
> however—of which I have been fully conscious since I
> found myself as a composer—is the brotherhood of
> peoples, brotherhood in spite of all wars and
> conflicts. . . . *The source must only be clean, fresh, and
> healthy!* [emphasis added][31]

Bartók's music is more abstract than that of Kodály, but his use of certain percussive qualities carries with them the influence of folk rhythms and tonalities. Kodály, on the other hand, achieved his greatest mastery in his oratorial works in which pentatonic melodies and Hungarian instrumental styles are combined. And while the composer managed to draw upon a variety of musical traditions, he still achieved a strong classical unity in his final works, particularly in his *Te Deum of Budavár*.[32]

Another way in which composers strive to overcome the strong musical legacy of past masters is by working closely with artists drawn from related fields. One form of such collaboration has been between choreographers and composers. Both Aaron Copland and Igor Stravinsky enjoyed such collaborative efforts; Stravinsky recalled his work on *The Firebird* as follows: "Fokine taught me much, and I have worked with choreographers in the same way ever since. I like exact requirements."[33]

The story of an American collaboration between writer, choreographer, and composer is briefly documented in Leonard Bernstein's "West Side Story Log." The idea of creating a contemporary version of *Romeo and Juliet* was provided by the choreographer Jerome Robbins. Arthur Laurents was asked to write the book for this operatic musical, and Bernstein the music. At first, the collaborators experimented with the idea of religious antagonisms, but then settled on a different theme:

> We're fired again by the *Romeo* notion: only now we have
> abandoned the whole Jewish-Catholic premise as not
> very fresh, and have come up with what I think is going
> to be it: two teen-age gangs, one the warring Puerto
> Ricans, the other self-styled "American." Suddenly it all
> springs to life. I hear rhythms and pulses, and—most of
> all—I can sort of feel the form.
> (six months later)
> Chief problem: to tread the fine line between opera and
> Broadway, between realism and poetry, ballet and "just
> dancing," abstract and representational.
> (Washington, D.C., Aug. 20, 1957.)
> The opening last night was just as we dreamed it. All
> the agony and postponements and re-writing turn out to
> have been worth it.[34]

Themes and variations: It has been easier to identify some of the *sources* composers rely upon in their work than to gain actual descriptions of the composing process. There is a certain and understandable hesitation on the part of artists in penetrating the processes of their creativity. Nevertheless, it has been quite astonishing to me that when I was able to obtain self-reports—either through interviews or by the artist's describing his or her working approach in essays and autobiographies—I could identify certain parallels across domains of creative endeavors.

Such a parallel emerges when one examines the trajectory of a germinal idea to its full realization. The notion that a promising thought may not be effectively expanded right away was first suggested in this book in my discussion of Stephen Spender's essay "The Making of a Poem." It was there that he wrote:

> The method which I adopt therefore is to write down as
> many ideas as possible, in however rough a form,
> in notebooks (I have at least twenty of these, on a
> shelf beside my desk, going back over fifteen years).
> I then make use of some of the sketches and discard
> others.[35]

A similar observation was made by Aaron Copland in the course of our talk.

> Most composers keep a notebook in which they put down
> germinal ideas that occur to them, thinking, "Well, we'll
> work on that later."
>
> You can't pick the moment when you are going to
> have ideas. It picks you and then you might be
> completely absorbed in another piece of work.
>
> I think composers will tell you that they get ideas
> when they can't possibly work on them. They put them
> down where they can find them when they need to look
> for ideas and they don't come easily.

The web of ideas, which may be started at one time and then put aside until needed in a new composition, or reworked again in a new form, characterized Beethoven's processes of composing. According to his contemporary Ferdinand Reis, Beethoven always carried music-paper with him for capturing spontaneous and evanescent ideas wherever he was. He also kept extensive sketchbooks to work through and test out the variations and implications of a new notion. These sketchbooks have now been studied in depth by contemporary musicologists, and they have found evidence that a series of interwoven ideas connected Beethoven's compositions during the first few years of the nineteenth century. There is a "concept sketch" for a work in E-flat major in a notebook that precedes the "Eroica" (Beethoven's Third Symphony) Sketchbook. According to Lewis Lockwood:

> This concept sketch appears to include the following: a triadic opening section, which was probably a slow Introduction as in the Second Symphony, followed by a 3/4 Allegro in E♭; then an idea for a slow movement, marked Adagio C dur and having, remarkably, the theme that was later used for the slow movement of the Quartet Op. 135; then a Minuet and Trio. *That these ideas crop up directly following the end of his sketch work on the so-called "Prometheus" Variations Op. 35 suggests that at the moment Beethoven foresaw the possibility of another large-scale work in E♭ major, for which the "Prometheus" theme might also serve as Finale.* [emphasis added][36]

This method of generating first-phrase ideas that get shifted, rearranged, extended, or abandoned is one that is described in a number of these *Beethoven Studies*. Christopher Reynolds writes in his analysis of Op. 35, *Piano Variations:*

> In the first sustained work that he devoted to single variations Beethoven wrote down ideas for ten separate variations on the sixteen staves of K82v. Most are no more than four to five bars long, concern only the first phrase, and employ two staves. . . . At the present stage his principle aim was to get down *a varied series of ideas for further expansion, a source he could tap throughout the sketch process.* [emphasis added][37]

The French writer Romain Rolland also studied Beethoven's sketch books in preparing to write *Beethoven: The Creator*. He notes that in "Eroica," Beethoven broke with tradition and developed a second section to his symphony that is longer and more substantial than the usual connection between exposition and conclusion. But to accomplish such a densely structured middle section, Beethoven wrote innumerable sketches, which eventually provided him with a symphonic structure within

the symphony. These sketchbooks reveal a process of both rapid notation of ideas and the inclusion of place holders. The musicologist Tovey
described the process as "Beethoven working at top speed, putting down
any cliché that would mark the place where an idea ought to be . . . so
that the act of writing had the same continuity as the flow of his thoughts,
rather than tinker in isolated passages."[38]

In Modeste Tchaikovsky's recollections of his brother's methods of
composing, we find some interesting similarities to those of Beethoven.
Tchaikovsky went on long solitary walks in the country during which
he worked on his compositions:

> Most of the time during these walks was spent in com-
> position. He thought out the leading ideas, pondered
> over the construction of the work, and jotted down
> fundamental themes. In Klin there are carefully
> preserved many little exercise books, which he had used
> for this purpose. . . . The next morning he looked over
> these notes, and worked them out on the piano. . . . He
> always worked out his sketches on the piano, so that he
> should not trust entirely to his indifferent memory.[39]

Aaron Copland also spoke of differing phases in composition during
our conversation:

> Very often one gets a half a page of music that seems to
> have in it the possibility of further development. And
> you don't know where it may lead to, but then you get
> another section, and you don't know where that is
> supposed to be going, but you know that it seems to
> belong with the first idea.
>
> Sometimes the very nature of the musical idea dictates
> the kind of instrument you are going to use. It sounds
> so much like flute music, it has got to be in the flute. But
> there are other musical ideas that don't immediately tell
> you how you might clothe them orchestrally. In that case
> it is better not to decide too soon, because then you have
> the luxury of being able to later fit it where it works well.

Like most composers, Copland does much of his work on the piano:

Well, I work at the piano. . . . But something directs your
fingers. . . . Some musical idea in your head which does
not take reality or take form until you actually hear
it. . . . Then some other things. You don't make music
out of one chord, you hear it in terms of melodic
material. . . .

In music, aside from the individual sections, one of
the great problems is structuring. It is a very different
thing to write a two-minute song and a forty-minute
symphony. I am a composer, I know from my former
experience that I have been able to write pieces that last
forty minutes, therefore that gives me courage so I know
that I will be able to do it again.

Was there a difference between a composition that starts without any
obvious external demand and a commissioned piece, I asked Mr.
Copland.

My music starts with musical ideas. . . . Now somebody
comes along and says "We want to commission you to
write a piece for Lincoln's birthday next year."
Naturally, it starts you thinking in the direction of
Lincoln, what he was like, what the times were like,
what sort of music would be suggestive of him, his
personality, and his times.

You still have to find the musical ideas, a theme that
sounds like Lincoln to you. So that until these vague
notions are translated to actual notes and rhythms and
harmonies, they exist just in your head.

There are some interesting internal sources for new musical
compositions that Stravinsky described. He wrote that the idea for *Le
Sacre du Printemps* came to him while he was still engaged in work on
The Firebird. He first dreamt of a ritual during which "a chosen sacrifi-
cial virgin danced herself to death."[40] Before further musical work on
the piece, Stravinsky sketched the plan of action of the ballet with his
collaborator Nicolas Roerich. The titles of the dances followed, and the
work was influenced by their access to a great collection of Russian folk

art. Then, working on his own, the thematic ideas started to emerge, and Stravinsky expanded these on a small, muted piano.

> I composed from the *Augures printanières* to the end of the first part and then wrote the Prelude afterward. My idea was that the Prelude should represent the awakening of nature, the scratching, gnawing, wiggling of birds and beasts.[41]

After a period of intensive work, composers frequently let a piece alone in order, in Copland's words, "to renew his sense of objectivity." Stravinsky also worked in such cycles, and tended to return to his works even after they had been performed.

> I have twice revised portions of *Le Sacre*, first in 1921 . . . and again in 1943. . . . By 1921, however, my performance experience had led me to prefer smaller divisions. . . . The smaller bars proved more manageable for both conductor and orchestra, and they greatly simplified the scansion of the music.[42]

The mature Stravinsky was re-composing in a way that reminds one of his training, of the way in which Rimsky-Korsakov showed him several possible ways of orchestrating. The full orchestration of musical ideas requires a process akin to the editing carried out by writers, and akin to the constant tug-of-war between ideas and their realization, of which the painter Ben Shahn has written. While Beethoven's sketchbooks and the retrospections of Copland, Stravinsky, and Tchaikovsky provide us with some insight into the lengthy tug-of-war between musical themes and thoughts and their realization, it was Leonard Bernstein who used a linguistic analogy as a tool for examining musical compositions, and thus made the process accessible to the nonmusician.

In *The Unanswered Question*, Bernstein examined sounds, the *phonology* of music; musical structure, its *syntax*; and musical meanings, which he compared to the *semantics* of language. In the course of these dramatic Norton lectures at Harvard University, Bernstein played, spoke, and demonstrated his ideas about music, which he described as a metaphorical language created by transformations.[43] He showed the constituent elements of music: tones, overtones, scales, triads, pentatonic and chromatic scales. He demonstrated the sources of harmony with men's and women's voices an octave apart. He made the suggestions that musical motives correspond to the "noun phrase" in language, while chords are analogous to modifiers, and verbs are akin to rhythm. These comparisons lead him to a fuller explication of his central notion, the importance of transformations in musical language.

The lectures are replete with examples of the multitude of transformations that provide the trajectory from germinal ideas to compositions: these transformations include reversals, alliterations, oppositions, deletions, the many variations on the musical theme: "the idea of repetition is inherent in music even when the repetition is not there at all. In other words, the repetitive principle is at the very source of musical art (and of poetry.")[44] Bernstein's illustrations give weight to a comment made by Copland during my talk with him. When I asked him about the way he starts to compose, Copland did not answer right away. Instead, his friend Harold Clurman said:

> You play one measure or two, the beginning of a general
> idea. And then you play it over and over and over
> again. It was as if you were testing, where will this take
> me? Now is that true, at all?

Copland answered him:

> I think so, yes. It sounds rather dull the way you put it.
> But each time you repeat it, you have a different idea of
> where it might go. It is the process of saying, how will
> this first idea inspire me toward the next one.

Composing thus emerges as a process which demands—as do other forms of creative endeavor—an ability to synthesize germinal ideas with elaborative structures. The transformation of inner, frequently vague notions, into orchestrated works is powerfully evoked by these composers. They provide students of the mind with the traces of complex activities, which are but barely understood in our studies.

Musicologists are just starting to study the sketchbooks of composers, but their findings support the notion of a slow and complex dynamic between germinal notions—frequently emerging in the midst of ongoing work on the part of the composer—and their full elaboration. The similarities between the writing of a novel and the composing of a symphony are interesting in this regard: they both depend upon the creator's full mastery of his or her tradition, of a sense of purpose and will that comes from knowing that one can execute a large work, and of the pleasures of an adventure as a work finds its own shape in the process of creation.

Choreography

"A movement idea takes longer to establish itself in dance than in one's mind," commented New York University choreographer and teacher Linda Tarnay. We were talking outside the "Yard"—a large, wooden, performing studio on Martha's Vineyard—where she had just begun to work with a group of young dancers. Tarnay had come to the morning's rehearsal with a lot of notes; they represented some of her ideas for the new dance they were working on. As with most choreographers, Tarnay has to observe closely the impact of her imagined movements on the bodies of the dancers. As they experiment together, her ideas unfold and change. After the rehearsal, Tarnay explained some aspects of dance thinking to me: "The logic of a dance movement is different from the way verbal ideas are connected. One movement leads to another the way the body responds kinesthetically. Movements also have a spatial logic of their own."

In dance, the dramatization of human experience is enacted through movements, through a subjective and visual elaboration of the messages of the body. Our understanding of what choreographers attempt to communicate is based upon our own familiarity with our bodies, a source of knowledge that reaches back to infancy. The first "dance" is that of the infant and his or her caretakers: it consists of the finely tuned interactions when children convey their wants by crying, by their gestures and facial expressions, by the tension and relaxation of their muscles.[45] The adults who nurture and protect them read the meaning of their movements; they are helped in their efforts in making sense of these nonverbal messages through their own experience with the body as a vehicle of remembered experience. Similarly, we bring to the dance theatre our knowledge of the language of the body, of emotions etched in bones and muscles, *of movements as messages.*

No universal vocabulary of the dance exists. Each choreographer shapes, simplifies, and crystallizes movements in a unique manner, though dance shares with all languages the functions of representing and communicating a shared human heritage. When dance forms are too obvious, too closely modeled upon expressive movements and gestures, the choreographer's work becomes clichéd. The true power of the dance lies in its possibilities to explore a range of meanings different from those inherent in verbal and visual languages. The dance critic

John Martin wrote of dance as communication as follows: "Movement, then, in and of itself is a medium of transference of an aesthetic and emotional concept from the consciousness of one individual to another."[46]

The development of movement ideas: In the course of my talks with choreographers, I asked each of them to describe the sources of their dances, the way they started. Eliot Feld, a highly regarded choreographer of contemporary ballets, described the source of movement ideas in his work to me while his company was rehearsing at the Delacorte Theatre in New York. They were preparing for the open air performance of his ballet "Intermezzo," and Feld kept one eye on his dancers while he spoke: "I always start with music. The most important thing is how the dance fulfills the music emotionally . . . how I respond to it." Feld recalled the early stages of his work as a choreographer when his feelings for music were that of a man first in love. He was quickly and totally moved by music.

More recently, Feld had expanded the range of his dances, beyond his first, strongly romantic repertoire, and in the process his choice of and perceptions concerning music have also changed. At the time of our talk, Feld had just completed the dance "Excursions," based on Samuel Barber's music. "The music evoked certain American perceptions," he reflected, "a good-naturedness, banjo picking, Westerners, horses, plains. The beginning of this dance had to do with a train, I established certain rhythms in the dance that were trainlike. . . . It is like going backwards from the train to the person."

Feld, in contrast with many choreographers, avoids an elaborate, mental plotting of his dances.

> I do one piece at a time, one gets involved in the specif-
> ics. Suddenly, when you go through a million specifics,
> you go away and say "My God, there is really an art to
> it. It forms a whole, but you don't know how it
> happens. I think maybe that's talent. Maybe that's the
> way you can judge talent."

The contemporary ballet is based on a powerful foundation, he commented. Feld has internalized the works of Petipa, Fokine, Tudor, Graham, Humphrey, and Balanchine as part of his choreographic heritage. That is part of his and his generation's strength: "We always step on building blocks. . . . We are building higher and getting taller."

Sara Sugihara, whose roots are in the José Limón school of dancing, described a very different source for her choreography. She keeps a variety of notebooks in which she jots down technical ideas and creative ideas as well as musical themes. She often begins her work with a dramatic concept, such as "embracing mountain"; the tension inherent in such a contradictory notion stimulates her to enact it in movements, to search for (or compose) appropriate music, and to choose the right dancers and visual frames for the dance once it is ready to be performed.

The virtuoso dancer Miguel Godreau recalled how a certain piece of music had haunted him for years. While dancing with European companies, Godreau heard one of Ariel Ramírez's compositions, a Spanish mass entitled "Paz." He was deeply moved by the music and tried to convince some of his choreographer friends to use it for their work. None of them did. But once Alvin Ailey asked Godreau to choreograph a work for himself as a dancer, the young Puerto Rican "whirlwind" listened to the mass once more: "I closed myself up in the studio and said, 'I want to do this.' . . . I started working, working with the feeling of it, the tranquility of it. That is why the beginning is peace. Peace of mind, peace of body, peace of soul."

The danger of being carried away by music, of drafting one's work simply upon that of another, was recognized by Godreau. "Anyone can just dance to music," he remarked. "I simplified my movements and tried to make them more visual."

Choreographers bring a dual awareness to their work: they are stimulated and nourished by music—they experience it with their bodies—but they also see their dances through the eyes of the beholder, through the eyes of their audience. The choreographer best known for the visual purity of his dances and for his deep knowledge of music, is, perhaps, George Balanchine. In a thoughtful biography of this great figure of twentieth-century dance, Bernard Taper described how music had sustained Balanchine, even during some difficult periods of his career. One of these was in the thirties, when Balanchine and his young company were hired by the Metropolitan Opera. Taper wrote:

> On this occasion, as always, the chief stimulant and deepest fount of inspiration for Balanchine was music. He listened during the intense, excited conferences that would sometimes go far into the night, to the ideas propounded by Tchelitchev and Kirstein, but the voice to which he gave most heed when it came time to choreograph was that of Christoph Willibald Gluck—poignant, passionate, grave, and noble. For

> Gluck's music (for his opera *Orpheus and Eurydice*)
> Balanchine created in Kirstein's words, some of his
> "most accomplished erotic patterns, touching and
> electric encounters, and noble plastic groups."[47]

Although neither the ballet nor Balanchine's cooperation with the Metropolitan Opera was a success, this opera ballet introduced the New York public to Balanchine's work which decades later they were to admire greatly. In this as well as in his later work, music has been in Taper's words "the sustaining element in which he swims."

The composer Stravinsky, whose music has been used by a great number of choreographers throughout the world, most understandably cherished his collaborations with Balanchine. He wrote of their joint efforts in *Themes and Episodes:* "To see Balanchine's choreography of the *Movements is to hear the music with one's eyes.* . . . [emphasis added] The choreography emphasizes relationships of which I had barely been aware—in the same way—and the performance was like a tour of a building for which I had drawn the plans but never explored the result."[48]

Though Balanchine's choreography is profoundly musical, Merce Cunningham—another major figure in contemporary dance—focuses on the spatial logic of movements in his work. "The ideas of the dance come both from the movement and are in the movement," commented Cunningham to Rosner and Abt in the course of their interview with him.[49] Cunningham's abstract dances are structured around time and space; his dancers rely upon mathematical counting and their own inner rhythms with the help of which they learn their parts.

Some ideas in Cunningham's working papers were published in a recent article.[50] These documented how he plots his dances with numbers, stick figures, and vectors. These reveal the sudden juxtapositions in his dances, an important hallmark of his choreography. Chance elements also are included in Cunningham's dances; these provide a sense of the unexpected, of delightful surprises. He frequently plots the sequence of his dance fragments by tossing pennies: "The apparent discontinuity of his dances reflect his statement that 'anything can follow anything'—a Zen-inspired acknowledgment of the randomness of life."[51]

Cunningham is greatly admired by the current, younger generation of choreographers. His explorations of movement and space have influenced many among them. Nevertheless, his abstract, cerebral approach to the dance is seldom adopted in its entirety by other dance-makers. Most of them seem to aspire toward a broader synthesis of the musical, emotional, visual, and movement aspects of dance compositions.

The most sustained effort at synthesis of the dance with other art forms (music, sculpture, literature) is found in Martha Graham's work. The sources of her dance-dramas encompass Greek mythology, Oriental philosophy, English and American poetry as well as her own Puritanical roots. These traditions have contributed to her sustained exploration of the human psyche through the medium of the dance.

Graham's approach to her work is revealed in her program notes, in the many interviews she has given during the extraordinary span of her creative life, and most fully through her notebooks, which were published in 1973. The most complete set of notes is devoted to the dance-drama "The Dark Meadows of the Soul." In these nearly forty pages she quotes from Jung, Goethe, Plutarch, Virginia Woolf, Blake, and many others. The quotes are interspersed with planning notes identifying projected cycles of the work (these are changed many times), the choice of dancers, and personal recollections:

> I seem to feel in the first part—the opening—a memory
> of standing in the wind on top of the Mexican
> pyramid—And then to remember the descent
> afterwards—There was an awareness up there of ancient
> rites—sacrifices—sufferings—prayers—but enduring
> through all—the sun, the wind, the rain—[52]

In *Dance in America*, Walter Terry wrote of the meaning of this major composition of Graham's as follows: "These are the ancestral footsteps echoing into the future." Many of the themes that were first explored by Graham in this work, which she composed soon after the end of World War II, reappear in her later cycle of dances, "Night Journey," "Phaedra," and in "Clytemnestra." Once more in her notes concerning "Phaedra," one can observe how Graham pulls together into a "magic circle" of ideas quotes from others, her own characterization of Phaedra: "It is the time of drought with Phaedra. . . . It is the desperate time when the need is for renewal. . . ."[53] In addition, she plans several beginnings of the dance and indicates some step-by-step choreography. These are jotted down in condensed, "inner-speech writing." Some of her planning resembles that of Dostoevsky (see Chapter 4), who also used his notebooks as a chance to explore and develop as well as to abandon ideas during a major project.

One of the examples of dance notations to be found in the *Notebooks* is this:

Beginning
Phaedra on bed
  1) On chords
    P.r. knee up sharply
      straighten r. leg
  2) On chords
      r. knee up
      swing leg to back wide
      leg straight[54]

These verbal notations of movements are a different record of the inner workings of the mind from Cunningham's vectors and stick figures. Graham's thoughts appear to have a strong verbal cast; there are but few arrows in her *Notebooks*. The ones found indicate spatial directions for a dance-movement or the sequencing of dance segments. Graham's interweaving of language and movement in her choreographic planning is consistent with her reliance upon literature as the foundation of her creative imagination.

The audience who attends a Graham performance needs the opportunity to examine repeatedly the meanings implicit in her work. Interestingly, Graham herself finds new insights in viewing and participating in her dances. The following passage, written in her *Notebooks* one evening in October 1950, reveals such a discovery: "Tonight in 'Deaths and Entrances' while standing I suddenly knew what witchcraft is—in microcosm—It is the being in each of us—sometimes the witch, sometimes the real being of good—of creative energy—no matter in what area of direction of activity."[55] The dance that gave rise to these thoughts deals with the Brontë sisters, with the struggle of female liberation from madness and confinement.[56] Graham's work is motivated by a multitude of struggles in which dancers confront and overcome their origins and their limitations. Some dance critics have suggested that Graham's puritanical background motivated her exploration of the physicality of life and also provided her with the will and fierceness with which she pursues her demons and her heritage.

The sources of movement ideas are thus quite diverse. Graham and many other choreographers find their themes in the tensions of emotions; others are stimulated by music, or by the specificity of movements through space, or by beliefs and experiences that can only be understood through the communicative messages of the human body.

The art of dance resides in taking these sources and making something of them. It requires a deep knowledge and respect for form. In the words of Anna Sokolow—one of the most experienced American choreographers:

> Anyone . . . can have a good idea for a dance. In itself
> that's not enough. There must be form as well as
> concept; both matter—what you feel and how you
> express it. First, the choreographer sees his idea in terms
> of movement, as the painter sees his in terms of color,
> line, mass. This happens spontaneously. Movements are
> not intellectually contrived but are evoked by emotional
> images. The only intellectual process is the one that puts
> these spontaneously conceived movements into a form
> that works as a whole.

She later added in an essay written for *The Modern Dance: Seven Statements of Belief:*

> True form comes from reducing reality to its essential
> shape, as Cézanne did with the apple. In the hands of
> an artist, form is essential, exciting. There is nothing
> superfluous, because the artist has stripped his work to
> the bare essentials. And an audience responds to this
> purity, this inevitability of form, which is beauty.[57]

Dance—a public art: A successful choreographer creates a work that —in the words of Lee Connor, a dance-maker from New Mexico—leaves "an indelible branding impression upon memory." That result is the end-product of a complex process of switching between private and public elaborations of movement ideas. To make a dance, one needs dancers. Their varied physiques contribute to the unwinding, and to the expansion of movements first tried by the choreographer in privacy. When Balanchine had to spend a few months, in 1929, in a TB sanitarium, he was unable to choregraph. Bedridden and isolated, he was cut off from the stimulating presence of dancers "assembled in the mirrored studio, waiting, idle but expectant."[58]

The need for, as well as the problems faced by, this close collaboration on the part of choreographers and dancers also preoccupies Eliot Feld: "Choreography is the only art done publicly," he told me. "Every time that I get stuck, or don't know what to do, there is a whole roomful of people waiting. It is as though you composed with the whole orchestra there. Or wrote a play and had all the actors waiting for their lines."

Even Martha Graham, whose *Notebooks* reveal a very private creator, found her dance-vocabulary affected by the background and training of her dancers. Margaret Lloyd, author of *The Borzoi Book of Modern Dance*, made an interesting observation in this regard. When Erik Hawkins and Merce Cunningham became lead dancers in the Graham company in the thirties, they came with a background of having been members of Lincoln Kirstein's Ballet Caravan. Lloyd wrote: "The advent of these ballet-trained men brought a more active adaptation of ballet *pas* into the Graham technic—another proof that the living material a choreographer has to work with is bound to influence the use he makes of that material."[59] The collaborative aspects of dance composition reveal an important contrast between choreography and other art forms. Writers and painters work in privacy; they revise their attempts before exposing them to an audience, while the planning of a dance involves work with dancers, the viewing of one's ideas on their bodies.

Still, the extent to which choreographers involve their dancers in each stage of their creative efforts varies considerably. New York choreographer Daniel Nagrin relied strongly upon his dancers' improvisations in the generative phase of his work. But he also edited his dances slowly and carefully, and thus created a small but strong body of work. Lee Connor, who had studied with Nagrin, and was deeply influenced by this humanistic choreographer, does not encourage improvisation on the part of his dancers: "It is funny," he told me. "Improvisation was such an important formative thing for me, but I cannot bear to leave any aspect of my choreography out of my control. I make every single movement."

The communication of meaning through movement requires an ability to weave together physical, emotional, and intellectual aspects of one's understanding. While choreographers are rooted in a strong tradition, they also have a great need to transcend their joint past and to create a personal idiom, their own dance vocabulary; the challenge of such distinctiveness weighs heavily on young choreographers. Agnes de Mille, in her autobiography *Speak to Me, Dance with Me*, described her difficulties: "My taproot was in acting, which is of necessity based on immediate recognition. I was literal, somewhat derivative and repetitious, but always clear and emotionally charged. But I kept trying to find a gesture that was not literal, to become abstract without loss of emotional impact."[60]

Most contemporary choreographers share with de Mille this striving to avoid a literalness in dance that has characterized this medium during earlier periods. Gestures, mime, and elaborate theatrical backdrops were part of the scaffolding of dance performances in the past. One focus of choreographers at present is upon the unexplored expressive and representational means of the human body. The great American dance pioneers, Isadora Duncan and Martha Graham, proceeded in building their dance vocabularies from such an examination.

Duncan linked dance to the natural movements of running and walking, the uses of arms and hands for expression, and the equality of the body with the mind. Erik Hawkins—a great admirer of Duncan—expressed the significance of Duncan's approach as follows: "only when the body was rerecognized and freed could a new art of dance arise in the West."[61]

Martha Graham built her approach around the contractions and expansions of the body which accompany breathing. She amplified these movements which led her to discover a whole range of new leaps, elevations, turns, and falls. She also developed a new approach to gravity in her dances. While ballet has a largely vertical orientation, the Graham technique includes much work on the floor. It consists of a variety of horizontal and angular positions, all of which contribute to the strongly expressive, psychological dance idiom of this great pioneer.

Once a new dance idiom is performed, a choreographer may find that the audience reacts with confusion and lack of understanding. Some very basic movements *are* eloquent because they are based upon nonverbal gestures used in daily exchanges. However, a full reliance upon these in dance would result in pantomime and literalness. The choreographer Doris Humphrey wrote: "the rousing of action-memory in the onlooker, by whatever means, is the sole key to good theater."[62] Humphrey aspired in her own work to combine abstract explorations (she was particularly interested in the dynamics of balance and imbalance) with the choreographic extension of gestures to provide both novelty and familiarity to her dances.

"Good choreography fuses eye, ear, and mind" wrote the dance critic Arlene Croce.[63] Human verbal communication provides analytical precision in the realization of meaning, in contrast with dance, which is an assimilative form of communication. The expressive possibilities of movement reside in their lack of full conventionalization. These are evocative symbols and they leave part of the task of interpretation to each individual member of a dance audience. In verbal language, on the other hand, where the precision of a shared system of meanings makes communication easier, the challenge for writers consists in the use of words in a fresh way.

In describing dance, critics and choreographers rely upon a terminology borrowed from the analysis of verbal language. Terms such as *dance vocabulary* or *dance phrases* abound in their writings. Although these analogies are helpful, because dance is a communicative form of human behavior, the differences between dance and speech should not be ignored in the context of such verbal and written usage.

Foremost among these is the immediacy of movement, a presence that the choreographer Erik Hawkins describes with a reliance upon the philosopher Northrop's concept of the first function of art. Similarly, dance exists "in and of itself, before it communicates." Hawkins writes further: "When the choreographer sets out to do more—to use movements not for their own sake but for the sake of revealing some theme, some idea, some narrative—then he must make the movement into some language."[64] This aspect of dance corresponds to Northrop's "second function of art." Throughout Hawkins's long life as an artist, he has attempted to unite these two functions in his own choreographic work.

Choreographers within the modern and the ballet tradition both strive toward an integration of the expressive and communicative possibilities of the dance without losing the power and immediacy of movement. The balancing act that such dual objectives requires was described by Eliot Feld: "It is a mix. It is curious when you choreograph. There is a mind, a perception. But you must not assert that too strongly on music, or on the movement, or on the dancers, because then you are not responding to reality, to the dancers in a room at a given moment. . . . I may be forcing things to happen or I am not directing enough."

Too great a reliance upon thoughtful preparation may result in work that is predictable. In an attempt to avoid the controlling power of a rational mind and the memories of other dances, choreographers return constantly to a close study of movement, to the examination of the logic of movement ideas. The focus upon the immediacy of movement also protects them from the undue influence of their predecessors. Linda Tarnay described some of these concerns during our interview on Martha's Vineyard:

> In my desire not to duplicate the vocabularies of my
> mentors, Graham, Cunningham, Limón, I have reduced
> my own vocabulary to very simple movements: walking,
> running, gestures, every-day movements. Now I want
> to try to work back to more technically demanding
> work, but which is still comprehensible to the people
> watching it. There is, particularly in modern dance, a

tendency for people to move abstractly, and the
audience does not know what is going on. I have a very
strong desire to be clear and accessible to anyone who
sees the dance. But I have to challenge the dancers and
use the medium.

In *The Art of Making Dances*, Doris Humphrey had also explored some
of the issues of linking craft with intent in choreography. One of her
concerns was to look at movement or dance "words" and see how
they fit into larger units: "I have gradually learned that movements and
gestures, like tones in music and shades in painting, have certain family relations and as groups, have their own laws."[65] Humphrey discusses
the many ways—spatial, rhythmic, interpersonal—for extending movement ideas into designed compositions. Central to this effort is the concept of dance "phrases"; Lee Connor defined a phrase in a manner quite
similar to Humphrey during our conversation. Both of them link it to
the rhythms of breathing: "When I take a breath and start to move, I
construct a sentence. It is what happens when I exhale. A 'sentence' is
logical, it has integrity and consistency. It does something."

But in contrast with simple breathing, dance compositions require variations in their rhythms. "These breaths, of course, can and should vary
in duration," Humphrey wrote, "as they are not literally the length of
one breath of the body at rest, but rather like a spoken sentence, with
possibly a subclause or two; or, using another comparison, like a melodic line a flutist might play in one breath."[66]

Not alone in emphasizing the importance of physical phrasing, Doris
Humphrey would have agreed with the dance critic Edwin Denby who
found fault with many contemporary choreographers in this area: "The
moderns have always cultivated continuity in their intellectual concepts;
but they did not build their dances out of a continuity of expressions."[67]
So, too, Lee Connor recalled how at an early stage of his work with
his partner Lorne McDougall he ran into rather comic problems with
phrasing: "I would have her on my shoulder, or she would have her
legs around my neck and I would close my eyes and think about the
next thing. It was like one word and then another." Good composition
requires a careful understanding of dance logic, of phrasing. The best
examples of such logic are provided in some of Limón's pieces, Connor
recalled, and in the extraordinary work of Twyla Tharp, in whose pieces
the musical phrase and the use of gesture *begins, rises, arches, peaks,* and
falls. Connor's work reflects his musical training and his meticulous at-

tention to composition, which results in a strong and sustained line in his dances.

It is during rehearsals that choreographers have an opportunity to examine the physical and spatial realization of their movement ideas. The work on a new dance may start with a personal experience, with some powerful feelings and images. Linda Tarnay described the beginnings of her composition "Primavera" taking place during a particularly hard spring for her. She was watching the vines grow on her window sill; the shoots and flowers looked both tender and painfully beautiful in her wistful state. These images of spring gave rise to some more specific movement ideas, which she focused on for their action possibilities. Tarnay uses verbs as her "notebook of the mind": she remembers writing words such as "twist, climb, open, turn toward the sun, etc." when first planning the dance "Primavera." One of the solos of the finished composition succeeded, Tarnay feels, in capturing the raw and tentative nature of early spring and her own emotions during that season.

At the time of our conversation, Tarnay had just begun to work on another dance-composition. It was tentatively titled "The Voice of the Whale"; the title was borrowed from the music she planned to use. In this case she had but a few ideas dealing with the depth and dangers of the sea, but once she heard this particular composition, she knew that the choice of this theme was right for her. The decision was difficult because she had another dance, her signature piece, entitled "Ocean" in her repertoire, but she knew that aspects of this subject continued to draw her and that she had not yet fully explored them in her previous work.

The long span of work from first ideas to full realization involves both solitary and group endeavors. Choreographers move from being inside their work to stepping outside of it. Tarnay demonstrates some of the movement ideas to her dancers that she has prepared in advance, and then she watches them unfold into the studio as her dancers work with the ideas. She explained: "I made up all these movements, but I did not know whether it would look the way it felt to me while I was working by myself." She did not find it hard to start this new dance; the movements were effectively linked to the emotional theme she had in mind. The formal design of the work required that the dancers start in unison, to be followed by individual and pair dancing. Thus, the second dance section was the result of a certain internal logic of the dance, where the movements came first to her, and then she worked out their meaning in her mind.

Tarnay recalled an interesting coincidence in her work on this dance composition. One of the people she was sharing a house with on Martha's Vineyard, at the time she had started to work on "The Voice of the Whale," was reading Virginia Woolf's *The Waves*. (The presence of this book was similar to what Mann had described as his "magic circle" of materials when he was beginning a new project.) The choreographer found some of the ideas and phrases in Woolf's novel suggestive—the equating of the ocean with sleep, with forgetfulness—and she started to jot down phrases: "I sink, I turn, I float, I escape, I am turned." The notion of not being in control, of having something done to one became important to her as she was working on the dance. She shared some of these themes and images with her dancers, and their understanding and participation contributed to their ability to execute the composition.

A dance, then, is constructed from different sources: some images are drawn from literature, others from the careful observation of nature. Dancers are part of the process of construction—their bodies inspire different movements, their understanding contributes to the shadings of execution. At times, choreographers rely upon the thematic possibilities inherent in the music they select: the third movement of Tarnay's "The Voice of the Whale" was to depict a storm. The suggestion came from the violent rhythms of the music for this part.

The notion that dance is an assimilative art is based on this many-sided synthesis, on the integration of space, movement, form, and music with the choreographer's intentions. The complexity of the woven patterns of the dance are worked out in rehearsal, as dance is a public art.

This aspect of the dance—its public nature—reaches back to the many forms and functions of dance in tribal, nonliterate societies. The joining of human beings celebrating birth, preparing for war, engaged in healing the sick among them, honoring their gods, praying for rain or fertility, has been a joining in dance and music. And contemporary makers of the dance are nourished by this ancient knowledge, by a recognition that dance expresses not only their individual but their social experience. In her "Notes on the Dance" Katherine Dunham has written:

> The emotional life of any community is clearly legible in
> its art forms, and because the dance seeks continuously
> to capture moments of life in a fusion of time, space and
> motion, the dance is at a given moment the most

accurate chronicler of culture pattern. The constant interplay of conscious and unconscious finds a perfect instrument in the physical form, the human body which embraces all at once. Alone or in concert man dances his various selves and his emotions and his dance becomes a communication as clear as though it were written or spoken in a universal language.[68]

7 / Scientific Thinking

The apprenticeships of artists are individually constructed times of learning, while young scientists-in-the-making follow a more formal and structured process of socialization. But in both art and science, individuals bring their minds trained from childhood and their creative intensity to the challenging tasks of extending knowledge. The full mastery of the scientific methods of thinking, though, is not easily accomplished. While classroom lessons are an essential part of the apprenticeship process, the emerging scientist gains further insights into his or her future work by reading and by sharing knowledge with peers and with mentors.

In the sciences, the urge for understanding and for intellectual adventure motivate most young people. The French-American biologist, René Dubos, wrote that his first contact with scientific adventure was made in reading the work of Jules Verne:

> I am sure that his stories could not instill valid knowledge or critical judgment or scientific spirit in anyone, but they can certainly foster a taste for the unknown and a desire for adventure.[1]

Curiosity and passion are maintained and renewed in the course of a scientist's career through the pleasures of discovery and through the use of varied kinds of thought when confronted with a new and intriguing problem. Some scientists identify visual processes as crucial to their thinking, while others emphasize metaphoric or mathematical processes. Colleagues frequently debate their premises and their philosophical assumptions: Werner Heisenberg has evoked in *Physics and Beyond* the intense discussions between physicists in the nineteen-twenties as they were trying to resolve their theoretical uncertainties:

Bohr's discussions with Schrödinger began at the rail-
road station and were continued daily from early
morning until late at night. . . . It is hardly possible to
convey how passionate these discussions were, just how
deeply rooted the convictions of each, a fact that marked
every utterance.[2]

Some of the sources and characteristics of the scientific imagination
explored here are informed by interviews with mathematicians, physicists, biologists, and psychologists. These interviews, together with a
growing descriptive literature of the psychology of scientists and of the
discovery process, form the basis of this discussion of scientific thinking.

Scientific Beginnings

In most biographical accounts of a scientific career, an early interest in
the explorations of nature is mentioned as well as a taste for books, such
as the adventure stories written by Jules Verne. In describing her husband's childhood, Marie Curie wrote of young Pierre's fascination with
ponds: "with their characteristic vegetation and their population of frogs,
tritons, salamander, dragon-flies, and other denizens of air and water."[3]
The young Charles Darwin was also an enthusiastic observer and col-
lector of small creatures. Howard Gruber noted in his book on Darwin
that the great British evolutionist considered the habit of observation
"as the first real training or education of my mind."[4] And, in *Adventures of a Mathematician,* Stan Ulam recalled the beginnings of his interest in science around the age of nine, when he found a book on
astronomy: the pictures of the stars fascinated him, as did a remarkable
portrait of Sir Isaac Newton. His enjoyment of astronomy was further
heightened when he received a small telescope as a gift from one of his
uncles.

The sense of wonder and the future scientist's desire to go beyond
the surface of things was also evoked by Einstein in his "Autobiographical Essay." There he wrote of his feeling as a very young child while
watching a compass, that "something deeply hidden had to be behind
things."[5]

A fascination with patterns at a very early age was reported by the
mathematician Reuben Hersh, co-author of the award winning book
The Mathematical Experience: "I remember looking at the bathroom floor,
and observing the different patterns that I could see by combining larger

and smaller tiles. I also did arithmetic in my mind, rather obsessively, adding things endlessly, and also looking for patterns in numbers." Hersh was a rather quiet child who did not know anybody interested in mathematics among his parents' friends and associates; thus he did not talk to adults about his interest in patterns and numbers.

On the other hand, Peter Lax (a distinguished teacher at NYU's Courant Institute), Hersh's friend and mentor, is a member of a professional family. His uncle, a well-known engineer and mathematician, enjoyed playing number games with his young nephew. But it was through tutoring and formal instruction that Lax first recognized the depth of his interest in and talent for mathematics. He also enjoyed some of the popular books written for young people, a memory that surfaces in many autobiographical writings. Einstein, for example, recounted how after studying a popular book on geometry at age twelve, he again felt a deep sense of wonder: "This (geometrical) lucidity and certainty made an indescribable impression upon me,"[6] he wrote. At a similar age, Stan Ulam found a popular book on algebra in his father's library, and the well-written volume stimulated him to start working on equations by himself.

Mathematicians and physicists also have reported that in addition to their independent explorations and discoveries, they had found stimulation when more mature men and women offered to share their interests with them. The historian of science Gerald Holton described the way in which the great Italian physicist Enrico Fermi was "intellectually adopted" by one of his father's friends at the age of thirteen:

> Fermi himself had come from a closely knit family and was
> very attached to his brother and sister. His own fate was
> determined decisively by the decision of a colleague of
> his father, Adolfo Amidei. He had noticed the young
> boy in a manner which itself gives a glimpse into the
> structure of society at that time. Amidei recalled that in
> 1914 he and Alberto Fermi, his colleague in the Ministry
> of Railways, after leaving the office at the end of the day
> "walked together part of the way home, almost always
> accompanied by the lad Enrico Fermi, my colleague's
> son, who was in the habit of meeting his father in front
> of the office. The lad, having learned that I was an avid
> student of mathematics and physics, took the
> opportunity to question me. He was 13, and I was 37."
> Amidei's intervention not only provided Fermi with

books and someone to talk about science with, but also a mentor to help plan and shape his career.[7]

The European-born scientist and Nobel prize winner Albert Szent-Györgyi also described his first experience with science in the laboratory of his uncle, a well-known histologist and anatomist who worked in Hungary at the turn of the century. The role of friends and relatives in stimulating one's scientific imagination is also noted in a biographical account of Einstein's life written by his sister, Dr. Maja Winteler-Einstein. She suggested that Einstein's interest in mathematical problems was kindled by his uncle Jakob Einstein, who was an engineer. He showed the young boy of seven a demonstration of the Pythagorean theorem, which then emboldened the young Einstein to develop a proof of his own. He also received encouragement from another uncle, Cäser Koch, a grain merchant who presented the young boy with a steam engine:

> Its chugging operation made such a deep impression upon the boy, that 30 years later, in writing a nostalgic letter to his uncle Cäser, he drew a remarkably precise diagram of the little engine.[8]

Thus, part of the informal apprenticeships of the mind consists of far-ranging discussions among individuals with shared interests. Some of the partners in these conversations are of the same generation, others may be decades apart in age. The exchange of ideas with a person of greater experience gives the younger individual a sense of direction and hope. Recently the television commentator Bill Moyers made a similar observation after completing a documentary series on creativity:

> An amazing number of creative people have been touched and moved by another person at some point in their lives. It might have been a parent, a grandmother, or very often a teacher. That person has communicated to them a sense of "you matter" and made them aware of their own intrinsic worth as a human being.[9]

The mathematician Peter Lax recalled how his tutor R. Peter, the author of *Playing with Infinity*, served the role of a mentor to him. She had contributed to his realization at the young age of twelve years, that he wanted to become a mathematician. The adolescent Lax met a number of Hungary's leading mathematicians before his family decided to emigrate to the United States. The opportunity to show his work to established mathematicians, who encouraged him in his pursuits, also helped Lax once he emigrated. The letters he carried from Hungary opened new doors for him.

The search for a mentor is not always a conscious one among young people; it may occur in childhood, in adolescence, or even later in life. Among scientists, the role of a mentor becomes more apparent when a student enters graduate school. N. P. Davis reported in his biography of Ernest Lawrence how the young physicist followed William Swann, his professor and idol, from university to university. Frequently, the opportunity to work with a particular individual affects the young scientist's choice of a graduate program. The theoretical physicist Nina Byers made her decision to enroll at the University of Chicago based on just such considerations.

At Chicago I knew Byers and enjoyed renewing our friendship twenty-five years later in her sunny, Los Angeles home while working on this book. She recalled her student years to me:

> During the late fifties, the faculty at Chicago consisted of
> some of the absolutely first-rate theoretical physicists.
> During those crucial years, Enrico Fermi's way of
> thinking and his way of doing problems pervaded the
> whole place, so we all had a common language from
> Fermi.

Byers had hoped to study with Murray Gell-Mann, a young physicist, whose work was a continuation of Fermi's (Gell-Mann did receive the Nobel Prize in physics in 1969): "I wanted to work on something that was interesting to him, because he would then take more interest in what I was doing," she explained. But Gell-Mann left Chicago soon after Byers started there, and the young woman physicist was given another advisor. They did not develop an intense collaboration; this second advisor was an older man, raised in the more formal, European tradition of university studies. "I presented the problem and we discussed it, and then I went away and did my work. When I had something in a written form, he read it and commented on it." But even in this more formal process of dialogue, the senior scientist's style of thinking was revealed to the apprentice physicist.

I have sought to imagine some of these talks between Byers and her advisors. And I asked her whether she would describe what she had meant by the "common language derived from Fermi" that the Chicago physicists had shared. How did they communicate? Did they use mathematics as part of their discussions? "No, mathematics is a tool, like language is a tool," Byers answered. "One would not confuse language with thought, right? Similarly, we would not confuse mathematics with the way one conceptualizes a problem."

The delineation of relationships in the subatomic world of particle physics requires the flexible use of certain concepts. Some of these are the use of parameters, the examination of movement paths and the analysis of boundary conditions. Once a problem is represented more precisely by means of these concepts, the physicist may then use mathematics to further analyze his or her task. The use of these mathematical tools is frequently shared by scientists; in a good physics department many opportunities exist to exchange ideas. Colleagues might meet for lunch, or for tea in the late afternoon, and while eating they use whatever clean surface they can find—napkins, matchboxes—to discuss new approaches to unsolved problems. There is a community of individual interests shared through a common language of science.

But close collaboration among young peers, or the chance to work intensively with a mentor, does not always present itself in graduate school. The physicist Byron Goldstein found such a relationship only after his schooling was completed, during a postdoctoral summer seminar. Goldstein described his mentor, the chemist Bruno Zim:

> He is one of the last of the renaissance scientists. He developed a great deal of theory both in physics and chemistry, he has designed excellent instruments, he is very knowledgeable about applied issues—he can tell you about paints and shellacs—and the role of DNA in biology.

During a postdoctoral fellowship with Zim, Goldstein initiated some research at the interface of physics and biology, which still characterizes his work more than a decade later.

While trading of ideas and intense discussions are important aspects of the development of theoretically oriented scientists, the apprenticeship of experimentalists reveals a somewhat different direction. To them, it is the opportunity to work in close collaboration with more experienced individuals in a laboratory setting, which enables them to acquire the invisible tools of their discipline. It is through such interactions that a young person's visual and kinesthetic problem-solving skills are sharpened, that innovative approaches to instrumentation are acquired, and that the learner finds his or her analytical thinking is being challenged and developed.

The importance of tutorial learning has been recognized by a number of students of scientific careers. However, very few detailed studies have been done of the development of young scientists. One notable exception is the work of June Goodfield, whose recently published book *An Imagined World* spans a five-year period in the life of a gifted, young experimental biologist. A Portuguese physician, called Anna Brito in this book, collaborated with Goodfield in the documentation of her growth as a scientist through the differing stages of her work, including research that led to a new formulation of the critical role of iron in human immune systems.

After finishing her medical training in Portugal, Brito started her research career in a British cancer laboratory. She knew little English at the time, and not much more about scientific research. But from the very start of her apprenticeship, she showed the hallmarks of a good scientist: she had patience, she was imaginative, and she was determined to go beyond the simple collection of facts in her work.

Her first assignment in the cancer laboratory was the organization of slides obtained from the lymph nodes of mice. While arranging these according to the time sequence of their collection, Brito discovered that two different populations of lymphocytes were represented among the slides. One of these was "thymic-dependent," the other, surrounding the central core of the spleen, was "thymic-independent." While this discovery was later recognized as an important one by other biologists, Brito found herself quite lonely and isolated during her first year as a researcher. She did not receive much encouragement. Her supervisor believed that she needed to acquire additional skills as an experimentalist before her work could be trusted by others. Brito was determined, however, to prove herself; she used her first year to stretch her skills and deepen her knowledge of biology. As a novice, she also had the advantage over some of her more experienced colleagues of being able to approach her task with a very open mind, without the clutter of false preconceptions. In addition, she was not afraid of criticism (a fear that discourages many beginners from taking independent stands).

By the end of her first year, Brito was moved from her isolated corner into the center of the laboratory. Her work was presented at a national meeting; she had become a scientist. When years later Goodfield asked her what the process consisted of, she answered:

> Well, there's creative observation for a start. . . . There's
> the designing of good experiments, too. Then, there's
> the capacity to think up concepts to explain the patterns
> you are seeing. Above all, there is freedom, the
> knowledge that you are going to make mistakes and not
> being afraid. To be frightened . . . is to be in prison. By
> the end of that time I was dropping mistakes right, left,
> and center. I learned to love making mistakes.[10]

Although the course of the development of scientific talent is not well understood, some recurrent themes have emerged in the published literature. In my own interviews with scientists, these have included the role of wonder, an interest in observing nature, a playful and exploratory approach to ideas, a willingness to tolerate long hours of solitude, and the courage to make mistakes.

Scientists may be more knowledgeable than articulate about these sources of their scientific curiosity. That may be, as June Goodfield has suggested, because of the enjoyment of solitude in research work. Einstein wrote of the purity of absorption in creative endeavors:

> One of the strongest motives that lead persons to art and
> science is flight from everyday life, with its painful
> harshness and wretched dreariness, and from the fetters
> of one's shifting desires.[11]

At the same time, Einstein's life also illustrates the importance of close friendships and the willingness of a famous and revered man to work for a peaceful and just world.

In the course of scientific apprenticeships, young men and women develop both their ability to concentrate for many solitary hours and their ways of collaboration. Interaction with colleagues, relatives, and mentors contributes to the nourishing of their scientific curiosity and to their sense of determination. The processes of science-making—the acquisition of techniques, modes of judgment, and disciplinary traditions—are acquired from these individuals and it is only through close collaboration that the apprentice can learn of the more hidden processes of scientific thinking.

The Shaping of Abstraction

"The way I personally function is always based on seeing things and thinking about them," Brito told June Goodfield.[12] A similar observation was made by the biologist Agnes Arber in her book *The Mind and the Eye:*

> The close interlocking and interweaving of the data gained
> directly through the senses, with the concepts of pure
> thought, are peculiarly marked in the biologist's sphere
> of work . . . [and later] the goal of pure morphology
> might be described as the visual and conceptual
> interpretation of the perceived.[13]

The nature of the integration between observations and concepts is of great concern to both philosophers and scientists. A purely inductionist approach has been criticized by the British philosopher of science Karl Popper, who argued that "we can never free observation from the theoretical elements of interpretation. We always interpret; that is, we theorize, on a conscious, on an unconscious, and on a physiological level."[14] The leap from experience to concept, though logically discontinuous, is "channeled and guided," wrote Gerald Holton, whose research in scientific thinking is strongly based on his studies of Einstein.

> One such guide, at least for Einstein himself, was the fact
> that he attained concepts for use at the A (axiomatic)
> level by *a form of mental play with visual materials* [and]
> . . . by a powerful iconographic rationality which he
> added to the more conventional semantic and
> quantitative ones.[15]

Einstein's famous letter describing his visual methods of thought was partially quoted in an earlier chapter on "Visual Thinking." In response to a questionnaire sent to him by the mathematician Hadamard, he described the role of images and signs as an important aspect of his thought, particularly in the early stages of working on a problem. Hadamard found a widespread reliance upon visual thinking among physicists and mathematicians. In his attempt to explore the hidden processes of mathematical thought, he found questionnaires and self-reports useful in his inquiry. He described the process: "Where information about the ways of thought is directly obtained from the thinker himself, who looking inwards, reports on his own mental processes."[16]

The method of self-reports, I have found, is an effective means of learning about scientific thinking: "I make abstract pictures," the physicist John Howarth told me in response to a suggestion that he specify the kind of visual images he evoked to solve the problem we were talking about, the thought processes involved in scientific thinking. Howarth described an image involving sets of index cards connected by wires with plugs on the ends:

> My natural mode of thought leads me to play with these images. I get inside them and wander about without any specific aim. Now I am looking at the wires and cards, the elements in the image. Only my visual sense is involved. I am not directing my attention, just watching what appears. The elements are taking on nonessential, or apparently nonessential qualities like colors. This kind of thing often leads to productive insights.

Mathematicians as well as physicists reported visualization of the type that Einstein had referred to. One of the mathematicians, Morris Kline, interviewed by Rosner and Abt for their book on *The Creative Experience*, described his thinking similarly.

> When one is mentally relaxed, ideas seem to come more freely as one works. In this state many possible approaches or at least ideas that should be looked into because they may bear fruit occur. As a matter of fact, these approaches and ideas are likely to occur with such rapidity and suddenness that one can't pursue each one seriously at the moment.[17]

These reports in which mature scientists described some of their rapid, creative processes of thought did not always follow the same order or the same relationship between observation and conceptual interpretation. One must ask: Are apprentice scientists similarly able to approach new problems by visualization and intuition?

The psychologist Jerome Bruner suggested that intuitive thinking (of the kind Einstein particularly believed in) depends upon familiarity with the field, a systematic integration of ideas which serves as background to novel thought. Individuals new to their discipline may therefore first require training in analytical and inductive thinking before they are able to use intuition in their problem-solving efforts.

There should be instruction in diverse problem-solving strategies just as there is instruction in varied laboratory techniques during the apprenticeship of young scientists; however, this is seldom the case. Instead young men and women are exposed primarily to what Medawar has called "the art of the soluble." Training consists in rules for precision, in the methods prevalent in one's field, and in ways of making public one's procedures and ensuring replicability of one's data. Generally, the work of students illustrates what Thomas Kuhn in *The Structure of Scientific Revolutions* called "normal science": "[it] consists . . . in extending those facts that the paradigm displays as particularly revealing, by increasing the match between those facts and the paradigm's predictions, and by further articulation of the paradigm itself."[18]

Most often apprentice scientists are taught to test hypotheses by conducting experiments, by applying careful controls to their observations, and by respecting facts while reaching for generalizations. It is less common for them to be taught about the intuitive and imaginative aspects of scientific thinking.

Some young scientists learn to think like their elders by trying to follow a project from its very inception to the end. Others study books on discovery, such as Hadamard's small but widely read volume on *The Psychology of Invention in the Mathematical Field*. In this volume, Hadamard draws greatly upon the lectures of the mathematician Jules Henri Poincaré, whose work on the unconscious and intuitive elements of thought has been frequently quoted. "The act of studying a question," Poincaré wrote, "consists of mobilizing ideas, not just any ones, but those from which we might reasonably expect the desired solutions."[19] He evoked an image of such a process as that of hooked atoms, which are motionless while the mind is at rest, but are drawn into vigorous movement—a sort of dance—which then provides the thinker with some fruitful new insights.

During our conversations, I asked Professor Howarth whether it was possible to help students to rely upon intuition as part of their preparation for becoming physicists. He answered:

> Intuitive solution of problems is important. Essentially it
> is finding the answer to a problem before you have
> solved it. Students are tempted to believe that physical
> intuition is something that you either have or don't
> have. We certainly all have different talents, but the
> process can certainly be encouraged—that's one of the
> things that teaching is about. Teachers can encourage
> the talent by example and by describing their own

approach to problem-solving. They can also take the time to explore the student's process with him or her.

In the classroom, Howarth, an inspired teacher, conveys the vividness with which he sees physical relations by demonstrating them. He also uses sketches, models, and films to provide visual counterparts to the laws of matter. These visual (two- and three-dimensional) representations are of importance in providing students with the means of possible solutions. But Professor Howarth cautioned: "No amount of visual imagery in your head will give you a complete answer. It can get you going and gives you the essence if you are lucky. But it still needs developing, and you ultimately write some equations." In contemporary physics, multiple approaches are necessary to represent and solve problems. The role of mathematics is stressed by W. I. Beveridge: "Physics has reached a stage," he wrote, "where it is no longer possible to visualize mechanical analogies representing certain phenomena that can only be expressed in mathematical terms."[20]

A flexible combination of visualization and mathematical approaches was described by the theoretical physicist James D. Finley III during my talks with him: "I don't think in words very much either," he remarked after reading Einstein's letter to Hadamard. "I think in a different language, I think in mathematics." And he elaborated:

> In quantum mechanics, particles have particular properties; they change in time. So when I think of a wave-pocket, I have a picture in my mind of a pencil. Yes, a pencil and a little bell curve that gets wider and wider along the pencil, and this generates a cone. So when I am calculating, I have all kinds of pictures of cones in my head which intersect.

Finley barely retains these pictures, however. They serve to sustain his attention while he is calculating. This combined method of problem-solving was suggested to Finley by one of his professors at the University of California. While these mental problem-solving tools are important, of even greater significance to scientific work are the concepts which lie, as it were, behind technique. Finley spoke of concepts "which engender language (including mathematics) out of which theoretical physics are born. They play a creative role."

The central aspect of scientific training resides, therefore, in the mastery of the conceptual schemes of one's discipline. The transmission of the governing notions of a field, at any one period, is accomplished through textbooks, lectures, journal articles, as well as in discussions between students and their teachers. It is more difficult to teach the way in which one expands knowledge.

Some apprentice scientists learn to think productively by carefully retracing an argument in published papers. These usually have a certain organization; they begin with a problem statement, followed by the articulation of specific hypotheses and the description of the research methods used in data collection. Most articles also include a presentation of the data collected and a discussion of its meaning. While such a transitional presentation provides a useful model of reasoning, it provides a somewhat idealized account of the actual sequence of research. Most published accounts exclude the many detours and fruitless approaches that characterize the actual progression of scientific work from first ideas to finished research.

It is in the course of collaboration that young scientists learn to avoid some of the more obvious cul-de-sacs and to use to full advantage associational, analogic, and deductive methods of thought. The combination of these varied methods leads to effective problem-solving and to discovery in the sciences, and the necessity to rely upon a breadth of approaches and the courage to deal with mistakes are among the qualities that Beveridge included in his characterization of successful scientists:

> The productive research worker is usually one who is not afraid to venture and risk going astray, but who makes a rigorous test for error before reporting his findings. This is so not only in the biological sciences but also in mathematics. Hadamard stated that good mathematicians often make errors but soon perceive and correct them, and that he himself makes more errors than his students.[21]

A fluency of ideas, the willingness to make mistakes as well as the mastery of the varied forms of systematic thought constitute the invisible tools of scientific thinking. In the never ending apprenticeship of scientific training, the thought activity of greatest importance is the pulling together into a whole—*the synthesis*—of bits and fragments of experience, which the thinker had previously known as separate. In discussing creativity in science and in the arts, Jerome Bruner quoted Poincaré, who "speaks of . . . combinations that 'reveal to us unsuspected kinship between . . . facts, long known, but wrongly believed to be strangers to one another.' "[22] Effective combinations require, in addition, the skills of discernment and the lengthy labor of evaluation.

Goodfield has described this process of synthesis in brilliantly visual words:

> When a suggestion is first broached in science, however tentatively, it can be, and often is, bolstered by little pieces of information which up to that point may well have seemed extraneous. These can now be picked up and cemented in place. It is like creating a new design from existing odd pieces of colored glass. Indeed, Anna once gave a lecture called "The Stained Glass Window Lecture," explaining that all scientists have these little pieces of colored glass, intriguing bits of information or facts which they don't quite know what to do with. They leave them lying around until, prompted by a new idea or a new piece of information, they mentally sift them and select the ones that may help the pattern.[23]

The shaping of thought in the course of scientific training is hard to fully document. Perhaps the richest source of insights concerning this inner, hidden process is linked to the literature of discoveries.

Paths of Discovery

Bisociation: During the last three decades, the topic of scientific discoveries has preoccupied a large number of working scientists, historians, and cognitive psychologists. The best-known account of the discovery process is that of Arthur Koestler, described in his major work *The Act of Creation*. He viewed creativity in science as an example of "bisociation"—referring to a process which results from the combination of previously unrelated areas of knowledge—so that "each new synthesis leads to the emergence of new patterns of relations."[24]

The work of Sir Francis Crick and his collaborators, who identified the structure of DNA, is an excellent example of Koestler's theory. The Nobel prize-winning discovery has been described by the historian of science Robert Olby, and in the popular book *The Double Helix*, written by James Watson, the young American member of the team.

Crick's career as a physicist started with his studies at University College, to be interrupted by World War II, during which he worked for the British Admiralty, addressing problems of hydrodynamics and magnetism, which were of significance to the war effort. His interests changed after he read *What Is Life?* by Erwin Schrödinger; he then decided to devote himself to "the chemical physics of biology."[25] The intellectual abilities of this young scientist were soon evident, according to Olby, who wrote of his work on proteins as a "very good example of that physical intuition which enables Crick to brush aside the complexities of a situation and the plethora of possible alternatives and to concentrate on finding a simple physical model."[26]

One of Sir Francis Crick's contributions to the group's efforts was his physical intuition and his ability to work with a minimum number of assumptions while approaching a problem. In our conversation, after a lecture he had given at the University of New Mexico, he emphasized that it was his and his collaborators' breadth of approaches that was crucial to their discovery. His statement confirmed a frequently noted aspect of creativity, that of the fluency of ideas and the flexibility of approaches that characterize scientifically creative individuals who are working together on a problem.[27]

The bisociation processes involved in the discovery of DNA's structure were multiple: they were the result of the successful collaboration of a microbiologist (James Watson), an X-ray crystallographer (Maurice Wilkins), and a physicist (Francis Crick). The work was also stimulated and supported by the availability in Cambridge and in London of a number of excellent chemists, for instance, Erwin Chargaff from Columbia University, with whom the members of the DNA team consulted informally. They were also helped—and spurred on—by Linus Pauling's research at the California Institute of Technology.

The weaving together of ideas, styles of work, and approaches that characterize different disciplines was an important aspect of this epoch-making discovery. Crick and Watson, while they came from different cultural backgrounds and differed in age as well, worked well together. They enjoyed their talks, and they were not afraid to criticize each other. Olby commented on this aspect of their collaboration:

> They compensated for each other's blind spots. But their collaboration involved far more than this. Alexander Humboldt expressed the essence of such work well when he said: "Collaboration operates through a process in which the successful intellectual achievements of one person arouse the intellectual passions and enthusiasms of others, and through the fact that what was at first

expressed only by one individual becomes a common intellectual possession instead of fading away into isolation."[28]

Perhaps this description characterized the collaboration among the three men, but it conflicted with the relationship that existed between them and Rosalind Franklin. No easy exchange occurred between her and Wilkins, with whom she had shared a laboratory. The very sad outcome of the failure of their relationship has been described; it illustrates the importance of personal and emotional factors (beside the intellectual ones) which influence contemporary group research endeavors.

Of particular interest to Koestler's analysis of "bisociation" are some aspects of the work conducted on the atom bomb in Los Alamos during World War II. N. P. Davis described Oppenheimer's role in fostering a collaborative atmosphere in his book *Lawrence and Oppenheimer*, particularly the ways in which he integrated individuals of differing expertise and temperament into single teams. He also provided for varied opportunities of lively and critical exchanges, which he considered a necessary part of the laboratory's work in the development of the atomic bomb.

One of the important issues facing the scientists in Los Alamos was to find a method to explode the bomb so that it would reach the critical mass necessary for a nuclear chain reaction. Ballistic experts were invited to give lectures and share their knowledge of different approaches. Years later, in the spring of 1983, one of the physicists present during these talks recalled the effect it had on him. Seth Neddermeyer, in reconstructing his thoughts while listening to these discussions, remembered that one of the ballistics experts objected to the way the word *explosion* was tossed about. Explosion would not do to describe the chemical violence that would drive together the parts of the critical mass in a fission bomb, he said. *Explosion* means driving apart. The proper word for driving together was *implosion*.

The expert's talk framed the pictures already forming in Neddermeyer's mind. It was as if Neddermeyer was visualizing the spheres of uranium and plutonium squeezed like an orange. Squeeze hard enough on anything hard and it will behave as thought it were soft. Squeeze it very evenly and very hard, and then what will it do? Neddermeyer said:

> I remember thinking of trying to push in a shell of material against a plastic flow, and I calculated the minimum pressures that would have to be applied. Then I happened to recall a crazy thing somebody had

published about firing bullets against each other. It may
have had a photograph of two bullets liquified on
impact. That is what I was thinking when the ballistics
man mentioned implosion.[29]

It was difficult for Neddermeyer to put into words the images and
unusual associations that preoccupied him while he was listening to
these lectures. The fact that his ideas were first greeted with a thinly
veiled ridicule by his more experienced colleagues contributed to his
discomfort in expressing himself. Although Oppenheimer was also du-
bious about Neddermeyer's suggestion, he did appoint him as head of
the Implosion Experimentation group, realizing the importance of exploring every possible idea in their pressured, difficult race against possible Nazi competition.

Both of these accounts of important discoveries demonstrate the role
of visualizing a solution by working with ideas that cut across disciplines and provide a bisociative solution. There have been widespread
discussions of these internal processes in the literature of discovery, while
somewhat less has been written on the role of analogies in scientific
creativity.

Analogy: The Japanese physicist Hideki Yukawa has described the
role of analogical thinking in science in his book *Creativity and Intuition:*

Suppose there is something which a person cannot understand. He happens to notice the similarity of this
something to some other thing which he understands
quite well. By comparing them he may come to
understand the thing which he could not understand up
to that moment. If his understanding turns out to be
appropriate and nobody else has come to such
understanding, he can claim that his thinking was
creative.[30]

Another analysis of analogical thinking is presented by the British
psychologist Sir Francis Bartlett:

The most important of all conditions of originality in experimental thinking is a capacity to detect overlap and
agreement between groups of facts and fields of study

which have not been before effectively combined, and to
bring these groups into experimental contact.

Bartlett provided a number of interesting historical examples of
analogical extensions in his analysis of experimental thinking. One of
these was the invention of mental chronometry:

> Helmhotz brought into the study of nerve conduction the
> very methods already established by astronomers to
> measure the difference between one "personal
> equation" and another. He adopted the method so that
> he could measure time differences of response. . . . He
> settled once and for all that discharge along the motor
> nerve takes a measurable time.[31]

The role of analogy was also frequently mentioned in my
conversations with scientists. The experimental psychologist Irwin Maltzman thus described the way he generated some of his new ideas:

> Most of the things that I think of that are any good hap-
> pen when I talk. For instance, when I give a graduate
> seminar and I pretty well know what I am going to talk
> about, I may get a new idea while I am lecturing. It
> might be triggered off by the overall topic or task which
> produces within me a wealth of associations.

A frequent use of analogies has also been described by the
mathematician Morris Kline:

> Many great mathematical papers have used ideas or meth-
> ods that had already appeared in the solution of other
> problems. Mathematicians do not always admit this
> though some have. However the major point is that
> reading related material may be the best way to get the
> mind started on a new channel of thought and because
> the reading is related, this new thought may be the
> right one.[32]

In laboratory experiments of thought, the role of analogies has recently
been scientifically examined. The technique used by John Clement, a
University of Massachusetts physicist, was basically an old one: it is

the method of thinking-aloud, which has been renamed protocol-analysis by the well-known researchers in artificial intelligence, Herbert Simon and Allen Newell. The subjects in Clement's research are scientifically trained individuals whose problem-solving approaches were video-taped. Among the problems he gave to these advanced graduate students and professors in technical fields were the "Spring Coils Problem," which required estimating how far coils will stretch under certain conditions.

Clement found "that spontaneously generated analogies were observed to play a major role in a number of solutions. For example, in solving a problem in a spring, several people first thought about the forces in a bending rod."[33] These inferences were not generated instantaneously. Some solutions took more than an hour and analogies were first suggested somewhat tentatively by the subjects. The analogies bore either a functional or structural similarity to the unsolved problems, and subjects needed to carefully examine the relationship between the given problem and their proposed solutions. This required a "cycle of conjecture, criticism, and modification that can produce successfully more powerful mental models," wrote Clements.[34] Interestingly, most of the analogies reported by his subjects were not deduced from formal principles; rather they revealed associational and inferential ways of proceeding.

One aspect of analogical thinking that emerges both from experimental investigations and from the accounts of creative thinkers is the role of experience. The physicist Byron Goldstein described the way in which experience guides a scientist in his or her choice of models:

> We started [Goldstein and his co-worker Carla Wofsy] by examining some published, experimental data on cell surface dynamics. The research revealed that structures on the cell surface that trap specific biological molecules had a certain concentration at the time the experiment started. As the experiment progressed the concentration dipped below the level where it would eventually stabilize. Although the published data was sketchy, it was possible to apply certain mathematical models to these findings. But a whole class of models had to be excluded, even though they appeared reasonable; the selection of what was appropriate was governed by our familiarity with fitting models to biological data.

The physicist's description provides an example of an inferential way of starting a scientific problem-solving process followed by the rigorous application of mathematical models. The mathematicians Davis and Hersh describe some aspect of intuitive thought as "convincing in the absence of proof. A related meaning is 'what one might expect to be true in this kind of situation, on the basis of general experience with similar situations or related subjects.' 'Intuitively plausible' means reasonable as a conjecture, i.e., as a candidate for proof."[35]

Reliance on such reasoning is the outcome of training, experience, and a certain fluency of ideas. In the course of scientific discoveries individuals may rely upon their large network of associations and their ability to generate analogies both within and across disciplinary boundaries.

From anomaly to integration: Analogical thinking is close to what Thomas Kuhn has described as normal science, the activity of puzzle-solving while confronted with a new problem. A more difficult process of discovery and theory construction takes place when a scientist identifies a basic anomaly that cannot be resolved by such methods. Kuhn describes this process:

> Discovery commences with the awareness of anomaly,
> i.e., with the recognition that nature has somehow
> violated the paradigm-induced expectations of normal
> science. It then continues with a more or less extended
> exploration of the area of anomaly. And it closes only
> when the paradigm theory has been adjusted so that the
> anomalous has become the expected.[36]

A carefully documented analysis of paradigm change is provided by Gerald Holton in his account of Einstein's development of relativity theory. One of the themes that has governed the work of this great physicist has been his view of nature as consistent. Holton commented:

> Einstein saw in the contemporary interpretation of Max-
> well's equations a discordant note that ran counter to his
> view of a basic symmetry and consistency in nature. The
> discordance concerned a phenomenon, discovered by
> Michael Faraday, that is the basis of a typical dynamo
> . . . (in some dynamos it is the   ·   : . . . in others it is
> the magnet that rotates and the wire is fixed). What
> caught Einstein's eye, however, was that the amount of

current produced was the same in both cases, given the
same relative speed between wire and magnet. . . .
Einstein produced a single formulation of
electromagnetic phenomena applicable to all situations
of relative motion.[37]

Einstein generally searched for the most universal principles. Though
he was influenced by experimental results in "his developing thought
processes" his efforts to resolve anomalies included thought experiments, the exploration as well as rejection of a diversity of ideas, and
the constant striving towards a creative *synthesis* of the totality of physical experience.[38]

Each creative individual follows a somewhat different path in the movement from anomaly to synthesis. It is not easy to reconstruct what Gerald Holton has called private science: "science-in-the-making, with its
own vocabulary and modes of progress as suggested by the conditions
of discovery."[39] But the importance of such reconstruction is vital to an
understanding of the process. Contemporary students of thought and
creativity rely upon the careful examination of private science—the letters, notebooks, and journals as well as published works—in tracing
the diverse paths of discovery.

It is by examining these sources that the psychologist Howard Gruber
developed his case study of Charles Darwin. The conflicts that beset
the evolutionary theorist illustrate well the differences between the emergence of a particular point of view—Holton's "private science"—and
the task of making it public. Darwin was confronted with great hostil-
ity toward his materialist conception of nature and his evolutionary theory. He was jolted into publishing his views by the development of A.
R. Wallace's somewhat parallel notions. The construction of a new point
of view as illustrated by Darwin's lengthy struggle is seen by Gruber as
a creative process situated in a human context and inseparable from
historical, cultural, and ideological currents. Gruber describes the process of construction "as tortuous, tentative, enormously complex, full
of unwarranted assumptions."[40] In the course of developing a new point
of view, the scientist works through many different processes of thought.
Some are quite straightforward and logical, while others entail ideas
tumbling over each other without any apparent order, as was revealed
in some of Darwin's notebooks. The case study of Darwin's work yields
information concerning the internal and external events that characterize the change in a governing paradigm in science, which could not be
obtained in any other way. Experimental studies conducted over short

periods of time in a controlled setting are valuable in testing some models of cognition, but these approaches are merely controlled pieces and hence fragments of the more complex and lengthy endeavors that characterize scientific discovery and theory-construction.

The construction of a new point of view can be the primary task of a single individual, or it can encompass a number of scientists or artists. In the 1920s, theoretical physicists confronted, as a group and individually, the challenge of going beyond the well-entrenched concepts of Newtonian physics. The development of subatomic physics required not only a new way of looking at physical phenomena; it required a new language.

In *Physics and Beyond*, Werner Heisenberg provided a fine reconstruction of the intense debates that accompanied the paradigm change from Newtonian to nuclear physics. One of the earliest conversations recalled by Heisenberg is between the Danish physicist Niels Bohr and himself, while he was still a student. Bohr, who was intrigued by the young man's questions following a lecture, tried to sketch for him some of the conceptual difficulties that he and his generation faced:

> We intend to say something about the structure of the
> atom but we lack the language in which we can make
> ourselves understood. We are in much the same
> position as a sailor marooned on a remote island where
> conditions differ radically from anything he has ever
> known, and where to make matters worse, the natives
> speak a completely alien tongue.[41]

Einstein, in his "Autobiographical Notes," also wrote about the difficulties faced by those who were attempting to "adapt the theoretical foundations of physics to this [new type of] knowledge."[42] The physicists of his generation felt as if the ground had fallen away and no firm foundation remained upon which they could build. Einstein wrote "that this insecure and contradictory foundation was sufficient to enable a man of Bohr's unique instinct and tact to discover the major laws of spectral lines and the electron shells of the atoms together with their significance for chemistry appeared to me like a miracle—and appears to me as a miracle today."[43]

In their efforts to construct a new conceptual framework, physicists were not only beset by the difficulty of leaving known territory (Heisenberg's metaphor) but they were also struggling with diverse approaches to theory construction. Many scientists tried to reduce known phenomena so that they could be explained (or just described) with the aid of a few simple concepts. At first Einstein was partial to such an approach in which he was greatly influenced by the writings of Ernest Mach and his notion of "thought economy." But as early as the turn of the century, he found that he could not integrate the important new findings "by means of constructive efforts based on known facts." He wrote, "The longer and more despairingly I tried, the more I came to the conviction that only the discovery of a universal formal principle could lead us to assured results."[44]

Einstein made a similar point to Heisenberg during one of their conversations in 1925. He explained that "it is the theory which decides what we can observe."[45] Although this approach surprised the younger man, the statement was valuable to him throughout his development as a scientist. Though Einstein's criteria for an effective theory were that a theory should not contradict empirical facts, at the same time he believed that facts could only provide "external confirmation" of theories. He argued that scientific thinking is constructive and speculative, and only in its end product does it lead to a system that is characterized by "naturalness" and "logical simplicity."[46] Gerald Holton, who examined Einstein's progression from an earlier Machian, positivistic point of view to his later notions of theory construction, concluded that his ideas entailed a creative synthesis "of the totality of physical experience in the field."[47]

One of the most complete descriptions of Einstein's epistemology was found by Holton in the physicist's letter to his friend Maurice Solovine. The letter started with a simple drawing consisting of (1) a straight line representing E (experiences), which are given to us, and (2) A (axioms), which were situated above the line but were not directly linked to the line. Einstein said:

> Psychologically the A rest upon the E. There exists, however, no logical path from E to A, but only an intuitive (psychological) connection, which is always subject to revocation. . . . From axioms, one can deduce certain assertions (S), which deductions may lay claim to being correct.

Einstein went further in explaining that assertions can be subjected to external confirmation, and they lead to "the logical simplicity of the basic premises."[48]

Theory construction at a period when one's conceptual framework is changing rapidly requires not only the development of a new language and new concepts but also a certain awareness of the nature of thought itself. It is significant that Niels Bohr, Albert Einstein, Werner Heisenberg, and Jacob Bronowski, to mention just a few twentieth century scientists, have all been interested in the human mind and the way in which it moves between fact and theory. Bronowski wrote of the search for unity in the variety of nature, and Kuhn has emphasized the resistance of the human mind to anomaly, to contradictions to expectations. "It is, I think, particularly in periods of acknowledged crisis that scientists have turned to philosophical analysis as a device for unlocking the riddles of their field," wrote Kuhn.[49] During such a period, scientists have to carefully examine the implications of a governing framework, and to speculate about the dynamics of human thought activity.

To Niels Bohr, the recognition that a conceptual conflict existed was crucial to its constructive use in theory building. The Viennese scientist Schrödinger and he argued about these issues, a debate that Heisenberg described in some detail. Schrödinger considered "the whole idea of a quantum jump as sheer fantasy," to which Bohr responded by emphasizing the need to think differently in light of these new findings:

> What you say is absolutely correct. But it does not prove
> that there are no quantum jumps. It only proves that we
> cannot imagine them, that the representational concepts
> with which we describe events in daily life and
> experiments in classical physics are inadequate when it
> comes to describing quantum jumps. Nor should we be
> surprised to find it so, seeing that the processes
> involved are not the objects of direct experience.[50]

Bohr's interests in the nature of thought and in the analysis of epistemological issues affecting science did not diminish in the course of his distinguished career. In an article entitled "Discussion with Einstein," he retraced some of the dialogues between the two of them devoted to these concerns. He first stressed the critical role of open debate in science in this article, and the stimulating role of such discussions during periods of paradigm change. Bohr then summarized some of the conceptual conflicts that emerged in the years between the two world wars in physics and described his point of view:

> Evidence obtained under different experimental conditions cannot be comprehended within a single picture,

but must be regarded as *complementary* in the sense that
the totality of the phenomena exhausts the possible
information about the objects.[51]

The importance of the notion of complementarity was seen by Bohr as
relevant to quantum mechanics as well as to domains outside of physics. Bohr welcomed the difficulties in physics and in psychology that
"originate in the different placing of the separation lines between object and subject in the analysis of the various aspects of psychical experience,"[52] and he drew an analogy between the two. In this conception,
Gerald Holton has suggested that Bohr was influenced by the ideas of
William James, particularly his notion of "flights" and "resting places"
in thought (a metaphor described in the "Visual Thinking" chapter).
Both Bohr and James valued the dynamics of thought. They wished to
propose a view of human mental activities that went beyond the simple dichotomies of object and subject, or theory and fact.

The path from anomaly to synthesis requires that the thinking scientist should be willing to confront and work with contradictions: that he
or she value debate as part of the means by which an individual or a
group of individuals construct a new conceptual framework or paradigm. The development of such a major conceptual shift includes periods of painful disagreement among colleagues, the viewing of familiar
phenomena in a different way, or as Kuhn has suggested, "when paradigms change, the world itself changes with them."[53]

While a single scientist may identify an important anomaly that may
lead to a paradigm change, only a group of scientists can actually achieve
the construction of a new paradigm. The part played by a group suggests that the view of creative work (whether in the arts or sciences) as
a solitary enterprise needs to be re-examined. In the well-documented
accounts of the most important paradigm shift in the twentieth century,
that of the move from classical to atomic physics, the role of a community of scientists as working with, and in opposition to, each other, is
dramatically revealed. The psychologist of thought may be richly rewarded in studying the ways in which these twentieth-century physicists went about their work. In their search they revealed as much about
their process of thought as about their concepts of nature.

The Scientific Mind at Work

The history of science is one of certain shared issues that confront a
generation of scientists. "While the individual scientist is the primary

repository of themata, they are also shared with minor variations by members of a community" wrote Gerald Holton.[54] In both the lives of artists and scientists, there is an important tension between the development of an individual's own style or voice and the disciplinary traditions that shape the creative individual. The shaping of a personal style to approach tasks within an intellectual discipline takes a long time. Its development is influenced by cultural and disciplinary traditions, by the tastes and talents of one's mentors, and by the person's intellectual and emotional socialization. Once an individual has developed a certain voice and is committed to certain themata, any great change in the climate of thought in the person's later years can still influence a talented individual's approach to his or her work. In this summary and highlight of some of the shared characteristics in the socialization of scientists—and their contrast with some patterns in the lives of artists—we are searching for an understanding of the work of the mind.

Are there diverse "languages of thought"? What do creative individuals have in common? These are the driving questions that motivate and sustain this inquiry.

Childhood: The Nobel laureate Saul Bellow remarked on the existence of a primitive commentator among children: "There is that observing instrument in us—in childhood at any rate," he told an interviewer from the *Paris Review*.[55] In their childhood, writers may try to capture their impressions in words, while the childhood impressions of painters have a strong visual primacy. The hold of childhood images was noted by several painters in their autobiographies (for instance, Gauguin and Kokoschka).

My conversations with scientists and mathematicians also revealed some of their strong childhood impressions. Mathematician Reuben Hersh spoke of noticing certain recurrent patterns around him, as when he was particularly intrigued by the geometric arrangements of the bathroom tiles in his parents' home. As children, many scientists recalled a similarly intense interest in observing the changing face of nature. Such a preoccupation can be the basis of a life-long enjoyment, as depicted by Albert Szent-Györgyi, the winner of the Nobel Prize in biology in 1937:

> I owe all my results to the fact that I love life, I live
> it trying to observe carefully every thing I see. . . . I
> always study living material: I examine it by touch, I
> watch it, and I observe every small thing about it.[56]

The need to explore, observe, and penetrate nature is shared by many young people. Future scientists are not easily satisfied in their preoccupation with the way nature works; they persist in their concerns with it. Is there a common home environment that stimulates such a powerful obsession? Vivian Gornick in her recently published *Women in Science* doubts it. She was unable to identify a common psychological, economic, or regional profile in the families of scientists. What she emphasized was another kind of similarity:

> What is true of all of them is a shared temperament of mind and spirit that defies analysis as to its origin but is invariably made substantive in the same way: Each of them had wanted to know how the physical world worked, and each of them had found that discovering how things worked through the exercise of her own mental powers gave her an intensity of pleasure and purpose, a sense of reality nothing else could match.[57]

Some writers on the background of scientists identified another common pattern. Anne Roe, whose pioneer study *The Making of a Scientist* appeared in 1954, found economic differences in the background of the sixty-four male scientists whom she had studied, but a shared emphasis on learning for its own sake was also present among the parents of her subjects.[58] A similar finding was reported by MacKinnon who studied creative architects. He found that "one or both of the parents (of this highly selected group of individuals) were of artistic temperament and considerable skill. Often it was the mother who in the architect's early years fostered his artistic potentialities by her own example as well as tuition."[59]

The majority of Roe's and MacKinnon's subjects were drawn from families involved in the life of the mind, but creative individuals also grow up in different kinds of families. Some of these individuals were encouraged in their explorations by neighbors; others benefited from the attentions of a teacher or a librarian. In any event, the role of an interested adult, or mentor, was important, as was noted by Bill Moyers in his television series based on interviews with creative individuals.

It is most likely that highly curious, intense, and independent children elicit an involvement, an interested response from those around them. The encouragement that they receive from caring adults is in turn an important part of the development of their sense of self, for an inner belief in one's self is a necessary strength in the pursuit of a creative life.

Apprenticeships: Transformation of childish wonder and intensity into a sustained career in the arts and sciences requires many forms of communal learning. One of these occurs in the context of apprenticeships between a young person and a more experienced individual who wishes to share his or her knowledge while working together. The beginner's choice of a language of thought, as well as of the ways one expresses thinking, is frequently shaped in the course of such interactions. Gerald Holton has suggested that the daily walks young Enrico Fermi shared with his father's colleague, Adolfo Amidei, an avid student of mathematics and physics, changed the young boy's fate. Fermi was thirteen years old when his father's friend adopted him intellectually. He was at an important stage of his life—he was starting to focus his talents and to explore possible future careers.

Learning by being with a knowledgeable partner is a more effective method of developing a particular language of thought than learning from books, classes, or science shows. The crucial aspect of these informal or formal apprenticeships is that they provide the beginner with insights into both the overt activities of human productivity and into the more hidden inner processes of thought. While a polished teacher or an effective science exhibit can offer a lot of information about the content of a discipline, it is only through close collaborations that the novice is likely to learn what the mentor may not even know: how he or she formulates a question or starts a new project.

Many such collaborations occur in laboratories where the opportunity to engage in research is critical in the young scientist's journey of self-discovery. The quiet hours spent in a laboratory provide the novice with a chance to become deeply absorbed in a problem and to test his or her skills with the equipment and the design of research projects. It is important to discover whether such a frequently lonely pursuit fits the needs of a scientist-in-the-making.

Einstein described some of the contradictory drives that impel a person into science:

> To begin with I believe with Schopenhauer that one of the
> strongest motives that lead persons to art and science is
> flight from everyday life, with its painful harshness and
> wretched dreariness. . . . With this negative motive
> there goes a positive one. Man seeks for himself, in
> whatever manner is suitable for him, a simplified and
> lucid image of the world, and so to overcome the world

of experience by striving to replace it to some extent by
this image.

He commented on how these motives were shared by creative
individuals in general:

> This is what the painter does, and the poet, the specula-
> tive philosopher, the natural scientist, each in his own
> way. Into this image and its formation, he places the
> center of gravity of his emotional life, in order to attain
> the peace and serenity that he cannot find within the
> narrow confines of swirling, personal experience.[60]

In recent decades, scientific work has become less solitary and very
competitive. Many young people are motivated to pursue a scientific
career, seeking a sense of order and peace through their abstract endeavors, but find themselves in large laboratories, competing against
their equally eager, driven contemporaries. One needs a strong ego and
an ability to withstand criticism of his or her first efforts in a field. The
support provided by a joint endeavor with a mentor can give a young
professional much-needed self assurance and an intimate view of scientific thinking. In the course of our talk, Reuben Hersh recalled how
much it had meant to him when Peter Lax, still a young professor at
New York University, offered to supervise Hersh's dissertation work.
The chance to work closely with him was of particular value, Hersh said,
as "Lax's way of thinking about what he does is so clear, original and
beautiful, and it is possible to get a glimpse into the inner processes of
his mind while working with him."

In the sciences as well as the arts, the ability to add new knowledge
to one's field requires the full internalization of the *meaning* of the achievements of the past. The task of interpreting and integrating major themes
and concepts in one's discipline is a very difficult one. It is much harder
than the mastery of research skills or the accumulation of facts. In establishing collaborative endeavors across generations, the mentor and
the apprentice teach each other the value of interpretation and synthesis.

Logic and Metaphor

Scientific thinking has been compared to problem-solving processes by
the cognitive psychologist Herbert Simon. To avoid inefficient trial and
error in solving a problem, humans rely upon analogies, upon meth-

ods and strategies that have yielded successful solutions in the past. If a novice scientist has the opportunity to monitor closely the problem-solving strategies of those with more experience, he or she is provided with living demonstrations of the use of analogies. While novices tend to pursue too many possible directions, the more experienced, on the other hand, avoid such laborious and diffuse efforts.

In one series of studies, the psychologist P. E. Johnson of the University of Minnesota worked with cardiologists who used both "top-down" and "bottom-up" thinking. In so doing, they placed a particular problem into a larger, hierarchically organized knowledge structure and worked "in a highly specific way, using [their] tremendous network of experiential associations."[61] Research scientists use similar approaches. They rely upon analogies that can generate many new associations when searching for an answer, for the truly outstanding members of a discipline can discern what Hersh called "the structure of structures."

An interesting and increasingly large literature is emerging devoted to the exploration of scientific thinking, such as the work of Tweeney, Doherty, and Mynatt. Some of these include computer simulation studies and the use of thinking protocols as developed by the psychologists Simon and Newell. And there is the work with experts in various fields: chess masters, lawyers, and chemists, as well as studies of hypothesis-generation and hypothesis-testing. But, while these efforts have made the processes of thought less elusive and helped teachers in many fields, they have given us little information concerning the origin and development of sustained, productive thinking in the arts and sciences.

What characterizes creative thought? Linus Pauling has suggested that one has to have many, many ideas and know how to choose from them. In addition to such fluency, I have found that an enchantment with the life of the mind characterized those creative scientists and artists who have contributed their ideas and experiences to this study.

In *An Imagined World* Anna Brito commented: "The greatest fun about ideas is to toy with them play with them . . . divorce them or abandon them."[62] The creative individual in the sciences resembles the artist in this regard. Both of them enjoy the pleasure and commitment involved in their preoccupations with their chosen field. And there is something childlike in the wonder and delight they feel in their work. Their mental life possesses an intense concern that at times borders upon the compulsive. To live inside an active mental world is to be both solitary and intensely social: to be engaged in shaping of new knowledge is to be part of the human enterprise while at times standing outside of its more mundane aspects.

Vivian Gornick depicts these individuals well:

> Scientists do what writers do. They also live with an
> active interiority, only the ongoing speculation in their
> heads is about the relation in the physical world rather
> than the psychological one. The natural biologist walks
> through a city park, across a suburban lawn, past an
> open shopping mall, and is half-consciously wondering:
> Why two leaves instead of three? Why pink flowers
> instead of white? Why does the plant turn this way
> instead of that way? Such rumination goes on without
> end in the scientist's mind, a continuous accompaniment
> to the rhythm of daily life. Whatever a scientist is
> doing—reading, cooking, talking, playing—science
> thoughts are always there at the edge of the mind. They
> are the way the world is taken in; all that is seen is
> filtered through an ever-present scientific musing.
>
> It is from this continuousness of thought and
> perception that the scientist, like the writer, receives the
> crucial flash of insight out of which a piece of work is
> conceived and executed. And the scientist (again like the
> writer) is *grateful* when the insight comes, because
> insight is the necessary catalyst through which the
> abstract is made concrete, intuition be given language,
> language provides specificity, and real work can go
> forward.[63]

The scientist's training allows him or her to test the value of an insight—a new pattern or set of connections—for its general concepts. And in the process of testing, other, more complex, anomalous, or disturbing patterns emerge that create a powerful tension between the varied aspects of the enterprise of extending knowledge. In our attempts to understand the creative mind, we frequently separate it into episodes, and we tend to observe and analyze the work in terms of polarities such as insight versus cumulative knowledge.

Metaphors, analogies, and the delineation of new patterns are the stuff of insights. These are then tested, and weighed for their levels of truthfulness by the application of the scientists' research. Logic and metaphor, quick thought and lengthy periods of evaluation characterize the creative endeavor, though the very act of writing and coupling such words demands a contradiction. At times the struggle with an idea is incredibly lengthy while its assessment—as in the case of building the model of the double helix—can be quite rapid.

The various shorthands of the mind can take the form of metaphor, or of an image of wide scope, a title, a poetic line—all of which become the basis of that lengthy tug of war between idea and its realization.

Conclusion: The Creativity of Thinking

The exploration of thinking and the depiction of creativity constitute joint endeavors in this work. The self-reports of artists and scientists provide critical insights into the many-sided, welded, inner stream of ideas. While experimental approaches are informative about short-term efforts at thinking and the many products of thought, they are of limited value in the examination of sustained and productive thinking. The latter is the focus of this inquiry. The issues and concerns raised in this volume are connected to the work of other contemporary students of creativity, such as Gerald Holton, Howard Gruber, and Frederic Holmes, who have chosen to look at the work of the mind from a genetic and historical perspective. They also used self-reports, notebooks, letters, and interviews as part of their methods in reconstructing the paths of discovery.

Three major themes have emerged in this examination of the processes of thought. The first of these is an inquiry into the growth in the mind of artists and scientists-in-the-making. How does a young person join wonder and skill, intensity and discipline, during the long trajectories of intellectual and artistic growth?

The second theme is devoted to the commonalities and differences among the languages of the mind. How does verbal thinking—what Vygotsky described as condensed inner speech—differ from thought-in-images? And what are the characteristics of movement ideas, condensed musical phrases, mathematical models; do they also constitute some kind of a shorthand of the mind?

The third theme addresses the difficult question of creative thinking;

how does it differ from ordinary problem-solving in science, or the work of the commercial artist?

The Scaffolding of Thought

One of the major challenges facing creative individuals is that of building upon the continuity of human knowledge while achieving novel insights. The shaping of a distinctive voice in the sciences and in the arts requires a profound knowledge of the conventions of one's discipline and of the invisible tools of the mind. Aaron Copland stressed this point in the course of our talk when he said that "in composition you do not proceed only from life, you proceed from models which are in your art." At the same time, the novice has to be careful to avoid repetition and re-discovery while immersing him- or herself in past achievements.

The lengthy period of human dependency provides for the social embeddedness of learning, for dialogues across generations during which children absorb their community's past. In reaching for their humanity, children make the ways of their kin their own. They master the values of their society and the knowledge of their parents. They also treasure their fresh discoveries, experiencing at a young age the productive interaction between the known and the new. In the homes of many creative individuals, such a tension is embraced by both parents and children; there are opportunities to focus childish intensity and wonder and there is encouragement in the pleasures of learning for its own sake.

Immersion and exploration characterize the early stages of development of the creative young person. Neruda recalled his hunger for books in his autobiography: "I gobbled up everything, indiscriminately, like an ostrich."[1] The painter and art educator Brent Wilson spoke of his great interest in pictures, and how *Life* magazine was one of his few sources for visual stimulation during his young years in a small town. Mozart wrote of his "bag of memories" accumulated during the childhood years of intense wonder, a source to which many creative people return again and again.

The recollections of those I have interviewed, together with the accounts of many others who have explored their early memories in letters, interviews, and autobiographies, demonstrate the impact of encounters with older creative people: the meeting between the young adolescent Enrico Fermi and his father's friend Adolfo Amidei is a good example. Immersion and exploration characterize these early stages of development of creative young people, and although they have not yet achieved a distinctive voice or mastered the discipline within their field of knowledge, their openness to experience and their accumulation of vivid impressions provide them with a lasting foundation.

These are the years when a creative child or adolescent is first noticed by others for his or her talent, and attention to a drawing, poem, or quick mind contributes to one's sense of direction. This interest is important during the long years in which the growing individual is in a contradictory process. On the one hand, to intensify an inquiry and develop a sense of commitment to a creative life, the learner needs models, teachers, and collaborators. On the other hand, the individual, while building upon the past, needs to transform it, and thus broaden his or her choices.

In linking their efforts with others, future scientists and artists learn to join their wonder and commitment with the necessary tools of their future craft or discipline. Some apprenticeships occur in one's home: the painter Raphael Soyer, the linguist Noam Chomsky, and the mathematician Norbert Wiener all learned about their future disciplines from their fathers.

On the outskirts of their small Russian hometown, the Soyer family enjoyed picnics, and while in the woods the children were encouraged to draw by their father. The elder Soyer was a poet whose enthusiasm for drawing stimulated his sons to observe, to read, to compare their work with published drawings and paintings. Noam Chomsky recalled growing up with the study of language. His approach to linguistics was influenced by his father, who was a student of medieval Hebrew grammar. The relationship between Norbert Wiener and his father reminds one of the intense shaping of a child's talent wrought by Leopold Mozart, the ambitious father of Wolfgang Amadeus. The immigrant Leo Wiener worked hard to achieve eminence in the United States. He started as a laborer but became a professor of Slavic languages at Harvard by the time he reached middle age. As a father he believed that children's intellectual talents could be stimulated and molded. He started his children on difficult lessons at a very young age, and he prodded Norbert Wiener's explorations of science and mathematics. Although he was demanding, he also shared with his children his enjoyment "in nature walks, the mushroom-hunting trips, the visits to foundaries, factories and museums and the travels to Europe."[2]

A rather different form of apprenticeship from that shared with a parent is the involvement of many creative young people with teachers from the past. Pablo Casals described as "the great event" of his life his discovery of Bach's *Six Suites for Solo Cello*. And for the rest of his life,

Casals started his day playing Bach. In a similar manner Jane Austen and Virginia Woolf were frequently mentioned by women writers as their distant teachers of previous generations.

The intense focus upon the work of an accomplished person or persons yields insights that are not easily acquired in the more traditional settings of learning. In school young learners are exposed to a diversity of ideas, traditions and techniques; but as Einstein noted, one can get drowned in details in the course of one's education and fail to learn how to concentrate effectively on important problems. Immersing oneself in the works of a predecessor and retracing his or her path, yields a useful counterpoint to the cafeteria of school learning for the person preparing for a creative life. Dialogues across generations are one form of focused learning and preparation in apprenticeship.

Less fully delineated settings that provide a crucial opportunity to the growing individual are those Paul Goodman and others called "communitas." The art educator Marjorie Wilson documented in a study of a high school art room areas and activities "which unite individuals in a common pursuit culminating in one large effort or product."[3] The opportunity to spend long, intense hours with a caring teacher and with peers in an art activity, or putting a school newspaper "to bed," or in rehearsing a play, forms the basis of relationships that can lead to a state of "communitas."[4] The lessons acquired in these settings go beyond those of craft or subject matter. When creative young people form a community—however temporary it may be—they become more aware of themselves, they profit from the criticism of their peers, and they learn new ways to claim their experience. In these contexts, they also go beyond the collection of raw materials for later accomplishment that characterizes the early years—what Maurois called "the gathering of one's honey"—and they start the exercise of sustained effort that distinguishes the young man and woman of serious purpose from the dilettante.

The processes of growth require resolution of the contradictory tensions between the social embeddedness of learning and the creative individual's drive toward a personal voice. When the young artist or scientist begins upon a unique path by declaring his or her identity (I am a writer, or I am a mathematician), he or she needs the assistance of others to overcome the limitations of a single view and to face public criticism or rejection. The demands of solitary work are coupled with those of participation with others in their creative fields throughout the life-span of gifted individuals.

These pressures are particularly evident among those engaged in changing a governing paradigm in their fields. The twentieth century physicists who were struggling to establish a new conceptual structure different from that of Newtonian notions formed a community that went beyond ordinary collegiality. They debated their new ideas during long walks, while visiting each other's homes, and in letters as well as at conferences—exchanges described by Heisenberg and further analyzed by some historians of science. These important documents highlight the role of closely knit groups during the construction of a new framework.

While physics underwent an important transformation during the early part of this century, so did painting. The Cubists led the paradigm shift away from Renaissance and Romantic conceptions, establishing a new field of vision for the representation of forms. The early French Cubist Georges Braque wrote of the powerful connection between the painters as they struggled with their emerging notions: "The things that Picasso and I said to one another during those years will never be said again, and even if they were, no one would understand them any more. It was like being roped together on a mountain."[5]

The powerful bond of which Braque wrote lasted but a few years in the lives of the Cubist painters. Once they had clarified their new premises and found a new visual language to convey their revolutionary insights, the relationship among them lost its intensity. To sustain such a tight connection between gifted individuals may be difficult over a long period of time; nevertheless, there are many records of lasting friendships and collaborations in the literature of creativity.

One such friendship was that of Einstein and the mathematician Marcel Grossmann. They first met as students at the Zurich Polytechnic Institute, where Grossmann was among the first to recognize Einstein's great talent. He also realized how much Einstein deplored ordinary schooling, and he helped him with the more trying courses and assisted him in finding a job after graduation. The two men continued corresponding when Einstein left Switzerland, and these letters allowed Einstein to test some of his ideas while they were still in a formative stage. In 1912, when the two men worked together, Grossmann provided the physicist with some important mathematical tools and thus contributed to Einstein's final formulation of his gravitational theory. Their friendship illustrates the continuing need of creative individuals to combine solitary labor with sustaining, nourishing connection with others.

Developmental views of creativity, such as I'm proposing in this volume, stress cycles of changing focus in the lives of the gifted. There are periods of stimulation and diversity; their antennae are reaching outward. At other times, the focus of attention is more internal. It may be upon the mastery of a difficult craft or upon "the lengthy, continuously reflective construction of a stable theoretical structure."[6]

In the psychologist Howard Gruber's view of creativity, which he calls "the evolving systems approach," the emphasis is upon regeneration:

> Not a system that comes to rest when it has done good work, but one that urges itself onward. And yet, not a runaway system that accelerates its activity to the point where it burns itself out in one great flash. The system regulates its activity and the creative acts regenerate the system. The creative life happens in a being who can continue to work.[7]

In my analysis of thought and creativity, I have emphasized the role of lengthy and varied apprenticeships, the impact of participating in a community, and the role of friendships and collaboration as part of an individual's ability to sustain his or her work and to develop an effective organization of knowledge and purpose. There has been, as well, an emphasis upon the evolution of different languages of thought, the differences between images, movement ideas, and inner speech. Now, in this concluding chapter, those themes will be linked to some of the common features of thinking and the way in which ideas are transformed from private to public forms, from condensed ideas to communicative expressions.

The Language of the Mind

Thinking—how shall I define it? It is a soundless dialogue, it is the weaving of patterns, it is a search for meaning. The activity of thought contributes to and shapes all that is specifically human. In building upon past knowledge, men and women transform the known—and the culturally transmitted means of knowledge—into new discoveries and into the ever-changing forms of thought and language.

Thinking is essential to life; yet, its exploration has been timidly pursued by psychologists, who struggle with constraints both methodological and theoretical. It is very difficult to examine complex inner processes with the scientific tools currently available. Much thinking about thought is therefore inferred from studies of products of thinking, but such studies yield limited and indecisive findings. These difficulties account for the preference of most students of behavior in choosing problems which are likely to yield clear-cut, if narrow, answers.

A major theoretical debate concerning the role of language in thought has long engaged and divided philosophers and social scientists interested in the mind. One dominant position within philosophy is clearly expressed by Hannah Arendt, author of *The Life of the Mind*, when she writes that the interconnectedness of language and thought "makes us suspect that no speechless thought can exist."[8] Psychologist Jean Piaget held a different position; he argued that "language does not constitute the source of logic but is, on the contrary, structured by it. The roots of logic are to be sought in the general coordination of actions (including verbal behavior), beginning with the sensorimotor level."[9] An even stronger position opposing a central role for language in thought is taken by the author of *Visual Thinking*, the Gestalt psychologist Rudolf Arnheim who suggested that language is essentially "stabilizing and conservative" while visual thinking provides "the patterns of forces that underlie our existence."[10] He maintains that

> Purely verbal thinking is the prototype of thoughtless
> thinking, the automatic recourse to connections
> retrieved from storage. It is useful but sterile. What
> makes language so valuable for thinking, then, cannot
> be thinking in words. It must be the help that words
> lend to thinking while it operates in a more appropriate
> medium, such as visual imagery.[11]

One current summary of the debate is offered by Morton Hunt in his excellent, popularly written book on thinking:

> Advanced thinking depends on the mental manipulation
> of symbols, and while nonlinguistic symbol systems
> such as those of mathematics and art are sophisticated,
> they are extremely narrow. Language, in contrast, is a
> virtually unbounded symbol system, capable of
> expressing every kind of thought. It is the prerequisite
> of culture, which cannot exist without it or by means of
> any other symbol system. It is the way we human
> beings communicate most of our thoughts to each other
> and receive from each other the food for thought. In
> sum, we do not always think in words, but we do little
> thinking without them.[12]

Though Hunt's statement of the role of language is persuasive, he minimizes the evidence provided by the self-reports of scientists who have emphasized the importance of visual thinking in their discovery processes. My own description of these reports was presented in the chapter on "Scientific Thinking," including the analysis by Gerald Holton of Einstein's "iconographic" cast of mind.

Rather than arguing for a universal role of language in thinking, some have suggested that different individuals rely upon one or another thought modality to different degrees. That position is supported by Anne Roe's findings. She determined that social scientists rely on verbal processes of thought while physical scientists favor visual thinking. The importance of visual thinking in scientific discovery was affirmed by T. H. Kruger, who, using a method of reconstruction, found that visual analogies played a critical role in the thought processes of engineers and physicists. In a study by British scientist Grey Walter and quoted in *The Natural History of the Mind*, written by G. R. Taylor, it is reported that fifteen percent of the population thought exclusively in visual terms, an equal percent in verbal terms, and the remaining majority used a mixture of these approaches.[13]

This issue has been of long-standing concern to me; it prompted my dissertation research more than twenty-five years ago and has been part of the motivation for writing this volume. Here I have chosen to gather indirect evidence concerning the contents and modalities of thought, relying upon the self-reports of experienced thinkers, and upon letters, notebooks, sketches, and diagrams frequently shown to me by those I have interviewed. In these drafts, scientists and artists reveal the importance of verbal *and* nonverbal notations of thought (the best known among them provided by Darwin's frequently drawn, irregularly-branched tree). These materials lend support to the assumption that a diversity of inner representational modes exists just as there are a diversity of expressive means by which thinkers convey their discoveries to others. The dichotomy between verbal and visual thinking, which is so prevalent in the popular literature at present, tends to oversimplify this diversity.

One dominant mode of thinking develops slowly, and it is linked to less dominant forms in the work of the creative individual. One example of such a connection between verbal and visual thought was described to me by the British writer Margaret Drabble. She relies strongly upon her inner voice while writing her novels; at the same time, she may visualize an event of her developing plot, usually when there is a sharp change in her narrative line. Many creative people similarly reported a unification of diverse thought processes as they developed their creative work.

The young person may at first exhibit a preference for learning by movement, sound, vision, or language. It is a preference shaped by many circumstances: the culturally available and patterned activities; the interests, experiences, and resources of one's family and schooling; the role of mentors and distant teachers. All of these contribute to both the content and form of knowledge in the developing individual. In turn these affect the growth of the dominant inner language of the mind.

Often it is difficult to specify the nature of a person's inner language. Its description and identification may be indirectly determined by how one gathers and remembers experience. These strategies then furnish them with valuable insights concerning the more hidden language of the mind. Rosemary Sisson, a scriptwriter for Masterpiece Theatre, recalled the training of her "mind's ear," including time spent acting, an experience she shares with many other dramatists and writers whose style bears the powerful echoes of spoken language.

These connections between recurrent experience, selective attention, and the reliance upon a particular inner language of thought and planning are not fully understood. I would suggest that the internalization of experience and of the modality-specific ways in which experience is shaped are not mirror images of the external communicative process. The notion that thought is but subvocal speech is strongly contradicted by the information provided by experienced thinkers. The internalization of speech requires a simplification and organization of one's experience; however, these are the precise methods of simplification that are related to the complex requirements of one's craft or discipline. As Stravinsky suggested:

> I believe that composers (and painters) memorize selectively whereas performers must be able to take in "the whole thing as it is," like a camera; I believe, in fact, that a composer's first impression is already a composition.[14]

One aspect of internalization is the way one links new information with existing inner structures and processes. The poet Stephen Spender wrote of the organization of these connective links, and his words quoted in an earlier chapter are also valuable as part of this summary:

> Memory is not exactly memory. It is more like a prong, upon which a calendar of similar experiences happening

> throughout years collect. A memory once clearly stated
> ceases to be a memory, it becomes perpetually present,
> because every time we experience something which
> recalls it, the clear and lucid original experience imposes
> its formal beauty on the new experiences. It is thus no
> longer memory but an experience lived through again
> and again.[15]

Stravinsky and Spender understood that there are no sharp differentiations between the processes of internalization of new experience and the familiar, well-honed ways in which creative individuals shape their own work. Their ability to nourish and sustain their work consists of many activities: among these are their knowledge of how to scan their surroundings for new stimulation and data, which as was seen in chapter six Thomas Mann called "the magic circle of books." Still another powerful description of mobilizing past knowledge, the accumulation of a lifetime of images, was given by Ben Shahn in his wonderful small book *The Shape of Content*. In describing the growth of "Allegory," one of his major paintings, he writes that a major theme helped to pull together images of diverse origins into a singular work.

These images may be kept solely in one's active memory. A scientist may remember, as Sir Francis Crick does, important conversations that have a bearing upon one's current research. Many individuals find it useful to keep records of these important components of their craft in a more permanent form, as does Stephen Spender who writes of his use of notebooks in which he has gathered promising poetic lines. One best-selling author told me that she starts a new notebook for each of her novels: she jots down names, short dialogues, impressions that strengthen the depiction of a place. While she is working on a book, her mind frequently runs ahead, and the notebooks become the repository of passages that may be useful at a later stage of her enterprise.

Notebooks such as these are indicators of the inner activities of the mind. They serve as fixed points on a lengthy trajectory. Laboratory notebooks are good examples. In addition to these notes on thinking, some individuals keep careful records of their actions in diaries, files, and tapes. Frederic L. Holmes, a historian of science, has found that, in contrast with published papers, private records indicate many "subtle shifts in objectives, in which the investigator departs from his initial research purposes, but with no distinct break in his investigative pathway."[16]

To comprehend the development of a line of argument in science, or the interplay between theories and evidence, the student of creativity needs to rely both upon published papers and private documents. Often the latter yield information about the thought activity itself. As Holmes, who had studied the notebooks of Claude Bernard, Hans Krebs, and Antoine Lavoisier, wrote, their notebooks affected his own ways of keeping notes on his thinking and made him aware of what he described as an "activated state"—a rapid flow of ideas which were provoked by the sustained immersion in a work—but which could stop just as rapidly as it had started. Note-taking, it would seem, is an important aspect of creative endeavor.

In some fields it is difficult to find published records of these rapid notes of thought, but one rich source of them is in the journals and diaries of writers, as was noted in the "Verbal Thinking" chapter. They exemplify the packed, telegrammatic nature of inner speech described by the Russian psychologist L. S. Vygotsky, who wrote: "Inner speech is to a large extent thinking in pure meanings. It is a dynamic, shifting, unstable thing."[17] It is a language of thought for the self; it is condensed and focuses upon the new in thinking, and only when it is expanded in form and made communicable to others does it lose its unstable, volatile, and internally creative character.

While inner speech—and "inner speech" writing of the kind recorded in Virginia Woolf's diary—has been studied by others, *condensed thought across several modalities* has not been noted before. Indeed, one of the most important outcomes of my work on this book, and the source of its title *Notebooks of the Mind*, is based on this realization. In Table 1 I have gathered a few examples of this condensed thought.

Darwin's frequently drawn image "is densely packed with potential meaning," wrote Howard Gruber in *Darwin on Man*. "Over the years, Darwin drew a number of tree diagrams both trying to perfect it and penetrate it—to learn what his own imagery would tell him."[18] The last phrase captures well the essence of these thought notations, the way a thinker telescopes a cluster of ideas into a symbolic form, only to find unpacking the symbol a promising and demanding task.

Once I had made the insight and realized that condensed thought is not limited to inner speech and to the inner processes of those who think in words, other examples of packed, symbolic representations for the self were easy to identify. Martha Graham's *Notebooks* are replete with shorthand notations of verbal and movement ideas; Cunningham's diagram reveals a similar combination of drawings of stick figures, ballet terminology in abbreviation, vectors, and so forth. His diagram (in Table 1) is particularly interesting as it links sequential and simultaneous

Table 1

Examples of Condensed and Generative Ideas
from Notebooks, Interviews, and Essays

I.

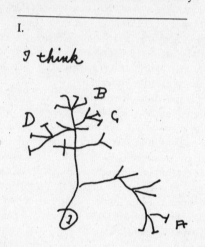

Darwin's Tree from Notebook B, in H. Gruber, *Darwin on Man* (1974)

II.
"This is going to be fairly short; to have father's character done complete in it; and mother's; and St. Ives; and childhood; and all the usual things I try to put in—life, death, etc. But the center is father's character, sitting in a boat, reciting 'We perished each alone.'"

Virginia Woolf, *A Writer's Diary* (1953).

III.
"When one is mentally relaxed, ideas seem to come more freely as one works . . . As a matter of fact, these approaches and ideas are likely to occur with such *rapidity* and *suddenness* that one can't pursue each one seriously at the moment. A good thing to do is to jot these ideas down so as not to lose sight of them."

Mathematician Morris Kline. Interview published in S. Rosner and L.E. Abt, eds. *The Creative Experience* (1970).

IV.

y
L
turn to ♀
LL
I & 8
triplet   g
L R L   arab
            L   R

Choreographer Merce Cunningham's working papers published in *New York Times*, March 21, 1982.

V.

"The method which I adopt, therefore, is to write down as many ideas as possible, in however rough a form, in notebooks (I have at least twenty of these, on a shelf beside my desk . . .) the best way of explaining how I develop rough ideas . . . is to take an example . . . For example no. 3 (never developed) is the one line: "A language of flesh and roses.""

Stephen Spender, "The Making of a Poem" in P.E. Vernon, ed., *Creativity*, (1970)

VI.

"Most of the time during these walks was spent in composition. He thought out the leading ideas, pondered over the construction of the work, and jotted down fundamental themes. In Klin there are carefully preserved many little exercise books, which he has used for this purpose. If in absence of mind Tchaikovsky had left his notebook at home, he noted down his passing thoughts on any scrap of paper, letter, envelope . . . which he chanced to have with him."

Modeste Tchaikovsky, *Life & Letters of Tchaikovsky*, p. 492.

processes, which is achieved by the combination of a visual and verbal shorthand.

Condensed notations occur in the notebooks of scientists just as they do in the diaries of writers and artists. For example, the physicist R. A. Millikan kept notebooks in which he organized his reading and noted important research topics such as the first of twenty-seven entries on May 21, 1898: "Resistance of air in its relation to the velocity of the (falling) moving body." Gerald Holton commented that this was "a major component of the problem that was treated a decade later in Millikan's work on the charge of moving droplets."[19]

Holton elaborates on the meaning of this condensed notation of promising research because he was familiar with the work of the physicists at the turn of the century, and he has also studied Millikan's work in depth. Without that background such notations, while *generative* for the self, would have little communicative value for others. Our insights concerning inner speech are derived from two major sources: the introspections of experienced thinkers and the quick notations of thought in inner speech writing, in diagrams, and sketches which are frequently included in the external records kept by those whose notebooks of the mind are rich in innovative and creative thought.

In summary, creative thinking is that search for meaning which encompasses rapid bursts of ideas embedded in the sustained thought activities of the thinker. There is a continuing interaction between generative thought, which is often condensed, fluctuating, and unstable, and communicated thought, which is expanded and organized for maximum impact. The way communicated thought is expressed varies across domains; writing requires a carefully organized *sequence* of ideas, while painting is characterized by a weaving of patterns into a *simultaneous* form. The most diverse languages of the mind are in their externalized forms, but they share some critical common attributes in their inner, generative processes.

A Passion for One's Task

Is creative thinking indistinguishable from ordinary thought? And are creative individuals bestowed with hereditary gifts or are they but more effective practitioners of ordinary human gifts shared by all of us?

The argument for a continuity of thinking activities is most strongly presented by behaviorist psychologists. D. E. Berlyne, a Canadian student of behavior, argued that "creative thinking often receives special treatment as a phenomenon apart, but this practice seems unjustified."[20] He suggested that we view productive and reproductive thinking as forming a single hierarchy of solution strategies. The former stands high in such a continuum and requires considerable effort for production, while reproductive thinking is easily accessible as it is tied to frequently occurring situations.

A different point of view characterizes those who view creativity as talents determined by heredity. The work of Sir Francis Galton serves as a starting point in this tradition. In his *Hereditary Genius* (1869), he argued that one individual out of 4,000 is likely to become an "eminent" member of his society, and that eminent men were related to each other within a particular field. In the United States, L. M. Terman continued this tradition; he initiated a large-scale study of intellectually gifted individuals whose careers he and his coworkers followed for over thirty years. While high achievement was identified among many of those included in his sample, the work by Terman did not throw much light on the processes of creativity itself.

An emphasis upon motivation, childhood experiences, and the role of sexual fantasies was provided by Freudian students of creativity. Sigmund Freud believed that creativity consisted of the sublimation of instinctual energy, and that creative individuals' unfulfilled sexual curiosities were the basis of their drives to acquire knowledge. The implication of his argument was that creative individuals while similar to neurotics, are able to link their intellect powers with their emotions. This argument is not supported by most research. Morris Stein's summary of research on the personality traits of creative individuals reveals contradictory findings: "Some say that creative people are emotionally unstable, others that they are actually mentally healthier than less creative people in their same professions."[21]

The personality traits that have been found to be characteristic of a large number of creative individuals, such as perseverance, independence, nonconformity, and flexibility, are not traits that denote neurosis. But a certain intensity exists among individuals who are committed to a creative life that is central to their being. Whether this is part of a hereditary endowment or the consequence of early stimulation, I do not know. The psychiatrist-author of *Creativity: The Magic Synthesis*, Sylvano Arieti, suggests that:

> Another motivation of the creative person may stem
> from the fact that he is endowed with a very active or
> intense imagination on account of biological or other as
> yet undetermined reasons. Whereas the average person

very early in life learns to check his imagination and to pay more attention to the requirements of reality than to his inner experiences, the creative person follows a different course. He feels himself in a state of turmoil, restlessness, deprivation, emptiness, and unbearable frustration unless he expresses his inner life in one or another creative way.[22]

Creativity requires a *continuity of concern*, an intense awareness of one's active inner life combined with sensitivity to the external world. In this developmental account of creativity, I have emphasized the way in which intensity at an early age may be enhanced, shaped, and encouraged through the multiple apprenticeships of gifted individuals. Part of their self-discovery and choice of a creative life is linked to their pleasure in the sensual aspects of their metier. Marjorie Wilson described how high school art students played with the "languages and uses of art"; in a study of young adults at the Chicago Art Institute, Getzels and Csikszentmihalyi depicted the great rewards of art work: "Squeezing a tube of paint becomes a pleasurable sensation, the smell of pigments is exhilarating, and so is the yielding feel of the clay in one's hands."[23] And the painter Gene Newmann celebrated the sensual pleasures of his craft when speaking to me.

Intensity is then the one universal given in this account of creative thinking; its origins are usually found in childhood. All the individuals I interviewed recalled some recognition of their engagement with play, with ideas, with the world, and while still very young. Anaïs Nin recalled her joy in listening to musicians rehearsing in her parents' house, and how she had channeled her joy of music into writing. Jessica Mitford and Margaret Drabble recalled their joyous, literate childhoods, and how they first practiced writing with letters and family magazines while still quite young.

The early activities of immersion and exploration, of which I wrote more fully in the beginning of this chapter, are the first indicators of the intensity that remains a hallmark of the individual committed to a creative life. In conceiving of creativity as an evolving system, Gruber stresses that it is not a system that burns out, but that it is regenerative. A similar analysis is offered by Arieti, who views the creative process as an open system, where the initial conditions do not determine the final outcome. These characteristics of creativity—its developmental nature, the linking of overt and covert processes, and the construction of an open-ended and regenerative system—may also be seen in lives lacking the distinction of creative achievements. What is the difference?

The difference lies in the intensity and continuity of the creative individual's mental life. Work in the market place is discontinuous; one is given a task, which once completed leads to another, a discrete assignment. Daily thought, which accompanies these daily challenges, also has a certain discontinuity. Once we close the door behind our paid work, we also tend to close our mind to it. Indeed, ordinary, repetitive work needs to be extrinsically rewarded because it lacks the intrinsic rewards of sustained, continuous mental labor.

The tools and skills used for solving daily problems may not be so different from the tools and skills used by individuals engaged in creative endeavors. But their sustained commitment to their queries transforms the power of the tools and the magnitude of their achievement. Vivian Gornick describes this process in *Women in Science;* she calls it the "active interiority" of the creative:

> A scientist or a writer is one who ruminates
> continuously on the nature of physical or imaginative
> life, experiences repeated relief and excitement when
> the insight comes, and is endlessly attracted to working
> out the idea.[24]

The strength of such sustained concern is not a deadly, willful thing. It is linked to childhood play and wonder and to the pleasures of one's craft. It is born of and is sustained by a variety of productive tensions. In Einstein's life, the questions he asked about space and time reached back to his early years and were childlike in their simplicity. But the answers were wrought through his inordinate ability to concentrate and to stay with issues, even when they were abandoned by other members of his discipline. While the internal preoccupation with ideas, images, and fundamental queries is continuous in the lives of creative individuals, breaks, unproductive periods, and disappointments occur in their external lives. But their need to create continues. Thomas Mann wrote to his daughter Erika after a difficult year: "I am very glad that I am writing again. I really feel like myself and know something about myself only when I am doing something; the intervals are gruesome."[25]

Thomas Mann's creative life is well documented because he was willing to answer queries about his way of working. In *The Story of a Novel*, he re-created the construction of *Dr. Faustus*. He realized the importance in creative work of nourishing the external and internal notebooks of the mind. In a letter to Viktor Polzer he described how he did this:

> For a longer book I usually have a heap of preliminary papers close at hand during the writing; scribbled notes, memory props, in part purely objective—external details, colorful odds and ends—or else psychological formulations, fragmentary inspirations, which I use in their proper place.[26]

The act of thinking about one's task in many different settings makes the capturing of fleeting ideas necessary; but without the incredible discipline of the creative individual and his or her continuous seeking, thinking, and ruminating about the varied directions and meanings of a focused work, notes on thinking remain illusive. The recognition of the value of rapid thought processes is made possible by the fact that they are embedded in the thinking person's continuity of thought, as suggested by Gruber:

> Deep understanding of a domain of knowledge requires knowing it in various ways. This multiplicity of perspectives grows slowly through hard work and sets the stage for the re-cognition we experience as new insights.[27]

The full realization of generative ideas requires a sustained, often painful, dialectic between condensed inner thoughts and realization. In the course of resolving such tension, the poet and novelist May Sarton has written "tension between idea and image has to do with the depth and complexity of the image. . . . The problem of course is to keep one's excitement, not to lose the zest in the process (of working and reworking).[28]

The ability to apply and extend productive ideas only succeeds when an individual can join these with a profound knowledge of his or her craft or the tools of a discipline. But tools are both external and internal: an individual's self-knowledge, an awareness of the specificity of one's talents, the rhythms of one's cycles of work, and the need for sustenance and support, all contribute to the realization of thought. As I wrote at the beginning of this work, "A new work of an artist may start with a phrase or a scientist may start with an image, which often represents that nucleus of understanding which unfolds through labor, craft, inspiration, and the careful nurturing of time that separates the beginner from those with experience."

In addition, self-knowledge without a life-long direction and purpose restricts the creative individual's ability to make lasting contributions. Bronowski wrote of knowledge in *Ascent of Man:*

> Knowledge is our destiny. Self-knowledge (an under-
> standing of man himself) at last bringing together the
> experience of the arts and the explanations of science,
> waits ahead of us. . . . Above all, it [knowledge] is a
> responsibility for the integrity of what we are, primarily
> of what we are as ethical creatures.[29]

Great art and great science are gifts of the individual to the society in which he or she is born and with which the struggling, solitary, trium-phant being is inextricably joined.

Appendix 1

LIST OF INTERVIEWS

James Aronson—journalist
Jeanne Bamberger—psychologist and musician
Basil Bernstein—sociologist
Albert Bharucha-Reid—mathematician
Judy Blume—author
Hedda Bolgar—psychologist
Barry Brukoff—photographer
Nina Byers—physicist
Henri Cartier-Bresson—photographer
Harold Clurman—dramatist
Joseph Concha—poet
Lee Connor—choreographer
Aaron Copland—composer
Sir Francis Crick—biologist
Hugh Delacey—philosopher
Dorothy Dinnerstein—psychologist
Margaret Drabble—novelist
Sandra Edelman—poet

Susanna Egri—choreographer
Alfred Eisenstaedt—photographer
Eliot Feld—choreographer
Andrew Ferguson—film-maker
Martine Franck—photographer
James D. Finley, III—physicist
Miguel Godreau—choreographer
Byron Goldstein—physicist
Vicky Gomez—student poet
Richard Gregory—psychologist
Shelley Grossman—photographer
Beatrice Harris—psychologist
Eric Hawkins—choreographer
Reuben Hersh—mathematician
Vivian Horner—linguist
John Holt—author
Enid Howarth—humanist
John Howarth—physicist
Henry Jaglom—film-maker
Suki John—choreographer
Peter Lax—mathematician
Eli Levin—painter
Berni Lujan—student/poet
Irwin Maltzman—psychologist
Karen McKinnon—poet
Elissa Melamed—writer
Jessica Mitford—writer
Ann Moul—painter
Shelia Nevins—film-maker
Eugene Newmann—painter
Anaîs Nin—writer
Rai Okamoto—architect/city planner
Alex Pitcher—student/poet
William Rohwer—psychologists
Fritz Scholder—painter
Douglas Scott—student/poet
Herbert Simon—psychologist/economist
Rosemary Sisson—television writer
Shari Steiner—writer
George Stoney—film-maker
Sara Sugahara—choreographer

Constance Sutton—anthropologist
Linda Tarnay—choreographer
Stan Ulam—mathematician
Jenny Vincent—musician
Gerald Vizenor—writer
Gilbert Voyat—psychologist
Doris Wallace—psychologist
Douglass Turner Ward—playwright
Brent and Marjorie Wilson—art educators
Marta Weigle—folklorist
Malka Wexler—social scientist
Elaine Wickens—educator
Michele Zackheim—artist

N.B.: This is a list of individuals whom I have quoted extensively and many others who have furnished valuable background materials for this book.

Notes

Introduction to Revised Edition

1. Pal Turan, "A Note of Welcome," *Journal of Graph Theory* 1 (1977): 7–9.

2. Gerald Holton, *The Scientific Imagination: Case Studies* (Cambridge: Cambridge University Press, 1978), 231–232.

3. Ludwig Fleck, *Genesis and Development of a Scientific Fact* (Chicago: University of Chicago Press, 1979), 39. The term "thought community" was first presented by the Polish biologist, Ludwig Fleck, who also used the term "thought collective." He defined these as "a community of persons mutually exchanging ideas or maintaining intellectual interaction." In my usage of this term, I refer to groups of experienced thinkers who engage in intense interaction with each other while promoting significant changes in their disciplines. Some of the researchers who have contributed new approaches to creativity over the last decade include Teresa Amabile, Jerome Bruner, Mihaly Csikszentmihalyi, David Feldman, Howard Gardner, Howard Gruber, David Harrington, Ravenna Helson, Keith Sawyer, and Doris Wallace.

4. Jerome Bruner, *Acts of Meaning* (Cambridge: Harvard University Press, 1990), xiii.

5. T. Z. Tardiff and Robert J. Sternberg, "What Do We Know About Creativity?" in *The Nature of Creativity: Contemporary Psychological Perspectives*, ed. Robert J. Sternberg (New York: Cambridge University Press, 1988), 429–440.

6. Doris Wallace and Howard Gruber, *Creative People at Work* (New York: Oxford University Press, 1989).

7. Mihaly Csikszentmihalyi, "The Domain of Creativity" in *Changing the World: A Framework for the Study of Creativity*, eds. David H. Feldman, Mihaly Csikszentmihalyi, and Howard Gardner (Westport: Praeger, 1994), 136.

8. Ibid., 148–149.

9. Howard Gardner, *Frames of Mind: The Theory of Multiple Intelligences* (New York: Basic Books, 1983).

10. Howard Gardner, *Creating Minds: An Anatomy of Creativity Seen Through the Lives of Freud, Einstein, Picasso, Stravinsky, Eliot, Graham, and Gandhi* (New York: Basic Books, 1993).

11. Vera John-Steiner, "Cognitive Pluralism: A Sociocultural Approach," *Mind, Culture, and Activity: An International Journal* 2 (Winter 1995): 3–11.

12. Zenon W. Pylyshyn, *Computation and Cognition: Toward a Foundation for Cognitive Science* (Cambridge: MIT Press, 1984).

13. Antonio R. Damasio, *Descartes' Error: Emotion, Reason, and the Human Brain* (New York: Grosset/Putnam, 1994), 107.

14. Steve M. Kosslyn, *Image and Mind* (Cambridge: Harvard University Press, 1980).

15. Ibid., 9, xi–xii.

16. Howard Gardner, "Introduction to the Tenth-Anniversary Edition," *Frames of Mind: The Theory of Multiple Intelligences* (New York: Basic Books, 1983), xiv.

17. L. S. Vygotsky, *Thought and Language* (Cambridge: MIT Press, 1962).

18. David Feldman, *Beyond Universals in Cognitive Development, Second Edition* (Norwood, NJ: Ablex, 1994), 3.

19. Hannah Arendt, *The Life of the Mind*, vol. 1: *Thinking* (New York: Harcourt Brace Jovanovich, 1977), 99.

20. Ibid., 100.

21. Ibid., 12; Jerry A. Fodor, *Modularity of the Mind: An Essay on Faculty Psychology* (Cambridge: MIT Press, 1983).

22. Arendt, *The Life of the Mind*, 17, 162.

23. Gita L. Vygodskaia, "Remembering Father," *Educational Psychologist* 30 (1995): 57–59.

24. James V. Wertsch, *Voices of the Mind: A Sociocultural Approach to Mediated Action* (Cambridge: Harvard University Press, 1991), 93.

25. L. S. Vygotsky, "The Genesis of Higher Mental Functions," in *The Concepts of Activity in Soviet Psychology,* ed. James Wertsch (Armonk, NY: M. E. Sharpe, 1981), 137.

26. Barbara Rogoff, *Apprenticeship in Thinking: Cognitive Development in Social Context* (New York: Oxford University Press, 1990), 51–52.

Introduction

1. Hannah Arendt, *The Life of the Mind*, vol. 1: *Thinking* (New York: Harcourt Brace Jovanovich, 1977), 4.

2. Jerome Bruner, *Toward a Theory of Instruction* (Cambridge: Harvard University Press, 1966), 19.

3. Morton Hunt, *The Universe Within: A New Science Explores the Human Mind* (New York: Simon and Schuster, 1982), 17.

4. Stephen Toulmin, "The Mozart of Psychology," *New York Review of Books* 25 (September 28, 1978): 57.

5. Nevitt Sanford, "Social Psychology: Its Place in Personology," *American Psychologist* 37 (August 1982): 897.

6. Albert Einstein, Letter in *The Psychology of Invention in the Mathematical Field*, ed. Jacques Hadamard (Princeton: Princeton University Press, 1945), 142.

7. Stephen Spender, "The Making of a Poem," in *Creativity*, ed. P. E. Vernon (Harmondsworth: Penguin, 1975), 64.

8. Bruner, *Toward a Theory of Instruction*, 19.

9. P. B. Medawar, *Induction and Intuition* (Philadelphia: American Philosophical Society, 1969), 46.

Chapter 1

1. Richard I. Evans, *Jean Piaget, The Man and His Ideas* (New York: Dutton, 1973), 16.

2. Basil Bernstein, *Class, Codes and Control*, vol. 3: *Towards a Theory of Educational Transmissions* (London: Routledge and Kegan Paul, 1975), 2–3.

3. John Martin, *The Modern Dance* (New York: A. S. Barnes, 1933), 8–9.

4. Merce Cunningham, Interview in *The Creative Experience*, eds. Stanley Rosner and Lawrence A. Abt (New York: Grossman, 1970), 175.

5. Don Johnson, *The Protean Body: A Rolfer's View of Human Flexibility* (New York: Harper Colophon, 1977), 2.

6. Oscar Kokoschka, *My Life* (New York: Macmillan, 1974), 7–8.

7. György Képes, *Language of Vision* (Chicago: Paul Theobald, 1944), 15.

8. Richard Gregory, *The Intelligent Eye* (New York: McGraw-Hill, 1970), 10.

9. Ulric Neisser, *Cognition and Reality* (San Francisco: W. H. Freeman, 1976), 10.

10. Andrew Sarris, *Interviews with Film Directors* (New York: Avon, 1969), 168.

11. Stephen Spender, "The Making of a Poem," in *Creativity*, ed. P. E. Vernon (Harmondsworth: Penguin, 1975), 70.

12. Ibid., 64.

13. Ernest G. Schactel, *Metamorphosis* (New York: Basic Books, 1959), 237–38.

14. Anaïs Nin, *The Novel of the Future* (New York: Collier Books, 1968), 25.

15. Ibid., 5.

16. William Burroughs, Interview in *Writers at Work*, The Paris Review Interviews, Third Series, ed. George Plimpton (New York: Viking, 1967), 150.

17. Christopher Caudwell, *Studies in a Dying Culture* (London: John Lane, the Bodley-Head, 1938), 50.

18. Simone de Beauvoir, *Memoirs of a Dutiful Daughter* (Cleveland: World, 1959), 16, 19–20.

19. Saul Bellow, Interview in *Writers at Work*, The Paris Review Interviews, Third Series, ed. George Plimpton (New York: Viking, 1967), 183–84.

20. Gail Godwin, *Odd Women* (New York: Berkley Medallion, 1976), 1.

21. Joseph Church, *Language and the Discovery of Reality* (New York: Random House, 1961), 99.

22. Schachtel, *Metamorphosis*, 295–96.

23. Raphael Soyer, Interview in *The Creative Experience*, eds. Stanley Rosner and Lawrence A. Abt (New York: Grossman, 1970), 285.

Chapter 2

1. Albert Einstein, "Autobiographical Notes," in *Albert Einstein: Philosopher-Scientist*, ed. Paul A. Schilpp, 3d ed. (LaSalle, Ill.: Open Court, 1970), 5–7.

2. Andrew Sarris, *Interviews with Film Directors* (New York: Avon, 1969), 35.

3. Noam Chomsky, Interview in *The Creative Experience*, eds. Stanley Rosner and Lawrence A. Abt (New York: Grossman, 1970), 74–75.

4. Robert Craft, *Current Convictions: Views and Reviews* (New York: Knopf, 1977), 8.

5. See, for example, Anne Roe, *The Making of a Scientist* (New York: Dodd, Mead, 1952), and D. W. Mackinnon, "The Personality Correlates of Creativity: A Study of American Architects," in *Creativity*, ed. P. E. Vernon (Harmondsworth: Penguin, 1975), 289–312.

6. Julian Huxley, *Memories* (New York: Harper and Row, 1970), 2.

7. Ibid., 20.

8. Ibid., 26.

9. Ibid., 56.

10. Anne Sayre, *Rosalind Franklin and DNA* (New York: Norton, 1975), 30.

11. Lillian Hellman, *An Unfinished Woman* (Boston: Little, Brown, 1969), 11.

12. Sigmund Freud, "Creative Writers and Daydreaming," in *Creativity*, ed. P. E. Vernon (Harmondsworth: Penguin, 1975), 133.

13. Anne Roe, "A Psychologist Examines Sixty-Four Eminent Scientists," in *Creativity*, ed. P. E. Vernon (Harmondsworth: Penguin, 1975), 50.

14. Einstein, "Autobiographical Notes," 17.

15. Marie S. Curie, *Pierre Curie* (New York: Macmillan, 1936), 34.

16. Henri Troyat, *Tolstoy* (Garden City: Doubleday, 1967), 29.

17. Wolfgang Amadeus Mozart, "A Letter," in *Creativity*, ed. P. E. Vernon (Harmondsworth: Penguin, 1975), 56.

18. James Baldwin, *The Devil Finds Work* (New York: Dial, 1976), 22.

19. Diego Rivera, with Gladys March, *My Art, My Life: An Autobiography by Diego Rivera* (New York: Citadel, 1976), 41.

20. Ibid., 43.

21. Ibid.

22. J. Ma. Corredor, *Conversations with Casals* (New York: Dutton, 1956), 109.

23. Ibid., 27.

24. Somerset Maugham, *The Summing Up* (London: Heinemann, 1948), 20.

25. John Berger, *Towards Reality* (New York: Knopf, 1962), 151.

26. Ibid.

27. Lewis Funke and John Booth, *Actors Talk About Acting* (New York: Avon, 1969), 16.

28. Ibid., 114.

29. Howard E. Gruber, *Darwin on Man: A Psychological Study of Scientific Creativity* (New York: Dutton, 1974), 68.

Chapter 3

1. Anaïs Nin, *Diary*, vol. IV (New York: Harcourt Brace Jovanovich, 1967), 125.

2. Hermann Hesse, *Autobiographical Writings* (New York: Farrar, Straus, Giroux, 1973), 46.

3. Ibid., 47–48.

4. Donald MacKinnon, "The Study of Creative Persons," in *Creativity and Learning*, ed. Jerome Kagan (Boston: Beacon, 1967), 30.

5. Jacob W. Getzels and Phillip W. Jackson, *Creativity and Intelligence* (London: Wiley, 1962), 75.

6. Rollo May, *The Courage to Create* (New York: Norton, 1975), 83.

7. Daniel E. Schneider, *Psychoanalyst and the Artist* (New York: New American Library, 1962), 54.

8. Albert Rothenberg, *The Emerging Goddess* (Chicago: University of Chicago Press, 1979), 345.

9. Ibid., 131–32.

10. Anne Tyler, "Still Just Writing," in *The Writer on Her Work*, ed. Janet Sternburg (New York: Norton, 1980), 13.

11. H. E. F. Donohue, *Conversations with Nelson Algren* (New York: Berkley Medallion, 1965), 51–54 passim.

12. David King Dunaway, *How Can I Keep from Singing: Pete Seeger* (New York: McGraw-Hill, 1981), 187.

13. Werner Heisenberg, *Physics and Beyond: Encounters and Conversations* (New York: Harper and Row, 1971), 59–60.

14. Ibid., 80.

15. Howard E. Gruber, *Darwin on Man: A Psychological Study of Scientific Creativity* (New York: Dutton, 1974), 26.

16. Ibid., 91.

17. Dennis Gabor, Interview in *Scientists Face to Face*, ed. Istvan Kardos (Gyoma, Hungary: Corvina, 1978), 82.

18. Stephen Spender, "The Making of a Poem," in *Creativity*, ed. P. E. Vernon (Harmondsworth: Penguin, 1970), 71.

19. Ingmar Bergman, Interview in *Interviews with Film Directors*, ed. A. Sarris (New York: Avon, 1967), 41.

20. Spender, "Making of a Poem," 71.

21. Igor Stravinsky and Robert Craft, *Expositions and Developments* (Garden City: Doubleday, 1962), 50–51.

22. Spender, "Making of a Poem," 71.

23. Ulric Neisser, *Cognitive Psychology* (New York: Appleton-Century-Crofts, 1967), 199ff.

24. Stan M. Ulam, *Adventures of a Mathematician* (New York: Scribner, 1976), 181.

25. W. I. Beveridge, *The Art of Scientific Investigation* (New York: Norton, 1950), 60.

26. Ulam, *Adventures*, 182.

27. Paul Gauguin, *Intimate Journals*, trans. Van Wyck Brooks (Bloomington: Indiana University Press, 1968), 154.

28. Robert Goldwater, *Paul Gauguin* (New York: Abrams, 1928), 118.

29. André Maurois, *The Quest for Proust* (Harmondsworth: Penguin, 1949), 61–62.

30. Ibid., 126–27.

31. May Sarton, *Writing on Writing* (Orono, Maine: Puckerbrush Press, 1980), 26–27.

32. Peter Ilich Tchaikovsky, "Letters," in *Creativity*, ed. P. E. Vernon (Harmondsworth: Penguin, 1970), 58.

33. Ibid., 59.

34. Katherine Anne Porter, Interview in *Writers at Work*, The Paris Review Interviews, Second Series, ed. Van Wyck Brooks (New York: Viking, 1963), 159.

35. Thomas Mann, *Letters of Thomas Mann: 1889–1955*, trans. R. and C. Winston (New York: Vintage, 1975), 256.

36. Ibid.

37. Sarton, *On Writing*, 50–52.

38. Mann, *Letters*, 257.

39. Van Wyck Brooks, *Opinions of Oliver Allston* (New York: Dutton, 1941), 30.

40. Gail Godwin, "Becoming a Writer," in *The Writer on Her Work*, ed. Janet Sternburg (New York: Norton, 1980), 252–53.

41. Ibid., 253.

42. Howard E. Gruber, "The Evolving Systems Approach to Creativity," in *Towards a Theory of Psychological Development*, eds. Sohan and Celia Modgil (Windsor, Eng.: NFER, 1980), 269.

43. Mann, Letters, 291.

44. Ibid.

45. Isidor Chein, *The Science of Behavior and the Image of Man* (New York: Basic Books, 1972), 289.

Chapter 4

1. Diana Michener, "Catching the Sun," in *Working It Out*, eds. Sara Ruddnick and Pamela Daniels (New York: Pantheon, 1977), 152.

2. R. R. Holt, "Imagery: The Return of the Ostracized, *American Psychologist* 19 (April 1964): 254.

3. Albert Einstein, "A Testimonial from Professor Einstein," in *The Psychology of Invention in the Mathematical Field*, ed. Jacques Hadamard (Princeton: Princeton University Press, 1945), 142.

4. Albert Einstein, Unpublished papers, quoted in *New York Times*, March 27, 1972, 26.

5. Rudolf Arnheim, *Visual Thinking* (Berkeley: University of California Press, 1969), 227.

6. Ibid., 315.

7. Ibid., 244.

8. Arthur Koestler, *The Act of Creation* (New York: Macmillan, 1964), 176.

9. J. C. Gowan, "Incubation, Imagery and Creativity," *Journal of Mental Imagery* 2 (Spring 1978): 26.

10. Allan Paivio, *Imagery and Verbal Processes* (New York: Holt Rinehart, Winston, 1971), 5.

11. Martha Moore-Russell, "John Locke: The Development of a Philosopher as a Person-in-Society," presented at the Seventh Annual Symposium of the Jean Piaget Society, Philadelphia, May 21, 1977, 7.

12. Howard E. Gruber, "Darwin's Tree of Nature and Other Images of Wide Scope," in *On Aesthetics in Science*, ed. J. Wechsler (Cambridge: MIT Press, 1977), 127.

13. Ibid., 137.

14. Ibid.

15. György Képes, *Language of Vision* (Chicago: Paul Theobald, 1944), 23.

16. Janos Balazs, *A Hungarian Gipsy Artist* (Budapest: Corvina, 1977), 11.

17. Raphael Soyer, *Diary of an Artist* (Washington, D.C.: New Republic Books, 1977), 181.

18. Ibid.

19. Paul Gauguin, *Intimate Journals*, trans. Van Wyck Brooks (Bloomington: Indiana University Press, 1968), 154.

20. D. W. MacKinnon, "The Personality Correlates of Creativity: A Study of American Architects," in *Creativity*, ed. P. E. Vernon (Harmondsworth: Penguin, 1970), 304.

21. Martha Kearns, *Käthe Kollwitz: Woman and Artist* (Old Westbury: Feminist Press, 1976), 18.

22. Judy Chicago, *Through the Flower: My Struggle as a Woman Artist* (Garden City: Doubleday, 1975), 3.

23. Jacob Getzels and Phillip W. Jackson, *Creativity and Intelligence* (London: Wiley, 1962), 76.

24. Jacob Getzels and Mihály Csikszentmihályi, *The Creative Vision* (New York: Wiley, 1976), 209.

25. Marjorie Wilson, "Passage-Through-Communitas: An Interpretive Analysis of Enculturation in Art Education," Ph.D. dissertation, Pennsylvania State University, 1977, 82.

26. Ibid., 116.

27. Getzels and Csikszentmihályi, *Creative Vision*, 216–17.

28. Ben Shahn, *The Shape of Content* (Cambridge: Harvard University Press, 1957), 51.

29. Chicago, *Through the Flower,* 175.

30. Ibid., 176.

31. Ibid., 114.

32. Miriam Shapiro, "Notes from a Conversation on Art, Feminism, and Work" in *Working It Out*, eds. Sara Ruddnick and Pamela Daniels (New York: Pantheon, 1977), 303.

33. William James, *The Principles of Psychology*, vol. 1 (New York: Dover, 1950), 203.

34. Soyer, *Diary*, 190.

35. Shahn, *Shape of Content*, 29.

36. Ibid., 50.

37. Federico Fellini, Interview in *Behind the Scenes: Theatre and Film Interviews*, ed. J. F. McCrindle (New York: Holt, Rinehart and Winston, 1971), 170–71.

38. Anaïs Nin, *Diary*, vol. VII (New York: Harcourt Brace Jovanovich, 1976), 233.

39. Luis Buñuel, "Cinema, Instrument of Poetry," in *Luis Buñuel: A Critical Biography* by Francisco Arando, trans. by David Robinson (New York: DeCapo Press, 1967), pp. 274–75.

40. John Berger, *Success and Failure of Picasso* (Harmondsworth: Penguin, 1965), 54–55.

41. Képes, *Language of Vision*, 68.

42. Arnheim, *Visual Thinking*, 38.

43. Agnes Arber, *The Mind and the Eye* (Cambridge: Cambridge University Press, 1964), 125.

Chapter 5

1. Virginia Woolf, *A Writer's Diary* (New York: Harcourt Brace Jovanovich, 1953), 292.

2. Henry Miller, Interview in *Writers at Work*, The Paris Review Interviews, Third Series, ed. George Plimpton (New York: Viking, 1967), 174–75.

3. L. S. Vygotsky, *Thought and Language*, trans. E. Hanfman and G. Vakar (Cambridge: MIT Press, 1962), 148.

4. F. Dostoevsky, *The Notebooks for "A Raw Youth,"* ed. Edward Wasiolek (Chicago: University of Chicago Press, 1969), 24.

5. Ibid.

6. Vygotsky, *Thought and Language*, 45.

7. F. Dostoevsky, *The Notebooks for "The Possessed,"* ed. Edward Wasiolek (Chicago: University of Chicago Press, 1968), 37, 41.

8. H. D. Thoreau, *A Writer's Journal*, ed. Laurence Stapleton (New York: Dover, 1960), 191.

9. Gertrude Wyatt, *Language Learning and Communication Disorders in Children* (New York: Free Press, 1969), 15ff.

10. Jean Piaget, *Six Psychological Studies* (New York: Vintage, 1968), 88ff.

11. Ruth Weir, *Language in the Crib* (The Hague: Mouton, 1962), 120.

12. Jean Piaget, *The Language and Thought of the Child*, trans. M. Gabain (New York: New American Library, 1974), 31.

13. Howard Gardner, *Art, Mind and Brain: A Cognitive Approach to Creativity* (New York: Basic Books, 1982), 158ff.

14. Joseph Concha, *Lonely Deer: Poems by a Pueblo Boy* (Taos, New Mexico: Taos Pueblo Council, 1969).

15. Kenneth Koch, *Wishes, Lies and Dreams* (New York: Chelsea House, 1970), 26.

16. Stephen Spender, "The Making of a Poem," in *Creativity*, ed. P. E. Vernon (Harmondsworth: Penguin, 1970), 26.

17. Ibid., 66.

18. Koch, *Wishes, Lies and Dreams*, 35.

19. Pablo Neruda, *Memoirs* (New York: Farrar, Straus, Giroux, 1977), 20.

20. Hermann Hesse, *Autobiographical Writings* (New York: Farrar, Straus, Giroux, 1971), 5.

21. Neruda, *Memoirs*, 21.

22. Jean Rhys, *Smile Please* (New York: Harper and Row, 1979), 43.

23. Jean Paul Sartre, *The Words* (New York: Fawcett World Library, 1964), 25.

24. Neruda, *Memoirs*, 21.

25. Nikos Kazantzakis, *Report to Greco* (London: Faber and Faber, 1973), 79.

26. Thomas Mann, *The Story of a Novel* (New York: Knopf, 1961), 38.

27. Malcolm Cowley, "How Writers Write," in *Writers at Work*, the Paris Review Interviews, Second Series, ed. Van Wyck Brooks (New York: Viking, 1963), 7.

28. Jorge Luis Borges, Interview in *Writers at Work*, The Paris Review Interviews, Fourth Series, ed. George Plimpton (New York: Viking, 1976), 124.

29. David Perkins, *The Mind's Best Work* (Cambridge: Harvard University Press, 1981), 49.

30. Ibid., 52.

31. Anthony Burgess, Interview in *Writers at Work*, The Paris Review Interviews, Fourth Series, ed. George Plimpton (New York: Viking, 1976), 332.

32. H. E. F. Donahue, *Conversations with Nelson Algren* (New York: Berkley Medallion, 1963), 68.

33. Thornton Wilder, Interview in *Writers at Work*, The Paris Review Interviews, First Series, ed. Malcolm Cowley (New York: Viking, 1959), 114.

34. Mann, *Story of a Novel*, 37–38.

35. Ibid., 82.

36. John Steinbeck, *Journal of a Novel* (New York: Viking, 1969), 3.

37. Katherine Mansfield, *Journal of Katherine Mansfield*, ed. J. M. Murray (New York: Knopf, 1946), 43–44.

38. Mann, *Story of a Novel*, 17.

39. Mansfield, *Journal*, 45.

40. Steinbeck, *Journal of a Novel*, 12.

41. Ibid., 18.

42. Ibid., 66.

43. Mann, *Story of a Novel*, 89.

44. Gustave Flaubert, "Letter to H. A. Taine," in *Novelists on the Novel* (New York: Columbia University Press, 1959), 155–56.

45. Arthur Miller, "Death of a Salesman," in *Playwrights on Playwriting*, ed. Toby Cole (New York: Hill and Wang, 1960), 275.

46. W. B. Yeats, "Language, Character and Construction," in *Playwrights on Playwriting*, ed. Toby Cole (New York: Hill and Wang, 1960), 47.

47. Harold Pinter, Interview in *Writers on Writing*, The Paris Review Interviews, Third Series, ed. George Plimpton (New York: Viking, 1967), 353.

48. John Gassner, "Introduction," in *Playwrights on Playwriting*, ed. Toby Cole (New York: Hill and Wang, 1960), xvii.

49. Catherine Patrick, "Creative Thought in Poets," in *Archives of Psychology* 78 (1935).

50. Perkins, *Mind's Best Work*, 39–40.

51. Albert Hofstadter, "On the Dialectical Phenomenology of Creativity," in *Essays in Creativity*, eds. Stanley Rosner and Lawrence A. Abt (Croton-On-Hudson, N.Y.: North River Press, 1974), 116.

52. Hannah Arendt, *The Life of the Mind*, vol. 1: *Thinking* (New York: Harcourt Brace Jovanovich, 1971), 99.

53. Ibid., 100.

Chapter 6

1. Albert Rothenberg, *The Emerging Goddess* (Chicago: University of Chicago Press, 1979), 248.

2. Leonard Bernstein, *The Unanswered Question* (Cambridge: Harvard University Press, 1976), 424.

3. Ray Jackendorff, "Generative Music Theory and its Relevance to Psychology," unpublished manuscript, 2.

4. H. Gordon, "Degree of Ear Asymmetries for Perception of Dichotic Chords and for Illusory Chord Localization in Musicians of Different Levels of Competence," *Journal of Experimental Psychology* 6 (1980): 520.

5. Howard Gardner, *Frames of Mind: A Theory of Multiple Intelligences* (New York: Basic Books, 1983), 126.

6. Joseph Szigeti, *With Strings Attached: Reminiscences and Reflections* (New York: Knopf, 1967), 8.

7. Igor Stravinsky and Robert Craft, *Expositions and Developments* (New York: Doubleday, 1962), 39.

8. Dimitri Shostakovich, *Testimony: The Memoirs of D. Shostakovich* (New York: Harper and Row, 1979), xxii.

9. Pablo Casals, with Albert E. Kahn, *Joys and Sorrows* (New York: Simon and Schuster, 1970), 30–35 passim.

10. Gardner, *Frames of Mind*, 121.

11. Aaron Copland and Vivian Perris, *Copland: 1900 through 1942* (New York: St. Martin's, 1984), 25.

12. Ibid., 29.

13. Ibid., 68.

14. Ibid., 62.

15. Shostakovich, *Testimony*, 61–74 passim.

16. Igor Stravinsky, *An Autobiography* (New York: Norton, 1963), 20.

17. Stravinsky and Craft, *Expositions and Developments*, 51–52.

18. Leonard Bernstein, *Findings* (New York: Simon and Schuster, 1982), 332.

19. Ibid., 339–40.

20. Gardner, *Frames of Mind*, 114.

21. Stravinsky, *Autobiography*, 21.

22. Shostakovich, *Testimony*, 230.

23. Robert H. Shauffler, *Beethoven: The Man Who Freed Music* (Garden City: Doubleday, Duran, 1929), 63.

24. Maynard Solomon, "Beethoven's Tagebuch of 1812–1818," in *Beethoven Studies* 3, ed. Alan Tyson (Cambridge: Cambridge University Press, 1982), 230.

25. Bernstein, *Findings*, 286.

26. Copland and Perris, *Copland*, 72–74.

27. Ibid., 104.

28. Ibid., 95.

29. Ibid., 130–131.

30. Ibid., 279.

31. Bela Bártok, *Letters*, ed. J. Demeny, Sr. (New York: St. Martin's, 1971), 201.

32. Laszlo Eosze, *Zoltan Kodaly: His Life and Work* (London: Collet's Holdings, 1962), 162–163.

33. Stravinsky and Craft, *Expositions and Developments*, 147.

34. Bernstein, *Findings*, 146–47.

35. Stephen Spender, "The Making of a Poem," in *Creativity*, ed. P. E. Vernon (Harmondsworth: Penguin, 1970), 64.

36. Lewis Lockwood, "Eroica Perspectives: Strategy and Design in the First Movement," in *Beethoven Studies* 3, ed., Alan Tyson (Cambridge: Cambridge University Press, 1982), 101–2.

37. Christopher Reynolds, "Beethoven's Sketches for Variations in E flat Op. 35," in *Beethoven Studies* 3, ed., Alan Tyson (Cambridge: Cambridge University Press, 1982), 61.

38. Donald Francis Tovey, *The Integrity of Music* (London, 1941), quoted in Lewis Lockwood, "Eroica Perspectives," in *Beethoven Studies* 3, ed. Alan Tyson (Cambridge: Cambridge University Press, 1982), 102.

39. Modeste Tchaikovsky, *Life and Letters of Tchaikovsky* (New York: Vienna House, 1973), 20.

40. Stravinsky and Craft, *Expositions and Developments*, 159.

41. Ibid., 161.

42. Ibid., 168.

43. Bernstein, *Unanswered Question*, 175.

44. Ibid., 162.

45. Andrew Lock, "The Emergence of Language," in *Action, Gesture, and Symbol: The Emergence of Language*, ed. A. Lock (London: Academic, 1978), 3–18.

46. John Martin, *The Modern Dance* (New York: A. S. Barnes, 1933), 13.

47. Bernard Taper, *Balanchine: A Biography* (New York: Macmillan, 1974), 184.

48. Igor Stravinsky and Robert Craft, *Themes and Episodes* (New York: Knopf, 1966), 25.

49. Merce Cunningham, Interview in *The Creative Experience*, eds. Stanley Rosner and Lawrence A. Abt (New York: Grossman, 1970), 175.

50. "Merce Cunningham: The Maverick of Modern Dance," *New York Times Magazine*, March 21, 1982, 25.

51. Ibid., 68.

52. Martha Graham, *The Notebooks of Martha Graham* (New York: Harcourt Brace Jovanovich, 1973), 190.

53. Ibid., 81.

54. Ibid., 333.

55. Ibid., 87.

56. Arlene Croce, *After-Images* (New York: Knopf, 1977), 193.

57. Anna Sokolow, "The Rebel and the Bourgeois," in *The Modern Dance: Seven Statements of Belief*, ed. S. J. Cohen (Middletown, Conn.: Wesleyan University Press, 1965), 33–34.

58. Taper, *Balanchine*, 124.

59. Margaret Lloyd, *The Borzoi Book of Modern Dance* (New York: Knopf, 1949), 64.

60. Agnes DeMille, *Speak to Me, Dance with Me* (New York: Popular Library, 1973), 98.

61. Eric Hawkins, "Pure Poetry," in *The Modern Dance: Seven Statements of Belief*, ed. S. J. Cohen (Middletown, Conn.: Wesleyan University Press, 1965), 41.

62. Doris Humphrey, *The Art of Making Dances* (New York: Grove, 1959), 52.

63. Croce, *After-Images*, 322.

64. Hawkins, "Pure Poetry," 47–48.

65. Humphrey, *Making Dances*, 170.

66. Ibid., 70–71.

67. Edwin Denby, *Looking at the Dance* (New York: Popular Library, 1968), 293.

68. Katherine Dunham, "Notes on the Dance," 7 *Arts* #2, ed. Fernando Puma (Garden City: Doubleday, 1954), 76.

Chapter 7

1. Rene Dubos, *The Dreams of Reason: Science and Utopias* (New York: Columbia University Press, 1961), 6–7.

2. Werner Heisenberg, *Physics and Beyond: Encounters and Conversations* (New York: Harper and Row, 1971), 73.

3. Marie Curie, *Pierre Curie* (New York: Macmillan, 1936), 35.

4. Charles Darwin, *Autobiography* (London: Collins, 1958), 77.

5. Albert Einstein, "Autobiographical Notes," in *Albert Einstein: Philosopher-Scientist*, ed. P. A. Schilpp, 3rd ed. (LaSalle, Ill.: Open Court, 1970), 9.

6. Ibid.

7. Gerald Holton, *The Scientific Imagination: Case Studies* (Cambridge: Cambridge University Press, 1978), 193.

8. "The Einstein Papers: Childhood Showed a Gift for the Abstract," *New York Times*, March 27, 1972, 1, col. 1.

9. Bill Moyers, "Sources of Creativity," *For Members Only: A Newsletter for American Express Cardmembers*, November, 1982, 1.

10. June Goodfield, *An Imagined World: A Story of Scientific Discovery* (New York: Harper and Row, 1981), 30–31.

11. Gerald Holton, *Thematic Origins of Scientific Thought: Kepler to Einstein* (Cambridge: Harvard University Press, 1973), 377.

12. Goodfield, *An Imagined World*, 223.

13. Agnes Arber, *The Mind and the Eye* (Cambridge: Cambridge University Press, 1964), 124–25.

14. Karl Popper, "Is there an epistemological problem in perception?," in *Problems in the Philosophy of Science*, eds. I. Lakatos and A. Musgrave (Amsterdam: North-Holland, 1968), 163.

15. Holton, *Scientific Imagination*, 99.

16. Jacques Hadamard, ed., *The Psychology of Invention in the Mathematical Field* (Princeton: Princeton University Press, 1945), 2.

17. Stanley Rosner and Lawrence A. Abt, eds., *The Creative Experience* (New York: Grossman, 1970), 91.

18. Thomas Kuhn, *The Structure of Scientific Revolutions* (Chicago: University of Chicago Press, 1962), 24.

19. Hadamard, *Psychology of Invention*, 45–47.

20. W. I. Beveridge, *The Art of Scientific Investigation* (New York: Norton, 1950), 76.

21. Ibid., 80.

22. Jerome Bruner, *On Knowing: Essays for the Left Hand* (Cambridge: Harvard University Press, 1962), 19.

23. Goodfield, *An Imagined World*, 113.

24. Arthur Koestler, *Bricks to Babel* (New York: Random House, 1981), 344.

25. Robert Olby, "Francis Crick, DNA and the Central Dogma," *Daedalus* 99 (Fall 1970): 982.

26. Ibid.

27. See C. W. Taylor and F. Barron, eds., *Scientific Creativity: Its Recognition and Development* (New York: Wiley, 1963), and in particular F. Barron, "The Needs for Order and Disorder as Motives for Creative Activity," 159.

28. Olby, "Crick, DNA and the Central Dogma," 963.

29. N. P. Davis, *Lawrence and Oppenheimer* (New York: Fawcett World Library, 1968), 168–169.

30. H. Yukawa, *Creativity and Intuition* (New York: Kodansha International, 1973), 114.

31. F. Bartlett, "Adventurous Thinking," in *Creativity*, ed. P. E. Vernon (Harmondsworth: Penguin, 1970), 101, 104.

32. Morris Kline, Interview in *The Creative Experience*, eds. Stanley Rosner and Lawrence A. Abt (New York: Grossman, 1970), 93–94.

33. J. Clement, "Spontaneous Models in Problem-Solving: The Progressive Construction of Mental Models," paper presented at American Educational Research Association Meetings, New York, March 1982.

34. Ibid.

35. P. J. Davis and R. Hersh, *The Mathematical Experience* (Boston: Birkhauser, 1980), 391.

36. Kuhn, *Structure of Scientific Revolutions*, 52–53.

37. Walter Sullivan, "The Einstein Papers: A Flash of Insight Came After Long Reflection on Relativity," *New York Times*, March 29, 1972, 32.

38. Holton, *Thematic Origins*, 329.

39. Ibid., 387.

40. Howard Gruber, "Darwin's Tree of Nature and Other Images of Wide Scope," in *On Aesthetics of Science*, ed. J. Wechsler (Cambridge: MIT Press, 1977), 6.

41. Heisenberg, *Physics and Beyond*, 40–41.

42. Einstein, "Autobiographical Notes," 45.

43. Ibid., 43–45.

44. Ibid., 53.

45. Heisenberg, *Physics and Beyond*, 65.

46. Einstein, "Autobiographical Notes," 23.

47. Holton, *Thematic Origins*, 316.

48. Holton, *Scientific Imagination*, 97–98.

49. Kuhn, *Structure of Scientific Revolutions*, 87.

50. Heisenberg, *Physics and Beyond*, 74.

51. Neils Bohr, "Discussion with Einstein on Epistemological Problems in Atomic Physics," in *Albert Einstein: Philosopher-Scientist*, ed. P. A. Schilpp, 3rd ed. (LaSalle, Ill.: Open Court, 1970), 210, 224.

52. Holton, *Thematic Origins*, 139–42.

53. Kuhn, *Structure of Scientific Revolutions*, 111.

54. Holton, *Scientific Imagination*, 23.

55. Saul Bellow, Interview in *Writers at Work*, The Paris Review Interviews, Third Series, ed. George Plimpton (New York: Viking, 1967), 184.

56. Albert Szent-Györgyi, Interview in *Scientists Face to Face*, ed. Istvan Kardos (Gyoma, Hungary: Corvina Kiado, 1978), 314.

57. Vivian Gornick, *Women in Science: Portraits from a World in Transition* (New York: Simon and Schuster, 1983), 15.

58. Anne Roe, "A Psychologist Examines Sixty-Four Eminent Scientists," in *Creativity*, ed. P. E. Vernon (Harmondsworth: Penguin, 1970), 43–52.

59. D. W. MacKinnon, The Personality Correlates of Creativity," in *Creativity*, ed. P. E. Vernon (Harmondsworth: Penguin, 1970), 309.

60. Albert Einstein, quoted in Holton, *Scientific Imagination*, 231–32.

61. Morton Hunt, *The Universe Within: A New Science Explores the Human Mind* (New York: Simon and Schuster, 1982), 265.

62. Quoted in Goodfield, *Imagined World*, 230.

63. Gornick, *Women in Science*, 38–39.

Conclusion

1. Pablo Neruda, *Memoirs* (New York: Farrar, Straus, Giroux, 1972), 21.

2. Steve J. Heims, *John von Neumann and Norbert Weiner* (Cambridge: MIT Press, 1930), 9.

3. Victor Turner, quoted in Marjorie Wilson, "Passage-Through-Communitas: An Interpretive Analysis of Enculturation in Art Education," Ph.D. Dissertation, Pennsylvania State University 1977, 126–27.

4. Ibid.

5. Georges Braque, quoted in John Berger, *The Look of Things: Essays* (New York: Viking, 1971), 133.

6. Howard E. Gruber, "The Evolving Systems Approach to Creativity," eds. Sohan

and Celia Modgil, *Towards a Theory of Psychological Development* (Windsor, Eng.: NFER, 1980), 285.

7. Ibid., 270.

8. Hannah Arendt, *The Life of the Mind*, vol. 1: *Thinking* (New York: Harcourt Brace Jovanovich, 1976), 100.

9. Jean Piaget, "The Semiotic or Symbolic Function," in *The Essential Piaget*, eds. H. Gruber and J. J. Voneche (New York: Basic Books, 1977), 507.

10. Rudolf Arnheim, *Visual Thinking* (Berkeley: University of California Press, 1971), 315.

11. Ibid.

12. Morton Hunt, *The Universe Within* (New York: Simon and Schuster, 1982), 315.

13. G. R. Taylor, *The Natural Gift of the Mind* (New York: Dutton, 1979), 214.

14. Igor Stravinsky and Robert Craft, *Themes and Episodes* (New York: Knopf, 1966), 50–51.

15. Stephen Spender, "The Making of a Poem," in *Creativity*, ed. P. E. Vernon (Harmondsworth: Penguin, 1970), 71–72.

16. F. L. Holmes, "Laboratory Notebooks and Scientific Creativity," to appear in "Creative People at Work," eds. D. Wallace and H. Gruber, in press.

17. L. S. Vygotsky, *Thought and Language*, trans. E. Hanfman and G. Vakar (Cambridge: MIT Press, 1962), 149.

18. H. E. Gruber, "Cognitive Psychology, Scientific Creativity and the Case Study Method," in *On Scientific Discovery*, eds. M. D. Graek, R. S. Cohen and G. Cimino (Amsterdam: D. Reidel, 1980), 318.

19. R. A. Milliken Collections at the California Institute of Technology, quoted in Gerald Holton, *The Scientific Imagination* (Cambridge: Cambridge University Press, 1981), 31–32.

20. D. E. Berlyne, quoted in John Radford and Andrew Burton, *Thinking: Its Nature and Development* (Chichester: John Wiley, 1974), 99.

21. Morris I. Stein, *Stimulating Creativity*, vol. 1 *Individual Procedures* (New York: Academic, 1974), 40.

22. Arieti, Silvano, *Creativity: The Magic Synthesis* (New York: Basic Books, 1976), 30–31.

23. Jacob W. Getzels and Mihaly Csikszentmihalyi, *The Creative Vision: A Longitudinal Study of Problem-Finding in Art* (New York: John Wiley, 1976), 217.

24. Vivian Gornick, *Women in Science* (New York: Simon & Schuster, 1983), 40.

25. Thomas Mann, *Letters of Thomas Mann, 1889–1955*, trans. R. and C. Winston (New York: Vintage, 1975), 140.

26. Ibid., 257.

27. Howard Gruber, "On the Relation Between 'Aha Experiences' and the Construction of Ideas," in *History of Science*, vol. 19, pt. 1, n. 43 (March 1981).

28. May Sarton, *Writings on Writing* (Orono, MN: Puckerbrush Press, 1980), 16, 50.

29. Jacob Bronowski, *The Ascent of Man* (New York: Little, Brown and Co., 1973), 438.

Bibliography

Allott, Miriam, ed. *Novelists on the Novel*. New York: Columbia University Press, 1959. [Flaubert, "Letter to H. A. Taine"]

Aranda, Francisco. *Luis Buñuel: A Critical Biography*. Translated and edited by David Robinson. New York: Da Capo, 1976.

Arber, Agnes. *The Mind and the Eye: A Study of the Biologist's Standpoint*. Cambridge: Cambridge University Press, 1964.

Arendt, Hannah. *The Life of the Mind*. Vol. I, *Thinking*. New York: Harcourt Brace Jovanovich, 1977.

Arieti, Silvano. *Creativity: The Magic Synthesis*. New York: Basic Books, 1976.

Arnheim, Rudolf. *Visual Thinking*. Berkeley: University of California Press, 1971.

Balazs, Janos. *A Hungarian Gipsy Artist*. Budapest: Corvina, 1977.

Baldwin, James. *The Devil Finds Work: an essay*. New York: Dial, 1976.

Bartok, Bela. *Bela Bartok Letters*. Edited by J. Demeny. New York: St. Martin's, 1971.

Beauvoir, Simone de. *Memoirs of a Dutiful Daughter*. Cleveland: World, 1959.

Berger, John. *The Look of Things: Essays*. Edited by Nikos Stangos. New York: Viking, 1971.

———. *The Success and Failure of Picasso*. Harmondsworth: Penguin, 1965.

———. *Toward Reality: Essays in Seeing*. New York: Knopf, 1962.

Bernstein, Basil. *Class, Codes and Control*. Vol. 3, *Towards a Theory of Educational Transmissions*. London: Routledge and Kegan Paul, 1975.

Bernstein, Leonard. *Findings*. New York: Simon and Schuster, 1982.

———. *The Unanswered Question: Six Talks at Harvard*. Cambridge: Harvard University Press, 1976.

Beveridge, William Ian. *The Art of Scientific Investigation*. New York: Norton, 1950.

Bronowski, Jacob. *The Ascent of Man*. New York: Little Brown, 1974.

Brooks, Van Wyck. *Opinions of Oliver Allston*. New York: Dutton, 1941.

Bruner, Jerome. *On Knowing: Essays for the Left Hand*. Cambridge: Harvard University Press, 1962.

————. *Toward a Theory of Instruction*. Cambridge: Harvard University Press, 1966.

Casals, Pablo, as told to Albert E. Kahn. *Joys and Sorrows: Reflections*. New York: Simon and Schuster, 1970.

Chaikovskii, Modest Il'ich. *The Life and Letters of Peter Ilich Tchaikovsky*. Edited by R. Newmarch. New York: Dodd, Mead, 1974.

Chein, Isidor. *The Science of Behavior and the Image of Man*. New York: Basic Books, 1972.

Chicago, Judy. *Through the Flower: My Struggle as a Woman Artist*. Garden City: Doubleday, 1975.

Church, Joseph. *Language and the Discovery of Reality*. New York: Random House, 1961.

Clement, John. "Spontaneous Models in Problem-Solving: The Progressive Construction of Mental Models." Paper presented at American Educational Research Association Meetings, New York, March 1982. Mimeographed. University of Massachusetts Physics Department.

Cohen, Selma Jeanne, ed. *The Modern Dance: Seven Statements of Belief*. Middletown, CT.: Wesleyan University Press, 1965.

Cole, Toby, ed. *Playwrights on Playwriting*. New York: Hill and Wang, 1960.

Concha, Joseph. *Lonely Deer*. Taos, New Mexico: Pueblo Indian Council, 1971.

Copland, Aaron, and Perlis, Vivian. *Copland: Nineteen Hundred to Nineteen Forty Two*. Vol. 1. New York: St. Martin's, 1984.

Corredor, J[osep]. Ma[ria]. *Conversations with Casals*. Translated by A. Mangeot. New York: Dutton, 1956.

Craft, Robert. *Current Convictions: Views and Reviews*. New York: Knopf, 1977.

Croce, Arlene. *Afterimages*. New York: Knopf, 1977.

Curie, Marie S. *Pierre Curie*. New York: Macmillan, 1936.

Darwin, Charles. *Autobiography*. London: Collins, 1958.

Davis, Nuel Pharr. *Lawrence and Oppenheimer*. New York: Simon and Schuster, 1968.

Davis, Philip J., and Hersh, Reuben. *The Mathematical Experience*. Boston: Birkhauser, 1980.

De Mille, Agnes. *Speak to Me, Dance with Me*. New York: Popular Library, 1973.

Denby, Edwin. *Looking at the Dance*. New York: Popular Library, 1968.

Donohue, H. E. F. *Conversations with Nelson Algren*. New York: Hill and Wang, 1964.

Dostoevsky, Fyodor. *The Notebooks for "A Raw Youth."* Edited by E. Wasiolek. Chicago: University of Chicago Press, 1969.

————. *The Notebooks for "The Possessed."* Edited by E. Wasiolek. Chicago: University of Chicago Press, 1968.

Dubos, René Jules. *The Dreams of Reason: Science and Utopias*. New York: Columbia University Press, 1961.

Dunaway, David King. *How Can I Keep from Singing: Pete Seeger*. New York: McGraw-Hill, 1981.

Dunham, Katherine. "Notes on the Dance." In *7 Arts # Two*, edited by Fernando Puma, pp. 69–76. Garden City: Doubleday, 1954.

Eosze, Laszlo. *Zoltan Kodaly: His Life and Work*. London: Collet's Holdings, 1962.

Evans, Richard I. *Jean Piaget: The Man and His Ideas*. New York: Dutton, 1973.

Funke, Lewis, and Booth, John, eds. *Actors Talk About Acting*. New York: Avon, 1969.

Gardner, Howard. *Art, Mind, and Brain: A Cognitive Approach to Creativity*. New York: Basic Books, 1982.

———. *Frames of Mind: A Theory of Multiple Intelligences*. New York: Basic Books, 1983.

Gaugin, Paul. *Paul Gaugin's Intimate Journals*. Translated by V. W. Brooks. Bloomington: Indiana University Press, 1968.

Getzels, Jacob W., and Csikszentmihalyi, Mihaly. *The Creative Vision: A Longitudinal Study of Problem Finding in Art*. New York: Wiley, 1976.

Getzels, Jacob W., and Jackson, Philip W. *Creativity and Intelligence: Explorations with Gifted Students*. London: Wiley, 1962.

Godwin, Gail. *The Odd Woman*. New York: Berkeley Medallion, 1976.

Goldwater, Robert. *Paul Gaugin*. New York: Abrams, 1928.

Goodfield, June. *An Imagined World: A Story of Scientific Discovery*. New York: Harper and Row, 1981.

Gordon, H. "Degree of Ear Asymmetries for Perception of Dichotic Chords and for Illusory Chord Localization in Musicians of Different Levels of Competence." *Journal of Experimental Psychology: Human Perception and Performance* 6 (1980):516–27.

Gornick, Vivian. *Women in Science: Portraits from a World in Transition*. New York: Simon and Schuster, 1983.

Gowan, J. C. "Incubation, Imagery and Creativity." *Journal of Mental Imagery* 2 (1978).

Graham, Martha. The Notebooks of Martha Graham. New York: Harcourt Brace Jovanovich, 1973.

Gregory, Richard. *The Intelligent Eye*. New York: McGraw-Hill, 1970.

Gruber, Howard E. *Darwin on Man: A Psychological Study of Scientific Creativity*. New York: Dutton, 1974.

———. "On the Relation Between 'Aha Experiences' and the Construction of Ideas." *History of Science* 19 (1981):41–59.

Hadamard, Jacques. *An Essay on the Psychology of Invention in the Mathematical Field*. Princeton: Princeton University Press, 1945.

Heims, Steve J. *John Von Neumann and Norbert Wiener: From Mathematics to the Technologies of Life and Death*. Cambridge, Mass.: MIT Press, 1980.

Heisenberg, Werner. *Physics and Beyond: Encounters and Conversations*. Translated by A. J. Pomerans. New York: Harper and Row, 1971.

Hellman, Lillian. *An Unfinished Woman*. Boston: Little, Brown, 1970.

Hesse, Hermann. *Autobiographical Writings*. Translated by T. Ziolkowski. Denver: Lindley, 1972.

Holt, Robert R. "Imagery: The Return of the Ostracized." *American Psychologist* 19 (1964): 254–64.

Holton, Gerald. *The Scientific Imagination: Case Studies*. Cambridge: Cambridge University Press, 1978.

———. *Thematic Origins of Scientific Thought: Kepler to Einstein*. Cambridge: Harvard University Press, 1973.

Humphrey, Doris. *The Art of Making Dances*. New York: Grove, 1959.

Hunt, Morton. *The Universe Within: A New Science Explores the Human Mind*. New York: Simon and Schuster, 1982.

Huxley, Julian. *Memories*. New York: Harper and Row, 1970.

Jackendorff, Ray. "Generative Music Theory and Its Relevance to Psychology." Unpublished manuscript. Mimeographed. Brandeis University Linguistics Department.

James, William. *The Principles of Psychology*. Vol. I. New York: Dover, 1950.

Johnson, Don. *The Protean Body: A Rolfer's View of Human Flexibility*. New York: Harper Colophon, 1977.

Kagan, Jerome, ed. *Creativity and Learning*. Boston: Houghton Mifflin, 1967.

Kardos, István, ed. *Scientists Face to Face*. Gyoma, Hungary: Corvina Kiadó, 1978.

Kazantzakis, Nikos. *Report to Greco*. London: Faber and Faber, 1973.

Kearns, Martha. *Kathe Kollwitz: Woman and Artist*. Old Westbury: Feminist Press, 1975.

Kepes, György. *Language of Vision*. Chicago: Paul Theobald, 1944.

Kisselgoff, Anna. "Merce Cunningham: The Maverick of Modern Dance." *New York Times Magazine*, 21 March 1982, 22, section 6.

Koch, Kenneth, et al. *Wishes, Lies and Dreams: Teaching Children to Write Poetry*. New York: Chelsea House, 1970.

Koestler, Arthur. *The Act of Creation*. New York: Macmillan, 1964.

———. *Bricks to Babel*. New York: Random House, 1981.

Kokoschka, Oskar. *My Life*. Translated by D. Britt. New York: Macmillan, 1974.

Krueger, Theodore H. "Visual Imagery in Problem Solving and Scientific Creativity." Unpublished manuscript, copyright 1976. Printed by Seal Press, Derby, Connecticut.

Kuhn, Thomas S. *Structure of Scientific Revolutions*. Chicago: University of Chicago Press, 1962.

Lakatos, Imre, and Musgrave, A. E., eds. *Problems in the Philosophy of Science*. Amsterdam: North-Holland, 1968.

Lloyd, Margaret. *The Borzoi Book of Modern Dance*. New York: Knopf, 1949.

Lock, Andrew, ed. *Action, Gesture and Symbol: The Emergence of Language*. London: Academic, 1979.

Mann, Thomas. *Letters of Thomas Mann: 1889–1955*. Translated by R. and C. Winston. New York: Vintage, 1975.

———. *The Story of a Novel*. New York: Knopf, 1961.

Mansfield, Katherine. *Journal of Katherine Mansfield*. Edited by J. M. Murray. New York: Knopf, 1946.

Martin, John. *The Modern Dance*. New York: A. S. Barnes, 1933.

Maugham, W. Somerset. *The Summing Up*. London: Heinemann, 1948.

Maurois, Andre. *Proust: Portrait of a Genius*. Translated by G. Hopkins. New York: Harper, 1950.

May, Rollo. *The Courage to Create*. New York: Norton, 1975.

McCrindle, Joseph F., ed. *Behind the Scenes: Theater and Film Interviews from the "Transatlantic Review"*. New York: Holt, Rinehart, and Winston, 1971.

Medawar, Peter Brian. *Induction and Intuition in Scientific Thought*. Philadelphia: American Philosophical Society, 1969.

Modgil, Celia, and Modgil, Sahan, eds. *Toward a Theory of Psychological Development*. Atlantic Highlands, N. J.: Humanities Press, 1980.

Moore-Russell, Martha. "John Locke: The Development of a Philosopher as a Person-in-Society." Paper presented at the Seventh Annual Symposium of the Jean Piaget Society, Philadelphia, May 21, 1977. Mimeographed. Institute for Cognitive Studies, Rutgers University.

Moyers, Bill. "Sources of Creativity." *For Members Only: A Newsletter for American Express Cardholders*, Nov. 1982.

Neisser, Ulric. *Cognition and Reality: Principles and Implications of Cognitive Psychology*. San Francisco: W. H. Freeman, 1976.

———. *Cognitive Psychology*. New York: Appleton-Century-Crofts, 1967.

Neruda, Pablo. *Memoirs*. New York: Farrar, Straus, Giroux, 1977.

Nin, Anaís. *The Diary of Anaís Nin*. New York: Harcourt Brace Jovanovich, 1966–1980.

———. *The Novel of the Future*. New York: Collier Books, 1968.

Olby, Robert C. "Francis Crick, DNA and the Central Dogma." *Daedalus* 99 (1970):938.

Paivio, Allan. *Imagery and Verbal Processes*. New York: Holt, Rinehart, Winston, 1971.

Patrick, Catherine. "Creative Thought in Poets." *Archives of Psychology*, no. 178 (1935): 74.

Perkins, David N. *The Mind's Best Work*. Cambridge: Harvard University Press, 1981.

Piaget, Jean. *The Essential Piaget*. Edited by H. Gruber and J. J. Vonèche. New York: Basic Books, 1977.

———. *The Language and Thought of the Child*. Translated by M. Gabain. New York: New American Library, 1974.

———. *Six Psychological Studies*. New York: Vintage, 1968.

Radford, John, and Burton, Andrew. *Thinking: Its Nature and Development*. Chichester: Wiley, 1974.

Rhys, Jean. *Smile Please: An Unfinished Autobiography*. New York: Harper and Row, 1979.

Rivera, Diego, with Gladys March. *My Art, My Life: An Autobiography*. New York: Citadel, 1976.

Roe, Anne. *The Making of a Scientist*. New York: Dodd, Mead, 1952.

Rosner, Stanley, and Abt, Lawrence E., eds. *The Creative Experience*. New York: Grossman, 1970.

———. *Essays in Creativity*. Croton-on-Hudson, N. Y.: North River Press, 1974.

Rothenberg, Albert. *The Emerging Goddess*. Chicago: University of Chicago Press, 1979.

Ruddick, Sara, and Daniels, Pamela, eds. *Working It Out: 23 Women Writers, Artists, Scientists, and Scholars Talk About Their Lives and Work*. New York: Pantheon, 1978.

Sanford, Nevitt. "Social Psychology: Its Place in Personology." *American Psychologist* 37 (1982):896–903.

Sarris, Andrew, ed. *Interviews with Film Directors*. New York: Avon, 1969.

Sarton, May. *Writings on Writing*. Edited by C. Hunting. Orono, Me.: Puckerbrush Press, 1980.

Sartre, Jean Paul. *The Words*. New York: George Braziller, 1964.

Sayre, Anne. *Rosalind Franklin and DNA*. New York: Norton, 1975.

Schactel, Ernest G. *Metamorphosis*. New York: Basic Books, 1959.

Schilpp, Paul A., ed. *Albert Einstein: Philosopher-Scientist*. 3d ed. La Salle, Ill.: Open Court, 1970.

Schneider, Daniel E. *The Psychoanalyst and the Artist*. New York: New American Library, 1962.

Shahn, Ben. *The Shape of Content*. Cambridge: Harvard University Press, 1957.

Shauffler, Robert H. *Beethoven: The Man Who Freed Music*. Garden City: Doubleday, Doran, 1929.

Shostakovich, Dmitri. *Testimony: The Memoirs of Dmitri Shostakovich*. As related to and edited by Solomon Volkov. Translated by A. W. Bouis. New York: Harper and Row, 1979.

Soyer, Raphael. *Diary of an Artist*. Washington, D. C.: New Republic Books, 1977.

Sprigg, Christopher St. John [Caudwell]. *Studies in a Dying Culture*. London: John Lane the Bodley-Head, 1938.

Stein, Morris I. *Stimulating Creativity*. Vol. I, *Individual Procedures*. New York: Academic, 1974.

Steinbeck, John. *Journal of a Novel*. New York: Viking, 1969.

Sternburg, Janet, ed. *The Writer on Her Work*. New York: Norton, 1980.

Stravinsky, Igor. *An Autobiography*. New York: Norton, 1962.

Stravinsky, Igor, and Craft, Robert. *Expositions and Developments*. Berkeley: University of California Press, 1981.

———. *Themes and Episodes*. New York: Knopf, 1966.

Sullivan, Walter. "The Einstein Papers: Childhood Showed a Gift for the Abstract." *New York Times*, March 27, 1972, 1, col. 1.

————. "The Einstein Papers: A Flash of Insight Came After Long Reflection on Relativity." *New York Times*, March 28, 1972, 32.

Szigeti, Joseph. *With Strings Attached: Reminiscences and Reflections*. New York: Knopf, 1967.

Taper, Bernard. *Balanchine: A Biography*. Revised and updated. New York: Macmillan, 1974.

Taylor, Calvin W., and Barron, Frank, eds. *Scientific Creativity: Its Recognition and Devlopment*. Selected papers from the proceedings of the first, second, and third University of Utah Conferences: "The Identification of Creative Scientific Talent," New York: Wiley, 1963.

Taylor, Gordon R. *The Natural History of the Mind*. New York: Dutton, 1979.

Thoreau, H. D. *A Writer's Journal*. Edited by Laurence Stapleton. New York: Dover, 1960.

Toulmin, Stephen. "The Mozart of Psychology." *New York Review of Books*, 28 September 1978, p. 51. [Review of L. Vygotsky, *Mind in Society* and *The Psychology of Art.*]

Troyat, Henri. *Tolstoy*. Translated by N. Amphoux. Garden City: Doubleday, 1967.

Tyson, Alan, ed. *Beethoven Studies III*. Cambridge: Cambridge University Press, 1982.

Ulam, Stanislaw M. *Adventures of a Mathematician*. New York: Scribner, 1976.

Vernon, Philip Ewart, ed. *Creativity: Selected Readings*. Harmondsworth: Penguin, 1975.

Vygotsky, Lev. S. *Thought and Language*. Edited by G. Vakar. Translated by E. Hanfmann. Cambridge, Mass.: MIT Press, 1962.

Wallace, Doris, and Gruber, Howard E., eds. "Creative People at Work." In preparation.

Wechsler, Judith, ed. *On Aesthetics in Science*. Cambridge, Mass.: MIT Press, 1977.

Weir, Ruth H. *Language in the Crib*. The Hague: Morton, 1962.

Wilson, Marjorie. "Passage-Through-Communitas: An Interpretative Analysis of Enculturation in Art Education." Ph.D. dissertation, Pennsylvania State University, 1977.

Woolf, Virginia. *A Writer's Diary*. New York: Harcourt, Brace Jovanovich, 1953.

Writers at Work: The "Paris Review" Interviews. First through fourth series. New York: Viking, 1959 (Malcolm Cowley, ed.); 1963 (Van Wyck Brooks, ed.); 1967 (George Plimpton, ed.); 1976 (George Plimpton, ed.).

Wyatt, Gertrud L. *Language Learning and Communication Disorders in Children*. New York: Free Press, 1969.

Yukawa, Hideki. *Creativity and Intuition: A Physicist Looks at East and West*. Translated by J. Bester. New York: Kodansha International, 1973.

Index